Building
Reading
PreK–3

SECOND EDITION

Pamela Nevills • Patricia Wolfe

Building the Reading Brain
PreK–3

SECOND EDITION

CORWIN PRESS
A SAGE Company

For information:

Corwin Press
A SAGE Company
2455 Teller Road
Thousand Oaks, California 91320
www.corwinpress.com

SAGE Ltd.
1 Oliver's Yard
55 City Road
London EC1Y 1SP
United Kingdom

SAGE India Pvt. Ltd.
B 1/I 1 Mohan Cooperative
   Industrial Area
Mathura Road, New Delhi 110 044
India

SAGE Asia-Pacific Pte. Ltd.
33 Pekin Street #02-01
Far East Square
Singapore 048763

Printed in the United States of America

Library of Congress Cataloging-in-Publication Data

Nevills, Pamela.
  Building the reading brain, preK–3 / Pamela Nevills, Patricia Wolfe. — 2nd ed.
     p. cm.
  Earlier ed. entered under: Wolfe, Pat.
  Includes bibliographical references and index.
  ISBN 978-1-4129-6325-1 (cloth)
  ISBN 978-1-4129-6326-8 (pbk.)
    1. Reading (Early childhood) 2. Reading, Psychology of. I. Wolfe, Pat. II. Title.

LB1139.5.R43W65 2009
372.4—dc22   2008034491

This book is printed on acid-free paper.

13   10 9 8 7 6 5 4 3

Acquisitions Editor:	Jessica Allan
Editorial Assistant:	Joanna Coelho
Production Editor:	Jane Haenel
Copy Editor:	Adam Dunham
Typesetter:	C&M Digitals (P) Ltd.
Proofreader:	Sue Irwin
Indexer:	Jean Casalegno
Cover and Graphic Designer:	Rose Storey

Contents

Acknowledgments

I am indebted to the many researchers and authors who have spent their careers studying the processes of developing competent readers. The seminal work of Marilyn Jager Adams is essential for anyone attempting to understand the vast amount of research that has taken place over the past three decades.

Marie Clay's studies and the resulting Reading Recovery program have given us invaluable information regarding the teaching of reading, especially to those who experience difficulty. The brain-imaging work of Sally Shaywitz and Susan Bookheimer has provided us with an exciting new neurological perspective, an ability to see what is happening in the brain as a person reads.

Kay Soper, reading specialist in the Napa Valley Unified School District, graciously read several chapters of the book and provided excellent feedback.

My good friend and colleague Robert Sylwester also read the book and gave his usual succinct and helpful suggestions.

—Pat Wolfe

Many contributed to the original and updated messages contained within these pages. I was initially encouraged by colleagues at the West End SELPA, San Bernardino County, California, who expect all children will make appropriate academic gains, especially in reading. Teaching struggling readers through a reading academy in the Central School District provided real-time classroom issues, challenges, and limitations. Student teachers attending the University of California, Riverside, deepened my understanding of what beginning teachers want and need to become reading teachers. And finally, my friends at Central School in the Ontario-Montclair school district diligently went through the book with me chapter by chapter to glean classroom strategies for making their kindergarten through sixth-grade students the best readers they can be.

Teaching friends Royene Higashi and Pat Holt and special educators from the Alta Loma School District contributed examples of classroom experiences and helped take research review to a practical level. Support with current, research-tested information comes from an avid reader and active thinker, Kevin Feldman. Cooperative teachers in the University of California, Riverside, opened their classrooms to student teachers and to me, providing a living laboratory of progressing readers. Grandsons Nathan and Neil gave willingly of their time for me to experience outcomes of reading development in young minds. A word of gratitude also goes to my husband, Neil Nevills, who listened to my excited dissertations and understood the dedication of time required to produce a manuscript. A special word of thanks to my coauthor and friend, who said to me 15 years ago, "Pam, you really need to start reading about how the brain is involved in learning."

—Pamela Nevills

PUBLISHER'S ACKNOWLEDGMENTS

Corwin Press gratefully acknowledges the contributions of the following reviewers:

Gail Hardesty
Mentor, Early Reading First
Chicago Public Schools
Chicago, IL

Katherine Taddie Kelly
Reading Interventionist
Waco ISD
Waco, TX

Sandra Kraynok, NBCT
Kindergarten Teacher
Rock Cave Elementary School
Rock Cave, WV

Kathy Lineberger
Media Specialist
Winston-Salem/Forsyth County Schools
Winston-Salem, NC

Rebecca Wood
Reading First Program Manager
West Virginia Department of Education
Charleston, WV

About the Authors

Pamela Nevills is first and foremost a teacher, working with learners from multiages—primary grades through postgraduate students. She supervises student teachers and teaches methods classes at the University of California, Riverside. Previous positions include teaching, staff development, and administrative positions. She has participated on and been honored by local and state advisory committees. As a two-time panel member for reading textbook selection for the state of California, she is well versed with state and national content standards. She is a national and international speaker and consultant on topics that include Brain Development From Birth through Adulthood, The Brain and Reading, School Designs for All Readers, and Adult Learners.

Writing is a recent addition to Pam's work. She is published through the state of California, the Journal of Staff Development, and she regularly contributes to organizational newsletters. Her passion about the brain and reading developed from a childhood love affair with books and encouragement from a dear friend, Pat Wolfe.

Pamela can be reached at 1619 Tecalote Drive, Fallbrook, CA 92028; phone: (760) 723–8116; e-mail address: panevills@earthlink.net.

Patricia Wolfe is an independent consultant who speaks to educators in schools across the United States and internationally. Her professional background includes public school teaching at all levels, staff development trainer for the Upland School District, Director of Instruction for the Napa County Office of Education, and a lead trainer for the International Principal Training Center in Rome and London.

Her staff development experience includes workshops in Madeline Hunter's Elements of Effective Teaching and Clinical Supervision, Anthony Gregorc's Mind Styles, Carolyn Evertson's Classroom

Management and Organization, and Peer Coaching. She has been featured in a number of videotape productions and satellite broadcasts.

Wolfe's major interest over the past 20 years has centered on the educational implications and applications of current neuroscience, cognitive science, and educational research for teaching and learning. She can be reached at Mind Matters, Inc., 555 Randolph Street, Napa, CA 94559; phone and fax: (707) 226–1777; Web site: www.patwolfe.com.

Introduction

When Corwin Press notified us regarding the need to revise *Building the Reading Brain*, we knew there was no denying the proliferation of information available about the wonders of the reading brain since the original publication. As the revision was underway, it was simply too easy to infuse new information with the strong, vital concepts from the first edition. Although the original book can still stand on its own for its bold message, it is lacking in current research that extends understanding and forcefully addresses teaching decisions and practices vital for children to learn to read and learn to read well.

The previous and new reader of this book is directed to what is different about the second edition through a series of specific examples. First, every reader will notice the introductory summary at the onset of each chapter. This summation allows readers to capsulize the chapter's information to determine the depth with which to read the chapter, peruse for later in-depth reading while going directly to the needed information in another chapter, or to share information with colleagues in a study group. The reader will notice the updated and impressive current research supporting the mainstream threads throughout the chapters for best methods and practices for teaching and their validation from neuroscience. Included in this edition, also, is information about neurons, the brain's nerve cells and work crew. An exciting, relatively new discovery, mirror neurons, is investigated for the vital role in the learning process these neurons play beginning at birth. Another addition features the decoding reading pathway. Notice the specification that the pathway is for decoding; there are other structures involved when we talk about reading comprehension, vocabulary development, or reading fluency. Recent studies using functional magnetic resonance imaging validate the importance of visual association (note visual, not auditory, areas), which are activated for advanced readers as they fluently traverse through a written passage. So while our originally defined pathways are still valid, they are now enhanced with additional areas of the brain supporting the reading process as it moves from simply identifying words to magnificently knowing words for their meaning.

A fifth area of expansion involves a look at sensory input into a child's brain. We look at expanded channels for information input and challenge teachers to check for understanding through a multiplicity of output products. Coupled with input and output channels, we turn to motivation to learn. Boldly, we state that teachers cannot make children learn. Children must be motivated to learn and willing to participate in the learning process with deep concentration. Readers will have some fun with this area and others that make teaching (according to the standards) exciting and captivating. Thinking about ways to motivate learners, what about children who are English learners? Yes, this edition has expanded information about our children who must become fluent English speakers. Surprise! They need to be engaged with language. Teacher talk and tell does not lead to language learning for their students.

Interestingly, Response to Intervention (RTI) is now common school campus vernacular. When the first edition of this book was printed, we referred to school level assessment teams, and Tier 1, 2, and 3 levels of intervention. Now this process is actualized by well-accepted RTI practices. Chapter 7 continues to have ways for doing RTI as well as current neuroscience research to validate the work of our schools. Simply put, most children who struggle with reading are not disabled. They have physiologically inadequate connections for the structures of the brain that can ensure successful reading. It is RTI practices, for the most part through general education programs, that force efficient reading pathways to emerge for use. And what is new about eye movements during automatic fluent reading? Scientists provide us with an astounding new look at how reader's eyes operate to provide the child's brain with the necessary information to read with understanding.

Finally, there is a plea to consider teaching outside the traditional curriculum and physical setting. Chapter 7 grapples with traditional teaching and the inferred benefits of expanded ways and places to reach a higher potential of the human brain. The statement, "We only use 10 percent of our brains," is simply not true. We use all areas of our brains, but to what percentage of our potential do we use this marvelous organ? It is intriguing to consider movement beyond our static way of looking at education.

The original purpose in writing this book was to bring to the field of developing literacy a focus that has become possible only through developments in neuroscience. Thus began the ambitious task to align new developments in neuroscience with the reading process. It is our hope that this work will continue to provide parents and educators with a better understanding of the ways they can help to leverage reading success.

First, chapters focus on the role of parents and caregivers as they work together with young children to build that most ancient and fundamental human communication bridge—spoken language. We offer parents and caregivers ways to build on children's natural proclivity for speech and to begin to nurture them in an appreciation and understanding of language, print, and books to support the process whereby children move from spoken language to understanding symbolic written language.

Next, by examining the neurobiology of language and the scaffolding it provides for the cognitive processes of reading, we hope to help educators use the best of what we know of how the brain learns and merge it with what we know from reading experts about the best reading instructional practices.

Looking through the new clarifying lens of brain imaging, we see how some children experience greater challenge in becoming readers, and we look at possible appropriate interventions for these children. From what we know of the brain, we have drawn conclusions about applications for classroom instructional decisions and practices that are in line with how the brain learns, how teachers can help to build the reading brain, and how they can differentiate instruction for struggling readers.

For the benefit of those people who work to ensure reading success—parents and families, caregivers for young children, nursery school teachers, preservice and in-service primary teachers, faculty study groups, staff developers, literacy coaches, and school leaders—this book is provided. To facilitate reflection, discussion, and application of the ideas offered, reflection prompts are included at the end of each chapter.

The chapters of this book are arranged to look chronologically at language and reading development. Parents, early caregivers, and teachers may choose to begin reading where they expect immediate application to their situations. However, note that Chapter 2, with its overview of how the brain processes language and reading, is particularly important as it provides a physiological foundation for the rest of the book.

Chapter 1 provides an introduction to the reading process and explains why reading is an "unnatural" act. It discusses the factors that influence whether or not children will become fluent readers. In Chapter 2, the authors explore the neurological processes involved in learning to read. The oral language pathway, which is hardwired in the brain at birth, provides the foundation for building the reading decoding pathway. However, some children's brains are hindered from making the transition from language to reading. This chapter includes a discussion of the biological and environmental causes of reading difficulties.

Because the brain uses the innate language pathway to learn to read, the development of language is an essential precursor to reading. Chapter 3 looks at how parents and caregivers can encourage and enhance oral language in their children from birth to age 3. It explains why reading to children and teaching them nursery rhymes helps to build the brain structures children will need in order to read. Chapter 4 continues this discussion with a focus on emergent literacy in preschool children. Discussed are developmentally appropriate activities and methods for continuing oral language development.

As children enter school, they are expected to be able to focus their attention on tasks that involve interpretation and the production of symbols from our oral language system. In Chapter 5, preparation for school tasks are identified as priming skills. Beyond the skills of attending and concentrating, the chapter provides a description of memory systems and concludes with rational and practical activities to maintain student motivation and to develop organizational skills. The kindergarten and first-grade child are the focus of Chapter 6. Here, the authors identify phonological processes and manipulations to reshape neural pathways in the brain for the oral reading process.

Primary-age children's brains are malleable and plastic; they are more open to learning than at any other time during formal education. When a child is not successful with school tasks for reading, early intervention is critical.

Chapter 7 identifies assessment and intervention issues for struggling readers. Comprehension and vocabulary development with a focus on second-grade children forms the essence of Chapter 8. The authors provide a discussion of what teachers can do to help children build extensive vocabularies, expand informational chunks for memory, and form connections among thoughts and concepts in novel and exciting ways.

Chapter 9 pulls all reading skills together with a focus on fluency. Fluency, as defined in this chapter, is observed when a child is able to read out loud with automaticity and comprehension. Fluent readers demonstrate speed, accuracy, and proper expression while they concentrate on meaning. Building the reading brain, a construction process for the school years, is finalized in Chapter 10. A 12-point list from the book's content provides a conclusive summary. Finally, it is acknowledged that it takes talented teachers, who understand how children learn to read, to orchestrate a delicate balance of instruction, student engagement, conversation, and reading practice so their students are able to read with a natural amount of effort and with obvious enjoyment.

1

On the Nature of Reading

Years of rigorous studies coupled with comprehensive reviews of research studies have resulted in an abundance of information about how children learn to read. This information and its implications have poured forth to our nation's teachers and parents. We know if we do not intervene when children struggle with oral language or phoneme awareness at the earliest possible grade, the child is most likely to be unsuccessful with developmental skills necessary for reading.

If the educational community knows early assessment and intervention are key to reading success, then why is it so difficult to teach the children, especially those who have been identified for special instruction, to read? While oral language develops naturally for most children, the reading pathway has no naturally designated neural mechanisms. Children must be taught to read. Some children seem to master this skill almost on their own, but most children need rigorous guidance to learn phonological skills and to be able to process parts of words, whole words, and phrases with automaticity. The English language follows many understandable rules; however, the many exceptions must make sense to the human brain, which is a pattern-seeking organ.

Skill development during the elementary years positions children to become fluent, accurate readers. The learning sequence begins with emergent literacy skills: knowledge about books and recognizing the alphabet. There is an acceptance that phonemic awareness provides the foundation for all following reading decoding skills. Children who are unable to hear and manipulate phonemes are likely to be unable to figure out orthography, or spelling patterns, for words. Many authors and researchers combine instruction, such as phonics, alphabetic principle, and word decoding, with sounds and letters under a large category called phonological processing. Vocabulary development, reading comprehension, and fluency are added to the instructional mix. Complex skills and concepts must develop individually and concurrently for each child to become a reader during the primary years.

THE IMPORTANCE OF LEARNING TO READ

Literacy is a relatively recent addition to human culture. Humans have used oral language for perhaps 4 million years, but the ability to represent the sounds of language by written symbols has been around for only 4,000 to 5,000 years. Until the 20th century, nearly every human on earth was illiterate. However, the expectation in today's society is that 100 percent of the population will be able to read and comprehend. We live in a society where the development of reading skills serves as the primary foundation for all school-based learning. Those who do not read well find their opportunities for academic and occupational success severely limited. Although the expectation that all children will read and comprehend is understandable, we are a long way from reaching this goal.

> We live in a society where the development of reading skills serves as the primary foundation for all school-based learning.

According to the National Assessment of Educational Progress (NAEP, 2007), 67 percent of fourth graders in the United States are reading at or above the basic level, whereas in 1997, 62 percent of fourth graders achieved that goal. This increase of 5 percent is significant and may be attributed to the extreme emphasis on the teaching of reading across the nation. However, those who do not rank at a basic reading level cannot read grade level materials. At the fourth grade, it means they cannot read and understand a short paragraph of the type found in a simple children's book (Lyon, 2001). A child who is not at least a modestly skilled reader by the end of third grade is unlikely to be a skilled reader in high school. In fact, research has shown that we can predict, with reasonable accuracy, students' future academic success by their reading level at the end of third grade (Slavin, 1994). The predictability of reading success or failure continues to be paramount in our

> According to the National Assessment of Educational Progress (NAEP, 2007), 67 percent of fourth graders in the United States are reading at or above the basic level, whereas in 1997, 62 percent of fourth graders achieved that goal.

determination to learn more about how children become proficient readers.

Lack of skill in reading also has a potent effect in other areas. Surveys of adolescents and young adults with criminal records indicate that at least half have reading difficulties. Some states actually predict their future need for prisons by fourth-grade reading failure rates (Lyon, 2001). Similarly, a high percentage of youth with a history of substance abuse have learning difficulties (National Center on Addiction and Substance Abuse at Columbia University, 2006).

An increasing proportion of children are labeled "learning disabled," with most being identified because of difficulties in learning to read. There are those who believe the special education population in our schools could be reduced significantly by giving more attention to early interventions designed to prevent reading problems (Kotulak, 1997). Although placement in special education programs for students with learning disabilities peaked in 1999 with a nationwide enrollment of 6 percent, there has been a slight downward trend recorded in 2002 of 5.9 percent and in 2003 of 5.8 percent (National Center for Educational Statistics, 2007). In spite of a possible downward trend in enrollment, there have not been significant gains in reading on national tests for fourth or eighth graders who are enrolled in special education programs (NAEP, 2007).

WHY LEARNING TO READ IS SO DIFFICULT

Our biological destiny is speaking, not reading. Speaking is a natural development; reading is an unnatural act. This means that almost every child will master speech just by spending time with people who already speak. Spoken language has become "hardwired" in the brain with structures built specifically for language. There are no naturally designated neural mechanisms for reading, however, so the brain must co-opt structures designed for other purposes. As the eye chases the words in a sentence across the page, the brain must continuously use neural systems designed by nature for entirely different survival tasks, such as looking for food or predators.

Even though reading is an acquired skill and not a natural process, most people do become fluent readers, but not without a lot of work. Learning to read is a long, gradual process that begins in infancy. Basic competency usually is not reached until middle childhood, well into the elementary school years. MaryAnn Wolf (2007), in her book, *Proust and the Squid: The Story and Science of the Reading Brain*, professes, "Unlike its component parts such as vision and speech, which *are* genetically organized, reading has no direct genetic program passing

> "Unlike its component parts such as vision and speech, which *are* genetically organized, reading has no direct genetic program passing it on to future generations" (Wolf, 2007, p. 11)

it on to future generations" (p. 11). Reading researcher Sally Shaywitz (2003), professor and director of the Yale Center for Learning and Attention, states, *"Speaking is natural, and reading is not.* Herein lies the difficulty. Reading is an acquired act, and invention of man that must be learned at a conscious level. And it is the very naturalness of speaking that makes reading so hard" (pp. 49–50).

Reading in any language poses a challenge, but reading in English is particularly difficult. For example, some language systems, such as the Japanese *katakana*, are based on a system where each syllable is represented by a written symbol. When these symbols are learned, the child can read with relative ease (Snow, Burns, & Griffins, 1998). Spoken English, on the other hand, has approximately 5,000 different possible syllables. Written English uses a system of letters—an alphabet—to make up a spoken syllable. A letter alone does not refer to anything. It must be combined with other letters to represent a meaningful unit or syllable. The child must learn this complex alphabetic system in order to be able to decipher written words.

Reading in English is further complicated by its orthography—the spelling of words. Alphabetical writing systems, like English, have what is described by Louisa Cook Moats (2000) as a *deep orthography*. Spelling units correspond to sounds, which are phonemes and syllables, and also to meaning, which are the morphemes in the language. So English is a morphophonemic system where words are not phonetically predictable from writing to speech.

English orthography is influenced by the spelling patterns of the languages of origin, Anglo-Saxon, Latin, and Greek. Each of the influencing languages had sounds, syllables, and morphemes that were systematically represented as the base of the language. However, when their influence came together for English, a mixed system resulted. The alphabet is simply insufficient for English spelling. The 26 letters from the Roman alphabet must be used to represent more than 40 phonemes of the English language (Moats, 2000).

> The alphabet is simply insufficient for English spelling.

In contrast, some languages, such as Spanish, have one sound for each letter. In English, one letter can represent several different sounds, depending on its placement in the word. It is understandably difficult to figure out the sound-symbol relationship when the sound of a particular letter changes in words that have the same root but different suffixes.

The sound of the *g* in the words *college, collegial,* and *colleague* is an example. Another complicating factor in English is the retention of historical spellings such as the *gh* in *ghost,* which is pronounced differently from the *gh* in *neighborhood* and the *ph* in *geography.* Other examples of spelling patterns that make the sound-symbol relationship so difficult to understand come easily to mind. Merely stating that spelling in English is unpredictable is an oversimplification of the reality of the language. Although teaching reading through a systematic phonetic program is essential, many other attributes of teaching reading, such as patterning, frequency of use, emotional impact of words, and oddity of spelling help children to make sense out of a seemingly irregular English language.

Some Learn to Read Easily, Others Don't. Why?

Most people do not remember more than the sketchiest details of the process they undertook in learning to read. They may remember the alphabet chart strung across the front of the classroom, their basal reader, the teacher writing a story as they dictated, or matching pictures to words on a worksheet. Nevertheless, they probably have no memory of how and when they finally made sense out of the written symbols to the point where they could read fluently and comprehend what they were reading.

What eventually happens to all fluent readers is that the process of decoding becomes automatic. They decode without conscious thought. This ability to carry out an act unconsciously occurs not only in reading but in many other habits and skills such as driving a car, tying shoelaces, playing the piano, or swinging a golf club. When someone first learns a skill, every aspect is consciously attended to. But over time, and with a great deal of practice, the brain "remembers" how to carry out all the procedures involved in the skill, allowing it to attend consciously to something else. This type of automatic processing is called *unconscious* or *implicit* *memory*. It comes into play in reading by allowing the reader to concentrate on the meaning of what is being read without having to think about deciphering every word. The downside to this unconscious memory is that knowledge about how this unconscious task is accomplished becomes very difficult to access. As a result, there has been no clear picture of the processes and procedures involved in learning to read. This lack of clarity about acquiring proficient reading habits partially explains the amount of intense debate over which teaching methods work best.

> What eventually happens to all fluent readers is that the process of decoding becomes automatic.

> But over time, and with a great deal of practice, the brain "remembers" how to carry out all the procedures involved in the skill, allowing it to attend consciously to something else.

To become a fluent reader, certain prereading skills need to be mastered, but emergent readers do not all learn these skills in the same way and at the same rate. A small percentage of children appear to learn to read on their own with no formal instruction before they enter kindergarten. Others learn to read fairly quickly once exposed to instruction.

However, too many children struggle throughout their school careers, continuing to read haltingly, and consequently lacking ability to fully comprehend what they are reading. Why this disparity? The answer to this question is complex. However, to begin to understand reading difficulties, two major factors, one biological and the other environmental or instructional, need to be explored.

Some Problems Have a Biological Basis

Neuroscience and educational research, when blended together, begin to give some rationale for struggling readers who have a biological or neurological difference from regularly progressing readers. We get a better understanding of neuroscience as it is defined as a science focusing on the nervous system. Neuroanatomy is the branch of neuroscience focused on the *structures* of the system, while the *functions* of the system are the focus of neurophysiology. Working together and uniquely separate, these two systems of study focus on the human central nervous system (the brain and spinal cord) and the peripheral nervous system (the cranial and spinal nerves to carry information from the brain and spinal cord). Neuroscientists use brain-imaging techniques, such as the **functional magnetic resonance imaging**, or fMRI, to examine brain activity when a task is processed and **computed tomography**, or CT, to provide detailed images of the anatomy and physiology of the nervous system. Obtaining a tentative picture of the brain components involved in reading gives a dynamic view of structures that have the potential to affect a child's ability to read.

> Neuroanatomy is the branch of neuroscience focused on the *structures* of the system, while the *functions* of the system are the focus of neurophysiology.

Dyslexia, a term coined by some researchers for specific reading disabilities, for example, appears to have a biological basis. While a complete composite of the specific structures involved in this disorder are often difficult to pinpoint, Bernard and Sally Shaywitz and their colleagues (2002) are beginning to make progress in identifying parts of the brain that play a role in this disorder. Specific research on dyslexia as a physiological disorder will be addressed later in this book.

Occasionally, adverse pregnancy or labor events can result in severe learning and/or reading problems for children (Berninger & Richards, 2002). Auditory and/or memory processing difficulties—found in an estimated 20 percent of all children—are additional causes of reading problems (Honig, 2001) and are most likely genetic factors resulting in some reading disabilities (Pennington, 1989; Scarborough, 1989). Hearing or visual impairment, verbal memory problems, and attention deficit hyperactivity disorder (ADHD) are other biological conditions that lead to risk factors for successful reading.

Looking at genetic and biological factors, we might assume that a child's intelligence quotient (IQ) would determine future reading success. This, however, does not appear to be the case. The results of a number of empirical studies on the correlation between IQ and reading achievement have shown that IQ is not a strong predictor of reading achievement, unless we are looking at children with severe cognitive deficiencies who usually develop very low, if any, proficiency in reading (Stanovich, Cunningham, & Cramer, 1984). Typically, IQ is more frequently used for entrance into a university than it is to predict school success. Regular educators and special educators alike identify children who test or respond at average or above intelligence ranges and also have difficulties with reading.

Care needs to be taken when attributing reading problems purely to biological factors. Discovering a child has a brain system that is not responding to instruction says little about the possibility for remediation. Young children's brains are remarkably plastic or open to change. The brain with its extraordinary ability to take in information and orchestrate complex behavioral responses is termed the "ultimate organ for adaptation" by the National Research Council, Institute of Medicine (2002). So researchers and educators alike realize the human brain's potential for remediation, and we are aware of biological factors that can be at the root of reading difficulties. However, the impressionable human brain can also be altered by the environment, in this case by the reader's experiences. The second set of factors influencing whether a child becomes a fluent reader leads to a discussion of environmental factors.

> Discovering a child has a brain system that is not responding to instruction says little about the possibility for remediation.

Other Problems Stem From Environmental Factors

Unfortunately, many children are capable of learning to read but do not make adequate progress because of their life's circumstances. Three major categories of circumstances influence whether children with no apparent biological deficits will reach their reading potential.

Instructional Factors

As a result of a massive effort, research-based guidelines and content standards for reading and language arts now identify specific information, concepts, and skills for children to master at each grade level. Reading First, now an initiative mature with age, is the portion of the federal government's No Child Left Behind Act that identifies five components for effective reading: phonemic awareness, phonics, reading fluency, vocabulary development, and reading comprehension. Alan Farstrup (2006), executive director of the International Reading Association, states, "Already, many students are benefiting from the additional professional development and resources made available to teachers through programs like Reading First. Recruitment of strong teacher candidates, excellent teacher preparation, and ongoing access to new research in support of best instructional practices are central elements in preparing students." In a previous strong statement for the success of the nation's students,

> "Instruction is the most important variable in achieving reading success" (Farstrup, 2000).

he applauds the alignment publishers have with reports, research, and recommendations. Additionally, he asserts that "teachers have heeded the call for reading reform and are teaching these components with vigor and sequence! Previous convictions about publishers not being informed of research or teachers following a potpourri of educational practices are no longer valid. Instruction is the most important variable in achieving reading success" (Farstrup, 2000).

So if it is not a lack of research-based, solid instruction, what is the cause for reading failure related to instructional factors? Studies have documented that the first-grade reader who makes poor reading progress continues to be a poor reader (Francis, Shaywitz, Stuebing, Shaywitz, & Fletcher, 1996; Torgesen & Burgess, 1998). Now, with appropriate instruction occurring in most public school classrooms, how can children continue to fail to become proficient readers? The response, quite simply, is that a lack of adequate instruction continues to be an environmental circumstance when children do not attend school consistently, change schools often, or are absent due to frequent illness.

Socioeconomic, Ethnic, and Second-Language Factors

Children of all social, ethnic, and economic groups experience reading problems. However, failure to read well, documented by national reading tests, is more common among nonwhite children, children who qualify for federal lunch programs, and nonnative speakers of English (NAEP, 2007). The reasons are complex. For example, Spanish-speaking students, who make up the largest group of limited-English-proficient (LEP) students in the United States, are particularly at risk. One obvious reason is the language difference itself, as evidenced by teachers who observe that when these students are taught to read in Spanish, many achieve excellent reading capabilities. However, this is not the only explanation. Children in good bilingual programs may still fall behind their English-speaking peers (Slavin & Madden, 1994). A thought worthy of study may be the confusion resulting from the English language as it is spoken at school and the language models children hear from the home environment when parents also attempt to learn English as a second language.

Low socioeconomic status (SES) also appears to play a role in reading achievement, although there is no consensus as to why. One possible explanation is that children with low SES tend to go to schools where there are fewer higher-achieving students and fewer educational opportunities. Another is that, unlike parents in middle-income homes, many low-SES parents provide fewer opportunities for informal literacy learning, a language-intense home environment, defined as visits to the library, joint book reading, play with print, independent reading, and frequent conversations with direct involvement with youth (Baker, Serpell, & Sonnenschein, 1995; Hart & Risley, 2003).

Early Language Development

As we shall see in Chapter 3, there is a close relationship between reading and language. In some children, inability to achieve reading proficiency seems to be attributable to a lack of exposure to language patterns and literacy-based interactions and materials during their early years (National Institute of Child Health and Human Development, 2000). Recent public concern focuses on television watching and impact on a young child's opportunity to experience language with real people. The American Academy of Pediatrics (AAP) recommends young children, under the age of two, have no television screen time and limits viewing of older preschool children to one to two hours a day of programs selected for their quality (Nemours Foundation, 2007). Current findings furthermore suggest that electronic sources can be excellent sources of education and entertainment for kids but caution that too much can have unhealthy side effects. Could it be that if children are not interacting with other people they are not experimenting with words and ideas?

> Recent public concern focuses on television watching and impact on a young child's opportunity to experience language with real people.

As with the development of all human abilities, genetic and biological factors cannot be dismissed or minimized in considering the ability to become a competent reader. However, whether a child becomes that reader is also dependent on the environment in which the child is raised. As author Ronald Kotulak (1997) so beautifully puts it, the genes are the building blocks of human development, but the environment is the on-the-job foreman.

THE BASICS OF READING

If teachers are asked to list all the skills a child needs to read, they might do so with some difficulty. As mentioned earlier, for nearly all adults, the act of reading has become an unconscious activity, its processes stored in a type of memory called *implicit* or *unconscious* memory. In the beginning, every step was a conscious process that had to be learned. Eventually, with a great deal of practice, reading gradually becomes a seamless, automatic activity carried out by the child's brain without conscious awareness.

> For nearly all adults, the act of reading has become an unconscious activity, its processes stored in a type of memory called *implicit* or *unconscious* memory.

As with any task that has reached the point of being cognitively automatic, the act of reading is difficult to explain (and equally difficult to teach) unless we break it down into its component parts. Many studies have focused on the act of reading, attempting to define each skill in the complex task of becoming a fluent reader who comprehends the meaning of print. The task is nearly impossible, as even before children learn to read in the conventional sense, most have developed complex neural networks of acquired information, word knowledge, skills, an oral language system, and the conceptual framework for projected reading success. A child's background for reading is inseparable from, but highly integrated with, skills training provided in a formal school system.

Emergent Literacy Skills

Some children on entering school and beginning formal reading instruction are more successful than other children. What are the prerequisite skills that make the difference? Although—as was mentioned earlier—biological factors are sometimes involved, many times the reason for differences can be traced to the amount of exposure to language children experience in the early years before they begin formal schooling.

The National Research Council coupled with other state agencies published a plethora of national reports emphasizing the importance of learning in the preschool years. High-quality preschool programs to prepare children to enter kindergarten ready to learn are unequivocally important, argue Head Start and Early Head Start proponents (McCardle & Chhabra, 2004). The National Reading Panel (Snow et al., 1998) states that reading is typically acquired relatively predictably by children who have normal or above-average language skills and have had experiences in early childhood that foster motivation and provide exposure to literacy in use.

Emergent literacy skills (sometimes called early childhood readiness skills or prereading skills) are terms used by researchers and educators to describe the skills acquired in early childhood that prepare future readers to gain the greatest benefit from formal reading instruction. These skills (e.g., knowledge about books, understanding how print works, being interested in reading and writing, playing with sounds and words, recognizing the alphabet, identifying common words from the environment) seem commonplace but appear to be highly predictable for reading ability. We realize, however, they are critical to reading. If ignored, they could put at risk a child who is tackling the difficult job of decoding print.

As we learn in Chapter 3, another milestone in language development is achieved when a young child begins to talk about what is being thought, including events and objects that are not visibly present. This language skill is termed **decontextualized text**. It is apparent as children increase the quantity of words they know and use in speaking. Additionally, as discussed in Pence and Justice (2008), the quality and depth of words they

> Another milestone in language development is achieved when a young child begins to talk about what is being thought, including events and objects that are not visibly present.

select to use when talking increases. These authors add another level of complexity for emergent literacy, **metalinguistic skills**, as children are observed to view language as worthy of their attention. Through planned and researched study, we learn that children who are able to focus their attention on reading and writing activities during the preschool years later achieve success in related school tasks (Justice & Ezell, 2004).

Reading Skills

Skill development for reading during the elementary years positions children to become fluent, accurate readers with keen dependency on the experiences they have during the preschool years. Educational use of terms to define the decoding process may appear to be confusing: *phonemic awareness*, *phonemes*, *phonics*, *phonological processing*, and *phonology*. There is a growing consensus that phonemic awareness provides the foundation for all reading decoding skills that follow. Children who are unable to hear and manipulate phonemes are also likely to be unable to figure out orthography, spelling patterns, for words. Many authors and researchers combine instruction, such as phonics, alphabetic principle, and word decoding, with sounds and letters under a large category called phonological processing. When vocabulary development, reading comprehension, and fluency are added to the instructional mix, we are aware of the complex reading system that must develop individually and concurrently for each child to become a proficient reader during the primary years.

Reading, Writing, and Literacy

The title of this book indicates that our primary concern is to understand how the brain of a child masters the processes of decoding print and eventually reads with fluency and comprehension. Chapter by chapter, we will continue scrutinizing aspects of learning to read with a focus on brain-related development. Most important, we consider how parents and teachers assist and support the learner with activities and information sensitive to and effective for the human brain to organize for reading. Notice, however, that learning to read without stumbling, while essential, is not sufficient. Literacy takes a variety of forms, from reading a listing in a phone book to researching and writing a dissertation.

Regardless of the difference in cognitive requirements of these activities, they all require the reader to move beyond decoding to understanding and often require being able to express that understanding in written form. Literacy is much broader than just being able to decode print. It involves writing, spelling, and other creative and analytical acts, such as speaking and listening. While it is not our primary emphasis, throughout this book we additionally address some of these broader literacy skills and examine what happens in the human brain to create a system capable of listening, speaking, reading, writing, and ultimately able to learn and remember.

REFLECTIVE QUESTIONS

1. Explain why reading in English is more difficult than reading in some other languages.

2. List and discuss at least two biological factors that can cause reading problems.

3. If you are reading this book as part of a study group, assign three people to make short presentations on three environmental factors that impact reading ability, instructional, socioeconomic, and early language development.

4. Many children come to school without the prerequisite skills for reading. What are these skills and how might educators influence their acquisition?

5. Assume you are making a presentation to parents of kindergarten and/or first-grade students. How would you explain emergent literacy skills, decontextualized language, and metalinguistic ability?

2

What Happens in the Brain When Children Read Words?

A serious desire to understand how children read must include efforts to gain basic knowledge of the brain's structures and their roles for learning. The human brain, weighing a little more or a little less than three pounds is divided into a right and left hemisphere. A huge band of nerve fibers, called the **corpus callosum**, joins the two hemispheres for communication. The outer quarter of an inch-thick layer, which allows us to process sensory data, communicate, think consciously, recall the past, and plan the future, is called the **cerebral cortex.** Within the cerebral cortex are four sets of lobes: **occipital lobes, parietal lobes, temporal lobes,** and **frontal lobes**. Other macrostructures located in the cerebral cortex are the **motor cortex** and the **somatosensory cortex.** The motor cortex allows us to plan and execute movement. The somatosensory cortex receives input from all the senses to signal what our body is experiencing.

While it is fascinating to be able to identify the large structures of the brain, teachers interested in understanding cognitive processes for reading eagerly examine more specific structures. Here is where we locate brain structures that connect highways of nerve cells, called neurons. Connective networks stimulate brain structures, such as **Broca's area** and **Wernicke's area**, to form well-used pathways that form naturally for oral language. The pathway for reading forms, not through a preprogrammed genetic mechanism, but through systematic instruction for reading.

Understanding how normally progressing readers develop skills provides a backdrop to understand struggling readers. Some children who have problems reading have a biological basis for their difficulties, while many others have what can be described as a "glitch" in the reading system, caused by genetic programming or environmental circumstances. Add the brain's systems for memory, and we begin to see how the complexities of the human brain can provide the foundation teachers and parents need to make good decisions about how to teach reading.

BRAIN BASICS

If educators are to make serious progress in understanding the developmental process experienced by children to read, efforts will need to be based on more than ideological debates on methodologies. A systematic study of the brain may offer the best hope. Since the 1980s, we have seen a tremendous explosion of research on brain structure and function. We've learned more about the human brain in recent years than in all of history.

> The breathtaking progress of scientific developments can be seen in brain-imaging techniques that show which parts of the brain are active when a person is engaged in various activities.

The breathtaking progress of scientific developments can be seen in brain-imaging techniques that show which parts of the brain are active when a person is engaged in various activities.

As we interweave neuroscience, genetic, and environmental influences, educators can benefit from interbehavioral conversations and begin to apply new understandings of how learning occurs in classrooms. Much research is based on human patients undergoing imaging for a variety of medical reasons. Other research is available based on animal studies to give insight into the complex nature of the human brain in a straightforward manner (National Research Council, Institute of Medicine, 2002). Whether information comes from animal or human models similar neural structures are studied. For educators to benefit from the current interplay between the science of neurology and the behavioral approach to education, a basic understanding of the human brain's structures and their roles is needed.

First, we will look at the overall structure (macrostructure) of the brain, then we will go deeper into the brain and look at the more specific brain structures and systems (microstructures) and how they connect to build a conductive pathway that allows a human brain to read.

Macrostructures

The human brain weighs only about three pounds, but its light weight belies its importance. All behavior that makes us human has its roots in the operations of the brain. A large fissure running from the back (posterior) of the brain to the front (anterior) divides the top of the brain into two hemispheres, a right and a left. Each hemisphere has its own specialties, but the hemispheres work in concert because they are joined by a huge band of nerve fibers called the *corpus callosum*. These specialties will be further delineated as we begin to look at the processes involved in language and reading.

> The human brain weighs only about three pounds, but its light weight belies its importance. All behavior that makes us human has its roots in the operations of the brain.

The outer one-quarter-inch-thick layer covering both hemispheres is called the *cerebral cortex*. (*Cortex* is the Latin word for "bark.") Within the cortex lie the abilities that make us uniquely human—the abilities to take in and process sensory data, communicate using language, be aware of what we are thinking (consciousness), recall the past and plan for the future, be aware of our emotions, create theories, move our body parts, and perform a myriad of other functions, including our ability to read. Each hemisphere is divided into four lobes (see Figure 2.1).

Starting at the very back of the human brain are the *occipital lobes*, which are primarily responsible for taking in and interpreting visual stimuli. The cortex covering the occipital lobes is often called the *visual cortex*. Between the occipital lobes at the back of the brain and the frontal lobes in the front of the brain, and behind the motor and sensory cortices, described below, are the *parietal lobes*. This pair of lobes additionally is located directly above the thalamus, defined later as the human brain's information relay system. The ideal placement of the parietal

Figure 2.1   The brain with the four lobes labeled.

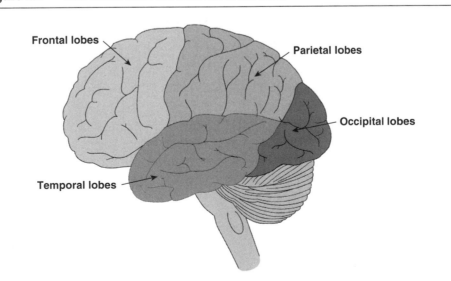

lobes allows them to receive tactile (pressure, temperature, pain) and other sensory information (visual and auditory). The parietal lobes are responsible for integrating all this information with the executive functions of the frontal lobes through working memory. In this case, information is maintained in mind while the child executes a particular task (Pence & Justice, 2008). Additional functions of the parietal lobes determine a general sense of well-being or discomfort and opportunity or danger. The ***temporal lobes*** are located on the sides of the brain above the ears. The cortex covering them is called the *auditory cortex*. The temporal lobes are responsible for taking in and interpreting auditory stimuli. Structures within the temporal lobes also control the production of speech and aspects of memory. Right behind the forehead and extending back over the top of the brain are the ***frontal lobes***. This area of the human brain encompasses slightly less than half (41 percent) of the cerebral cortex and is involved with conscious decisions and behaviors. Often referred to as the "chief executive officer" of the brain, the frontal lobes are responsible for problem solving, dealing with abstractions from sensory information, future planning, and other higher-order thinking skills. When a person is engaged in demanding cognitive tasks, neuroscientists see heightened activity in the frontal lobe area of the brain. Due to these intense activities science refers to the area covering the frontal lobes as the *association cortex*.

Two individual parts of the cerebral cortex deserve special attention (see Figure 2.2). Toward the back of the frontal lobes is a strip of cells called the **motor cortex**. It stretches across the top of the brain like a headband

Figure 2.2   The brain showing the motor cortex and somatosensory cortex.

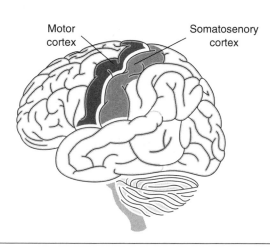

Motor cortex

Somatosenory cortex

and controls all motor functions except reflexes. Different sections of this strip govern the movements of specific muscles in the body with the amount of space on the cortex being directly related to the required preciseness of the area regulated. Immediately behind the motor cortex lies the *somatosensory cortex*. Just as the motor cortex sends messages out to the various muscles in the body about how and when to move, the somatosensory cortex receives information from the environment about temperature, the position of our limbs, sensations of pain, and pressure. As with the motor cortex, each part of the body is represented by a specific area on the surface of the somatosensory cortex.

Microstructures

Almost anything a person does, from moving a hand to picking up a glass to reading a book, requires unbelievable coordination among numerous small brain structures. As we begin to look at some of these microstructures of the brain, note that although each microstructure is addressed separately, none of them works alone. No one area of the brain is devoted to "comprehension" or "semantics"; rather, every task or function involves an interconnected group of structures. Each area within the group makes a specific contribution to the performance of the task. Therefore, trying to determine the exact functions of a specific part of the brain or the neural pathways involved in language or reading is a challenge.

> Almost anything a person does, from moving a hand to picking up a glass to reading a book, requires unbelievable coordination among numerous small brain structures.

For years, scientists have worked to understand the brain processes involved in language, but they were limited to studies of the brains of people whose language problems were caused by neurological disease, strokes, or other injuries that often caused some type of *aphasia*. (Aphasia is the partial or complete loss of abilities to comprehend or produce language following damage to the brain.) During the last two decades of the twentieth century, however, exciting new brain-imaging techniques have allowed scientists to picture the normal brain at work processing language.

Imaging techniques most frequently used by neuroscientists are positron emission tomography (PET), magnetic source imaging (MSI), and functional magnetic resonance imaging (fMRI). Simply defined, PET imaging traces the amount of glucose used by the cells of different structures of the brain as a person is engaged in various mental activities. It requires that radioactive glucose be injected into the bloodstream. MSI and fMRI, on the other hand, are less invasive as they do not require the injection of any substance. Rather, these imaging techniques measure the amount of oxygen being used by the cells, which are viewed as soft tissue in the brain. From this process, researchers can establish a correspondence between images of brain activation patterns and the psychological functions particular to a complex cognitive skill, such as reading. The functional aspect of fMRIs allows views of brain activity and changes during the imaged event. For educational purposes baseline activity is used to reveal malfunctions or deviations from anticipated rates of metabolism, which are low (hypoactivation) or are observed to be unusually high, which corresponds to hyperactivation (McCardle & Chhabra, 2004). Essentially, neurologists attempt to account for differences in reading performance by looking at the underlying brain circuits that support reading activities.

> Essentially, neurologists attempt to account for differences in reading performance by looking at the underlying brain circuits that support reading activities.

Although the way the brain works while normally processing language is not thoroughly understood, most researchers agree that there are numerous structures and areas central to language. As we described, reading and writing press into use the structures and pathways used to speak and understand language, so we will begin by looking at these structures.

Brain Structures Involved in Language

Oral language is a kind of code consisting of a set of spoken symbols that represent the words of the language. Once we break the code, we can understand the language. Language is a very complex code, however, requiring us to manipulate all its forms (words, sentences, and intonation) that refer to objects, actions, and thoughts (Caplan, 1995). What goes on in the brain when we select our words, activate the sounds for each word, select the correct order of words based upon underlying rules to form a sentence (the syntax), and finally determine the proper intonation to convey the meaning?

> Oral language is a kind of code consisting of a set of spoken symbols that represent the words of the language.

Auditory Cortex

Much language is generated in response to information coming into the brain from the environment, for example, during a conversation with another person. The first stepping-stone on the language pathway is for the brain to recognize that the stimulus being received is sound (see Figure 2.3a and b). The structures that make this preliminary distinction are the *thalamus* and the *auditory cortex*. The thalamus is the receiving point for all incoming sensory data (with the exception of smell), and its job is to act as a sort of relay station, sending messages to the appropriate part of the cortex for further processing. In this case, the sound stimulus is sent to the primary auditory cortex, which is located in the front of the temporal lobe.

Figure 2.3a   Diagram of the oral language pathway in the brain.

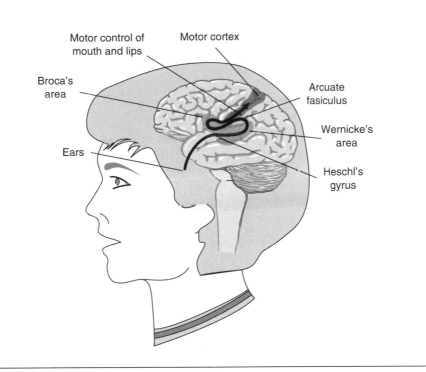

Heschl's Area

The thalamus and the auditory cortex appear to work in concert to determine if the incoming stimulus is language or some other type of sound such as environmental noise, music, or random sound. Analysis of the auditory input to recognize if it is indeed speech happens in Heschl's gyrus, the next step of the language pathway. This area, also referred to as the transverse temporal gyri, was named specifically for Richard L. Heschl, an Austrian anatomist who identified critical aspects of auditory processing in the temporal area. In this small left temporal region, the sounds are processed for speech, particularly hearing language. Note the use of the term *gyrus*, meaning a ridge in the folds of the brain. More than one gyrus becomes *gyri*, and a groove between gyri is called a *sulcus* (or a particularly deep groove is a fissure). These terms, gyrus and sulcus, are common in describing other areas of the brain as well. In relationship to identifying sounds as speech we are cautioned to not limit the activity to the left temporal lobe, as it appears that at least some aspects of speech processing occur bilaterally. Indications are that

> Analysis of the auditory input to recognize if it is indeed speech happens in Heschl's gyrus, the next step of the language pathway.

Figure 2.3b   Flow chart of the oral language pathway.

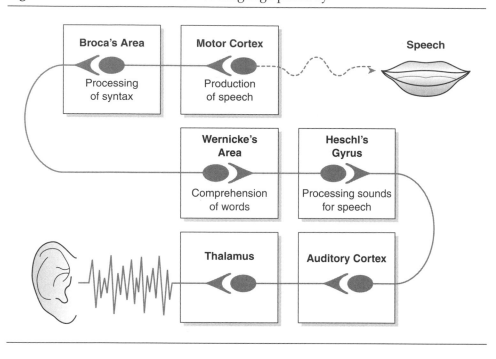

a rapid identification of sounds as language occurs in the left hemisphere, whereas the overall analysis of speech characteristics (distinguishing qualities, appearance) are right hemisphere temporal activities (Pence & Justice, 2008). Once the sounds have been identified as language, the next stepping-stone on the pathway is **Wernicke's area.**

Wernicke's Area

Named for its discoverer, Austrian neurologist Karl Wernicke, this group of cells is located at the junction of the parietal and temporal lobes in the left hemisphere very near the auditory cortex. (For about 9 out of 10 right-handed and nearly two-thirds of left-handed people, the major language structures reside in the left hemisphere [Restak, 2001].) The traditional view of Wernicke's area is that it is the semantic processing center and that it plays a significant role in the conscious comprehension of the spoken words by both the listener and the speaker. It appears to contain a sort of lexicon that stores memories of the sounds that make up words. It uses this internal "dictionary" to determine whether the incoming phoneme patterns or words are meaningful at this step of the language pathway.

In this sense, words are not understood until they are processed by Wernicke's area. People who have had damage to this particular area of the brain (called *Wernicke's aphasia*) have no difficulty speaking; however, much of their speech makes no sense. These people also lack the ability to monitor their own speech and do not appear to be aware that they are sub-stituting nonwords for real ones and that to the listener much of what they are saying is meaningless (Carter, 1998). Persons with Wernicke's aphasia also have difficulty comprehending what others are saying to them.

The Arcuate Fasiculus and Broca's Area

Our language pathway is not yet complete. There are two remaining stepping-stones, both controlled by the second major language area of the left hemisphere. The first is the **arcuate fasiculus.** Information leaving Wernicke's area needs to reach the frontal language regions of the brain for speech to occur. This feat is accomplished by means of a band of connect-ing neural fibers called the arcuate fasiculus. Damage to the conductive pathway of the arcuate fasiculus can result in what is called *conduction aphasia*, where people are not able to repeat what is said to them because the incoming words from Wernicke's area cannot be passed on to the area of the brain responsible for articulation.

The next stepping-stone on the language pathway is called **Broca's area**. This brain region was named for the French neurologist Paul Broca, who first discovered it in the late 1860s. Located in the left hemisphere at the back of the frontal lobe, Broca's area was originally thought to be primarily involved in language production. It has often been referred to as the expressive language center of the brain. Adjoining the section of the motor cortex that con-trols the jaw, larynx, tongue, and lips, Broca's area appears to convert words into a code to direct the muscle move-ments involved in speech production.

> Recent studies have suggested that while it does control production of speech, Broca's area—probably along with some of the surrounding cortical structures—has a second major language function, that of processing syntax, or assembling words into sensible phrases that are grammatically correct.

People who have damage to this area (called *Broca's aphasia*) produce a sort of halting, "telegraphic" speech using nouns, verbs, and adjectives while often omitting conjunctions and other parts of speech.

Recent studies have suggested that while it does control production of speech, Broca's area—probably along with some of the surrounding cortical structures—has a second major language function, that of processing syntax, or assembling words into sensible phrases that are grammatically correct. This ability to organize words is essential for meaning. A string of words becomes a sentence only when appropriate grammatical constructions are in place.

Language in the Right Hemisphere

Although the left hemisphere is nearly always dominant for lan-guage processing, this does not mean that the right hemisphere plays no role. Studies of persons with right hemispheric damage and of "split-brain" subjects (persons whose hemispheres cannot communicate with one another because the corpus callosum, the band of fibers connecting the two hemispheres, has been surgically severed) have shown that the right hemisphere can read and understand simple sentences. However, the major role that the right hemisphere seems to play is in the affect, or emotional aspects, given to spoken language. A stroke or lesion in the language areas of the right hemisphere does not affect the ability of a person to speak, but his or her speech is devoid of or limited in emotional content. Other right hemispheric functions, such as appreciating humor and recognizing metaphors, are also often affected by stroke or trauma.

A Caveat

Although the terms *Broca's area* and *Wernicke's area* are commonly used, these language areas are not neat modules with clearly defined borders. A danger exists of overstating the significance of a given cortical area for a particular function, as it may be that each area is involved in more than one language function (Frackowiak et al., 2004; Gazzaniga, 1998). The areas of the brain associated with language—its reception, comprehension, processing, and production—are still being studied. As mentioned earlier, it is difficult to map the detailed functions of the language system directly onto the brain's complex anatomical structures. Given these constraints, scientists have, however, produced a tentative architecture of the brain's language pathway that has fairly accurate validity and is useful in our quest to understand what goes on in the brain when we process both spoken and written language (Bear, Conners, & Paradiso, 1996) (see Figure 2.3a and b).

> A danger exists of overstating the significance of a given cortical area for a particular function, as it may be that each area is involved in more than one language function.

Brain Structures Involved in Reading

One of the miracles of the brain is that engaging in a conversation involves all the brain macrostructures and microstructures just described, but learning how to talk does not require an understanding of them or conscious attention to their processes. While reading these words, fluent readers are not conscious of the structures that are being activated to allow them to process and comprehend the print. However, for some children these processes are not automatic. It is critical for teachers of

> One of the miracles of the brain is that engaging in a conversation involves all the brain macrostructures and microstructures just described, but learning how to talk does not require an understanding of them or conscious attention to their processes.

these children to understand these underlying processes and how they come to be automatic (or don't). Without this understanding, teachers will not be able to comprehend or use the research on dyslexia and other reading research that is being conducted. Therefore, our next task is to examine the structures (in addition to the ones just discussed) that the brain uses to decode and comprehend print.

The Neural Pathway for Reading

As we have discussed, many of the structures used in reading are the same as those used for spoken language. However, print is a relatively recent invention and requires the brain to co-opt structures that were perhaps designed for other purposes. We will look at two additional areas of the brain that are infused into the pathway for reading: the *visual cortex* and the *angular gyrus*.

Visual Cortex

The human visual system is one of the most studied and best understood areas of the brain. Although a thorough discussion of this system is beyond the scope of this book, a basic understanding is necessary in order to appreciate its role in the reading process. Visual information is contained in the light that is reflected from objects. As light rays enter the eyes, they are transduced, or changed into electrical impulses, and are sent from the eyes through the optic nerves to the thalamus. The job of the thalamus is to relay this information to the primary visual cortex located in the occipital lobes. It is here in the visual cortex that the brain begins the initial step of reading by recognizing the visual pattern of a word (Gazzaniga, 1998). It does this by calling into use an already existing visual feature extraction system for visual stimuli in general. The brain has adapted this system to allow it to process letter strings, as well as other visual features. Even though the features of the word have been extracted, the string of letters has not been perceived as a word. That job falls partially to another structure, the angular gyrus.

Angular Gyrus

Located at the junction of the occipital, parietal, and temporal lobes, the angular gyrus is perfectly situated to be a bridge between the visual word recognition system and the rest of the language processing system. It is located near Heschl's gyri, which is a part of the oral language pathway. The letters of the written words appear to be translated in the angular gyrus into

> Located at the junction of the occipital, parietal, and temporal lobes, the angular gyrus is perfectly situated to be a bridge between the visual word recognition system and the rest of the language processing system.

Figure 2.4a   Diagram of the silent reading pathway in the brain.

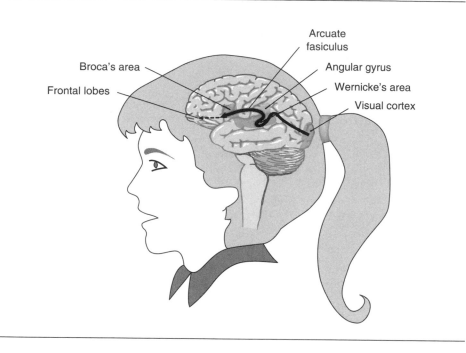

the sounds or **phonemes** of spoken language. This function of hearing sounds without letters attached occurred naturally for oral language, but it appears for the angular gyrus to become a step in the reading pathway sounds must be practiced, repeated, reorganized, and literally "played with." These activities recognized as phonemic awareness training stimulate the angular gyrus to become an accepted detour in the well-established oral language path.

Without this transformation, reading and writing would be impossible. Indeed, damage to the angular gyrus disrupts both reading and writing (Carter, 1998). Sally Shaywitz (2003), in discussing the neurobiology of reading and dyslexia, states that the angular gyrus is pivotal in carrying out cross-modal integration (auditory and visual) and mapping the sights of print onto the phonemic structures of language. In essence, the angular gyrus, in conjunction with Wernicke's area, is the "hub" where all the relevant information about how a word looks, how it sounds, and what it means is tightly bound together and stored (Shaywitz, 2003). From this point forward, processing of the written word follows pretty much the same pathway as spoken language, going from the angular gyrus to Wernicke's area, across the arcuate fasiculus to Broca's area, and, if reading aloud, to the motor cortex for the production of speech.

We can now add to the diagram the additional structures used in the brain for processing written language (see Figure 2.4a and b). Remember

Figure 2.4b Flow chart of the silent reading pathway.

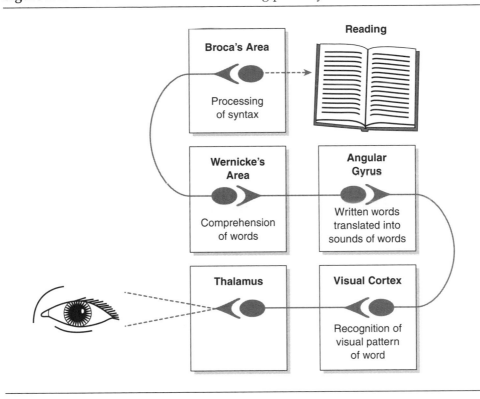

that the brain is a parallel processor, and the pathway for reading is not as linear as a drawing makes it appear. Also, the specific task affects which structures (in which hemispheres) will be activated. Reading aloud activates different structures from those used in reading silently (Bookheimer, Zeffiro, Blaxton, Gaillard, & Theodore, 1995; Eden, Turkeltaub, Weisberg, Flowers, & Basu, 2004). The Eden study refers to oral reading as story reading and states it is likely to demand activation of more brain regions used for semantic and syntactic language processing than is required for decoding words. Listening to text activates different parts of the brain than does word ordering or syntactic judgments during word decoding. Which pathways are activated may also depend on how practiced or automatic a task is. However, an understanding of the general functions of the structures involved in processing spoken and written language will allow educators to be more informed consumers of reading research and better able to understand how particular neural deficits affect children's ability to read.

> Listening to text activates different parts of the brain than does word ordering or syntactic judgments during word decoding.

READING PROBLEMS WITH A BIOLOGICAL BASIS

In Chapter 1, we discussed some of the reasons children fail to learn to read. As was mentioned, some problems stem from genetic or biological factors. Now that we have examined the structures and pathways the brain uses to read words, we can look at what happens when one or more of these systems fail to work normally. People whose reading difficulties stem from neurological sources are called *dyslexic* by scientific researchers, and it is a term used by educators for some reading problems based on word analysis or decoding. **Dyslexia** is a brain disorder that primarily affects a person's ability to read and write words (Bloom, Beal, & Kupfer, 2003). This disability is separate from intelligence.

Persons with dyslexia generally have normal or above-normal intelligence and their higher-order skills are intact. Their problem is not behavioral, psychological, motivational, or social. Dyslexia appears to be fairly widespread. Although reading experts may not all agree on the prevalence of this disorder, Shaywitz believes that it can be found in as many as 17 percent of school-aged children and as many as 40 percent of the adult population (Shaywitz & Shaywitz, 2001). Dyslexia can be either developmental or acquired as the result of some injuries to the brain such as trauma, tumor, or stroke. However, what both developmental dyslexia and acquired dyslexia have in common is a disruption in the neural pathways for reading. People do not outgrow dyslexia. Even though as adults they may become more proficient at reading words, they still have difficulty reading unfamiliar words and are not as fluent or automatic in their reading as a nonimpaired reader (Shaywitz & Shaywitz, 2001).

Visual Processing Problems

Because reading begins with visual input, any problem in the visual system can affect the ability to process print. A growing body of research shows that some poor readers may have subtle sensory deficits in visual processing (Berninger, 2002). These deficits may manifest as poor eye health, poor visual acuity, and/or slower than normal eye movements. Imaging studies of adults with dyslexia conducted at the National Institute of Mental Health (Eden et al., 2004; Eden et al., 1996) detected subtle deficits in the visual motion detection area of their brains, known as brain region V5/MT. Nonimpaired readers showed robust activity in this area, while persons with dyslexia showed almost no activity. This area of the visual cortex has connections to areas that are active in phonological processing, and it is possible that it plays an important role in the processing of written words.

Eden and others believe these findings indicate that dyslexia is a discrete brain disorder and that the source of some reading difficulties may stem from visual deficits rather than problems in the language-related areas. Still other studies are finding that minor differences in how the brain handles the visual processing of images, color, and contrast, as well as fast motion, can impede reading (Eden et al., 2004; Wolf, 2007).

MaryAnne Wolf (2007) identifies the cingulate gyrus located in the frontal lobes, below the deep fissure between the two hemispheres, as an area equipped for visual processing. It appears this portion of the executive system functions specific to reading by directing the visual system to focus and pay attention to the visual features of letters and words. A novice reader is directed to focus attention to specific intricacies of letter forms, making one a *b*, while with a slight change it becomes a *d* or *p* or *q*. Semantic processing for the meaning of words can also come from this analytical visual area as it looks for variances in word meanings and implications: For example, "How can it be that the nose runs and feet smell?"

> It appears this portion of the executive system functions specific to reading by directing the visual system to focus and pay attention to the visual features of letters and words (Wolf, 2007).

Auditory Processing Problems

Educators are often surprised to learn that in an fMRI or PET scan (which depicts activity levels in the brain) the auditory cortex is active even when a person is reading silently. This occurs because the brain is busy processing all the "sounds" associated with reading through an activity called subvocalization, just as it would be if the person were listening to someone speak (Bookheimer, Zeffiro, Blaxton, Gaillard, & Theodore, 1995). It is not surprising, then, that deficits within the auditory processing areas of the brain are another source of reading problems. These deficits can occur anywhere along the auditory pathway, with the most obvious being a hearing impairment or deafness.

Chronic ear infections (chronic otitis media) often lead to intermittent hearing loss in young children and may have a negative effect on language development and, consequently, on reading. Farther along the auditory pathway, other problems can occur. Recall that, in order to read, children must be able to process the auditory sounds of the language by identifying the sounds (phonemes), linking the phonemes, then associating them to the written words. In English, vowels change relatively slowly, but stop consonants, such as *b* and *p*, change more rapidly.

Researcher Michael Merzenich and his colleagues at the University of California at San Francisco have discovered that some poor readers do not process these consonant sounds quickly enough (Merzenich et al., 1996). This means that a person with this auditory processing deficit would not be able to clearly distinguish the difference between "bat" and "pat." Although the original research was conducted with adults, subsequent research has shown that children suffer from the same deficit (Temple et al., 2003). Using commercially available programs, such as Fast ForWord or Earobics that focus on auditory processing and oral language training, researchers have been able to train the brains of some dyslexic children to increase the speed and accuracy with which they process rapidly successive and rapidly changing sounds. Brain imaging scans of children who completed the Fast ForWord program showed that critical higher-order areas necessary for reading could be activated for the first time (Temple et al., 2003). Whether the training results in actual long-term changes in these higher-order areas or if the changes in the basic auditory system are providing information to the higher-order areas is not known at this point (J. Gabrieli, personal communication, April 6, 2003).

Problems in the Oral Language/Reading Pathways

> Although many reading difficulties can be attributed to visual or auditory processing deficits, more often the central difficulty appears to be a deficit in the system that integrates the sensory input from both the ears (auditory/temporal) and the eyes (occipital/visual) into a language system for reading.

Although many reading difficulties can be attributed to visual or auditory processing deficits, more often the central difficulty appears to be a deficit in the system that integrates the sensory input from both the ears (auditory/temporal) and the eyes (occipital/visual) into a language system for reading. The language/reading pathway of the brain can be conceptualized as a hierarchy of lower- and higher-level skills.

At the higher levels are the neural systems that process semantics (the meaning of the language), syntax (organizing words into comprehensible sentences), and discourse (speaking and writing). Underlying these abilities are the lower-level phonological skills dedicated to deciphering the reading code.

In simple terms, the lower levels handle decoding while the higher levels are dedicated to comprehension. This is a reciprocal process. As a person reads, the brain shifts back and forth between decoding and comprehension. As we have seen, scientists are now able to map the neural structures that process both the higher- and the lower-level skills involved in language and reading. Phonological processing occurs in the back of the left hemisphere (in most people) in the angular gyrus and Wernicke's area. The more skilled readers are, the more ease they have to activate this region. Higher-level comprehension skills are handled largely by the frontal regions of the left hemisphere in Broca's area and the frontal lobes. Problems or deficits in either of these areas appear to be central to many reading difficulties, including and beyond simple decoding.

The Glitch in the System

While educators have long known that poor readers have difficulty "sounding out" unfamiliar words or do so slowly and with difficulty, there has been little research to help them understand why these problems occur. With the advent of brain-imaging technology, this is changing. Sally and Bennett Shaywitz, pediatricians and neuroscientists at the National Institute of Child Health and Human Development (NICHD)–Yale Center for the Study of Learning and Attention and their colleagues have conducted some current, illuminating research.

Using fMRI, a noninvasive imaging technique, these researchers studied 144 children by scanning their brains while they read (Shaywitz et al., 2002). The children ranged in age from 7 to 18 years. Of the readers, 70 were dyslexic and 74 were nonimpaired. What they discovered is that brain activation patterns differed significantly between the two groups.

In nonimpaired readers, there is activity in both the frontal (Broca's area) and the posterior regions (Wernicke's area and the angular gyrus) in the left hemisphere of the brain. However, in the dyslexic readers, there is a relative underactivation in the posterior areas and a relative overactivation in the frontal regions. As Sally Shaywitz (2003) states, "It is as if these struggling readers are using the systems in front of the brain to try to compensate for the disruption in the back of the brain" (p. 81).

> "It is as if these struggling readers are using the systems in front of the brain to try to compensate for the disruption in the back of the brain" (Shaywitz, 2003, p. 81).

In other words, it appears that the dyslexic readers are using the frontal regions as a sort of "alternative backup" to try to decode, because the areas that would normally serve to interpret the written code are not working as they should. This pattern seems to be universal in readers struggling to decode words, no matter which language they speak or what their age. An earlier study conducted by the same team of researchers showed that this failure to activate the phonological processing area of the brain continues into adulthood if there is no reading intervention (Shaywitz & Shaywitz, 2001).

This research shows that there is a physiological basis, or "glitch" in the system, for some reading difficulties. As Sally Shaywitz states (2003), "Most likely as the result of a genetically programmed error, the neural system necessary for phonologic analysis is somehow miswired, and a child is left with a phonologic impairment that interferes with spoken and written language" (p. 68). For educational practices, this study indicates children who struggle to decode words do not have a genetic predisposition to activate the area of the brain that puts letters, sounds, and words together. Or they have not been exposed to enough practice and play with words and their sounds to build mighty neural connections to the areas of the brain that will make them successful decoders.

Another study led by Bennett and Sally Shaywitz and their colleagues (2002) compared the brain scans of 43 young adults who were impaired (dyslexic) readers with 27 *nonimpaired* readers. These two groups had been followed since elementary school and were from similar socioeconomic backgrounds and had comparable reading prerequisite skills when they began school. What the researchers discovered was surprising: There appeared to be two distinct types of brain problems in the dyslexic readers. One is predominantly genetic, as reported in the earlier study. These students, as we have seen, appear to have a genetically programmed glitch in their neural circuitry and enlist other parts of their brains to compensate. The result is they can read and comprehend, but they read slowly.

The findings from the second group are even more interesting. The researchers have determined that these readers have what they call "a more environmentally influenced" type of dyslexia. Their brains' systems for processing sounds and language were intact, but the brain scans of these readers showed that rather than using the usual language structures in the left hemisphere to process print, they created an alternate neural pathway, reading mostly with regions in the right hemisphere—areas not as well suited for reading. The portion of the right frontal lobe, which was activated in these readers, is an area that is primarily devoted to memory. These readers appeared to rely on memory to read. This rote-based type of learning can get the student to a certain point, usually the second grade, but eventually, words become too long and there is too much to memorize. The system fails. As Sally Shaywitz states,

> [These] persistently poor readers have a rudimentary system in place, but it's not connected well. They weren't able to develop and connect it right because they haven't had that early stimulation. If you can provide these children early on with effective reading instruction, these children can really learn to read. (Shaywitz et al., 2002)

> Researchers, using . . . brain imaging, may be able to neurologically validate effective strategies for helping struggling readers as they observe changes that take place in the neural systems for reading as the result of specific reading interventions.

These exciting findings have major implications for those who study and teach reading. Researchers, using their understanding and background in brain imaging, may be able to neurologically validate effective strategies for helping struggling readers as they observe changes that take place in the neural systems for reading as the result of specific reading interventions. These interventions and the implication for educational practice will be discussed in later chapters.

ATTENTION AND MEMORY SYSTEMS

Thus far, we have been examining the physiological structures the brain has adapted to allow us to read. Attention and memory systems are a bit more difficult to localize in the brain than are the sensory processes. However, an understanding of how the brain's memory systems function is essential to understanding the reading process, since successful reading relies on these systems.

As we know, phonemic awareness and phonological processing are necessary components to decode words, but they are not sufficient. In addition, we previously identified that the beginning reader must be able to concentrate on different shapes and combinations of letters through focused attention (concentration) and hold a visual image in memory. What does it mean to pay attention or to have a good memory? Actually, it can mean many things. First, let's look at a model that is commonly used to differentiate among the three major memory systems of the brain.

Sensory Memory

Figure 2.5 depicts how the brain takes in or discards incoming information, manipulates it, and stores it. The first box in the diagram is labeled Sensory Memory and defines the initial stage of information processing, taking in sensory data, and determining what to keep and what to drop. Sensory memory can be thought of as the brain's attention system, which can function both consciously or unconsciously. Because much of the sensory stimuli impinging on the body—the feeling of clothing against the body, for example—is not relevant at any given moment, perhaps 99 percent or more is immediately discarded. A sensory system able to focus on letters and words rather than on random stimuli provides the initial step in becoming a reader.

> Sensory memory can be thought of as the brain's attention system, which can function both consciously or unconsciously.

Many factors influence a child's ability to focus attention. Inability to concentrate on a task can be the result of hunger, fatigue, and other physical factors as well as the emotional state of the child, environmental noise and/or temperature, or an inappropriate level of difficulty of the material. Given the right conditions, however, most children have little or no difficulty paying attention to relevant stimuli, but some do. Possibly the most well known, but still inadequately understood, biological condition to

Figure 2.5 Diagram of information processing model.

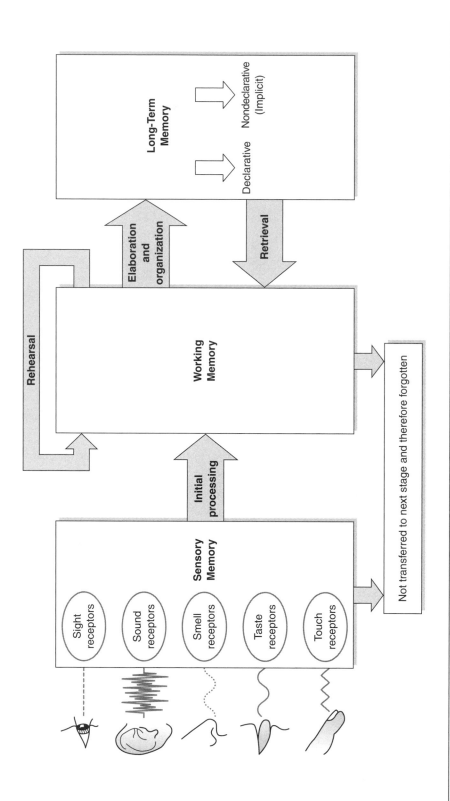

impact focused attention is attention deficit/hyperactivity disorder (ADHD). ADHD is a label given to a neurobiological disorder some children have that interferes with their capacity to attend to tasks selected by others and regulate their behavior to be appropriate in different environments. Although ADHD and reading disability are distinct disorders, there is good evidence that they can occur together. According to researcher Sally Shaywitz, reading disability is relatively common in children with attention problems. Shaywitz estimates that this occurs in 31 percent of first-grade children, becoming a more serious problem for reading as the child grows older. She estimates that over 50 percent of ninth-grade students diagnosed with ADHD have a reading disability (Shaywitz, Fletcher, & Shaywitz, 1994). This disorder is contained to some degree by medication and/or behavioral therapy.

> ADHD is a label given to a neurobiological disorder some children have that interferes with their capacity to attend to tasks selected by others and regulate their behavior to be appropriate in different environments.

Coupled with information from Shaywitz, a study by researchers from the National Institute of Mental Health and McGill University used imaging techniques to study children with ADHD. Their findings are refreshing for parents, educators, and students alike. The areas of the brain needed for attention to appropriate sensory stimuli and an ability to modulate motor activity are normal for children diagnosed with ADHD at the preschool and kindergarten age. However, the significant outcome from the study is that these brain systems develop more slowly than they do in other children. Furthermore, authors of the study, which analyzed measures of social and intellectual development from over 16,000 children, suggest that children who have attention and behavior concerns in kindergarten can be "worked around" in the classroom. The behaviors did not correlate with academic success by the end of elementary school for three out of four students (Carey, 2007).

Working Memory

The filtering of stimuli that occurs in sensory memory happens so quickly and efficiently that it is an unconscious process. The brain is continuously taking in sensory stimuli, assembling and sorting the data, and directing only some of it to conscious attention. MaryAnn Wolf (2007) describes working memory as our cognitive blackboard or scratch pad. Although conscious processing represents only a small part of information processing, without it readers would not be able to retain the first part of a sentence they are reading to its end. Working memory allows the brain to hold on to visual or auditory information for a short time, approximately 18 seconds. However, the brain can retain the information longer by rehearsing it. Researcher Alan Baddeley (1986) coined the term "articulatory loop" to describe this type of rehearsal.

Think about a child who is given several directions at a time or who is trying to remember a series of letters to spell a multisyllabic word. Most children mentally repeated the directions or the letters of the word over and over using their own articulatory loop, often by subvocalizing the information, as well. When a memory is retained through rehearsal strategies, a strong neural foundation is formed. The term *long-term potentiation* (LTP) is used when neurons, the brain's cells, form strong chemical connections among communication networks (Nevins, 2007). For readers, LTP is critical to memory required for reading with automaticity. Future chapters will deal with teaching decisions and learning strategies that force long-term potentiation as information, skills, and concepts move from practice in working memory into long-term memory for conscious or unconscious recall.

> Although conscious processing represents only a small part of information processing, without it readers would not be able to retain the first part of a sentence they are reading to its end.

This verbal or subvocalized rehearsal appears to be essential for comprehension of what is being read. According to research, skilled readers cannot remember—or comprehend—a complex sentence when they are prevented from subvocalizing its wording (Baddeley, 1986). The chemicals in the brain that allow memories to become hardwired are not activated (Nevins, 2007). While children can be observed repeating songs and phrases, this is generally not done with a conscious understanding of the need to rehearse to remember information. This understanding of the need to rehearse information to remember it often does not occur spontaneously until around age 7 or 8. However, children can be taught to do this earlier (Kail, 1984). Younger—and poorer—readers often do not engage in this type of rehearsal. This is especially true for children in homes where parents do not automatically or intentionally use rehearsal strategies.

It is easy to imagine how a young child without a habit to practice language skills, and with a slow-to-develop or dysfunctional verbal memory system, could be negatively affected in reading development. However, the problem may not necessarily be in the articulatory loop. Other aspects of working memory may be completely normal but still work against the reading process. (Remember that even the brain that works normally was not designed for reading.) To understand these, we

> It is easy to imagine how a young child without a habit to practice language skills, and with a slow-to-develop or dysfunctional verbal memory system, could be negatively affected in reading development.

need to become familiar with several other characteristics of a normal working memory that affect the ability to decode and comprehend print.

Solitary Focus

The human brain can focus on only one train of thought at a time. This brain feature, often referred to as the cocktail party effect, points to the conflict the brain has when interesting, important verbal stimuli come from two or more sources, such as when one is at a cocktail party. The brain has a problem: It can pay conscious attention to only one conversation at a time. People can *do* two things at the same time if one is automatic. This phenomenon is familiar. Who hasn't arrived at a familiar location without being aware of driving there? The procedure of driving was so automatic that you were able to think through a problem, develop a grocery list, or even plan a meal at the same time you were driving.

> People can *do* two things at the same time if one is automatic.

Think about children who are still in the process of sounding out unfamiliar words as they are reading. In all likelihood, their train of thought—comprehending what they are reading—is lost when they stop to decode. This would also be true of an adult who is learning to read a second language. It is not that the child or adult has a dysfunctional working memory; it is a normal phenomenon of a brain that is functioning as it is designed to do, by focusing on decoding rather than on comprehension.

Educators need to be aware of this processing limitation when working with a beginning reader. After an unfamiliar word has been deciphered, it is generally wise to have the child reread the sentence, checking to make certain that its meaning is understood. Otherwise, some children may come to view reading as a sort of "performing art," not realizing that we read for meaning.

The Capacity of Working Memory

The ability to retain information in working memory is essential for reading. Readers must be able to remember what they have previously read in order to make sense of what they are presently reading. Therefore, it is important to be aware that memory capacity is developmental and that the age of the children determines how much information they can hold on to at a time.

Researcher Pascual-Leone (1970) theorizes that the number of items held in working memory varies with age. According to Pascual-Leone, in a test requiring a subject to recall strings of digits, the typical 5-year-old can recall two digits. The number of digits children can recall accurately increases by one every two years until a mental age of 15, when the adult capacity of seven is reached. At each age level, normal variance is plus or minus two bits of information. However, emergent readers are not recalling digits but engaging in the very complex task of learning to read. The capacity of working memory is relative to the requirements of the reading task. These include the following:

The amount of effort children are having to invest

The speed with which the individual words are decoded

Whether children are engaging in verbal rehearsal

The length and complexity of the sentences

What this adds to our efforts to understand reading is that the greater effort readers must invest in the individual words, the less processing "space" they will have to recall the preceding words or phrases when it is time to put them all together. The child's brain could be thought of as being on cognitive overload. One research study found that poorer third-grade readers could not remember as many as three words back in a clause (Goldman, Hogaboam, Bell, & Perfetti, 1980).

Chunking as a Way of Increasing the Capacity of Working Memory

Most adults have the ability to hold on to seven bits of information. However, it is easy to think of an example of a string of digits longer than seven that can be recalled without difficulty. How does this happen? The answer is in the definition of a bit. When a certain configuration of numbers or letters is processed many times, the brain eventually stores that particular configuration as a single bit of information.

Let's say, for example, that a beginning reader is introduced to an unfamiliar word such as *cap* and is able to read it by pronouncing each letter sound or phoneme. This act requires using three bits of working memory. However, with repeated exposure to the word *cap*, it is recognized as a word, not three separate letters, and the reader no longer has to decode it. It has become automatic and is now stored in working memory as one bit or chunk of information.

> Our ability to chunk information into larger and larger bits is one of the marvelous qualities of our brains that allows us to read fluently and eventually comprehend what we are reading.

Michael Pressley (1998) puts it very well in his book *Reading Instruction That Works: The Case for Balanced Teaching:*

In fact, decoding and comprehension compete for the available short-term capacity. When a reader slowly analyzes a word into component sounds and blends them, a great deal of capacity is consumed, with relatively little left over for comprehension of the word, let alone understanding the overall meaning of the sentence containing the words and the paragraph containing the sentence. In contrast, automatic word recognition consumes very little capacity and thus frees short-term capacity for the task of comprehending the word and integrating the meaning of the word with the overall meaning of the sentence, paragraph, and text. Consistent with this analysis, uncertain decoders comprehend less than do more rapid, certain decoders. (p. 67)

Our ability to chunk information into larger and larger bits is one of the marvelous qualities of our brains that allows us to read fluently and eventually comprehend what we are reading. When we see how the brain links separate bits of information into larger wholes, we see why repeated exposure to a common vocabulary is essential.

Long-Term Memory

Now that we have looked at how the brain encodes incoming information (sensory memory) and manipulates it (working memory), we are ready to look at the third part of our model, long-term memory. **Long-term memory** explains how the brain stores that information.

There are actually two types of long-term memory: declarative and nondeclarative. Declarative memory is just what its name says, recalled information that can be declared, such as names, events, concepts, and other types of learned data. To bring these data to mind requires conscious thought. Nondeclarative memory, on the other hand, consists of habits and skills that have been practiced to the point that they can be performed unconsciously. For this reason, declarative memory is often called *conscious* or *explicit memory* and nondeclarative labeled *unconscious, procedural, automatic*, or *implicit memory*.

To read fluently with comprehension requires both declarative and nondeclarative memory skills. At this point, we focus on nondeclarative memory as it relates to reading. Our conscious working memory, as we have seen, is limited in the amount of information it can handle. One way to reduce this overload is to get certain procedures or skills to the automatic level. In the case of reading, decoding is what we want to become an automatic or unconscious activity. As has been pointed out, unless this occurs, most or all the space in working memory is used for deciphering the print and little or none is left for the higher-level skills involved in comprehending what is being read. Reading the words in this sentence relies on automatic processing so that the reader can focus on the meaning. However, if this sentence contained an unfamiliar word or one in another language, automatic processing would be disrupted while the reader decoded the word. How do fluent readers reach the point of decoding automaticity? What is necessary to assist the beginning reader in reaching this point? Obtaining automaticity in any skill is not as much a matter of the person's innate ability or intellectual prowess as it is of the amount and type of practice in the skill. While

> Obtaining automaticity in any skill is not as much a matter of the person's innate ability or intellectual prowess as it is of the amount and type of practice in the skill.

long, tapered legs might be an asset to becoming an expert gymnast, they would be of little value unless the person practiced long and hard under expert guidance. The same is true of becoming an expert reader. No matter what our IQ, we do not have brains that can remember most words after seeing them once. For readers to obtain automatic word recognition, a great deal of the right kind of practice under the expert guidance of an adult or teacher is also necessary.

First, the grapheme-phoneme (letter-sound) relationships need to be matched and experienced so frequently that they begin to be seen automatically as units. As readers put more and more of these units together into words, the same rehearsal with words is necessary. (Second-language learners often do the opposite of the procedure. They take the pieces they understand and put them into the language structure.) This is accomplished by frequent retrieval of these words in normal reading activities. Gaining automaticity in reading is not a simple or quick process, but when teachers understand the process and provide beginning readers with many opportunities for rehearsal, it happens with nearly all children.

Understanding the systems in the brain that are involved in learning to read is a necessary, but not a sufficient, component in our quest to build a reading brain. We now need to look at how an understanding of brain processes can assist us in determining the best methods to use as we guide children on their journey to becoming readers. In the next chapter, we will look at how the foundations for reading are set in the years from birth to age 3.

REFLECTIVE QUESTIONS

1. Assume a colleague has asked you how an understanding of the brain will help her teach reading. How would you respond?

2. Explain the statement, "Reading is an unnatural act for the brain."

3. Discuss the role the right hemisphere normally plays in language.

4. If you are reading this book as part of a study group, ask two people to diagram and explain the differences between the language pathway and the reading pathway.

5. Make an outline for a short faculty presentation about Sally Shaywitz's research and her findings about the "glitch in the system" that causes some children difficulty in learning to read.

3

Building a Foundation for Reading

Birth to Age 3

During the first few years of life, the brain is wiring itself at a tremendous pace to learn to speak. Trillions of connections are formed as the infant attempts to understand sounds, particularly those of people. Parentese, language with accompanying emotional emphasis, has elongated vowels, repetitions, and overpronounced syllables. It is a natural inclination for infants to learn language and it is a natural act for adults to use Parentese with babies.

As areas of the motor cortex mature, around 2 to 3 months, the baby begins to vocalize. Phonemes from the language the child hears are produced prior to 10 months of age. Repetition of sounds and reinforcement of sounds affects the sounds a baby learns to form. At 18 months, many children begin adding vocabulary at a rate of one new word every two hours or so. At this stage of brain development, metabolic activity and neural connections are higher than at any other time during life. Between 2 and 3 years simple phrases are formed. Additionally, the child experiments with plurals and past tense.

Parents and family have a profound influence upon children, not only for their vocabulary, but also for quality and quantity of literary experiences they provide. Oral language development is so important. It can be predicted at age 3 if a child will have problems with reading in elementary school.

Parents who are aware of the important role they play in the child's eminent reading ability make a conscious effort to "talk, talk, talk" to their young children. They encourage vocabulary development and build background information and vocabulary critical for comprehension through story reading. Even nursery rhymes relate to the development of abstract word processing skills.

Eventually, pre-school-age children show an interest in writing as they go through stages of early scribbling, controlled scribbling, a pictorial stage, and finally the letter stage. There is no way to underestimate the importance of learning to talk and communicate through language. Building a strong foundation at the toddler age is critical to reading success during the school years.

READING RELIES ON EARLY LANGUAGE SKILLS

In a sense, learning to read begins at birth. We don't mean that as soon as a child is born parents should buy a book on how to teach a baby to read. However, one basic element underlies reading: language skills. Since we now know that learning to read depends on well-developed language structures, as well as on the type of life experiences the child has, the process actually does begin at birth.

Not too many years ago, the conventional wisdom was that babies are cute creatures who are not capable of a great deal of learning in the very early years. Research has proved conventional wisdom to be wrong (Gopnik, Meltzoff, & Kuhl, 2000). In the first few years of life, the brain begins to wire itself at a furious pace. Trillions of connections (synapses) are made between the 100 billion neurons the infant has at birth. The experiences of the infant help define which neural connections are made. This is especially true for the language centers in the cortex. For example, at birth the human brain has the language capacity to pronounce the sounds of over 6,000 languages, including the umlaut *ö* in German, the 10 *t* sounds of Hindi, and the trilled *r* of Spanish. Babies are born primed to be multilingual. However, the sounds children hear repeatedly in their natural environment strengthen particular connections in the brain, while connections for sounds that are not reinforced, particularly in languages that are foreign, eventually fade away (Kuhl, Williams, Lacerda, Stevens, & Lindblom, 1992).

How does the infant, whose name reflects an inability to speak (*in fantis* means "not speaking"), come to be a proficient speaker? Interestingly, infants begin to practice their native language long before they speak it. They are somehow computing the frequency of the sounds they hear and becoming

> The experiences of the infant help define which neural connections are made.

attuned to these sounds. This amazing ability can most likely be attributed to the brain's neural plasticity. The brain is the only organ in the body that remains plastic throughout life and sculpts itself through its experiences. This marvelous capacity allows the brain to adapt and change its neural patterns in response to its environment. Neuroscientists are fond of saying, "Neurons that fire together wire together." The synapses that are reinforced are more likely to remain, while those that are not are likely to atrophy.

> This marvelous capacity allows the brain to adapt and change its neural patterns in response to its environment.

In looking at the development of language, we often focus on the period beginning with the child's first recognizable words at around 1 year of life. However, every day of that preceding year, a variety of language-related mechanisms have been working to prepare the child for speech. In fact, the journey toward language begins *before* birth. Studies have shown that a baby is born recognizing its mother's voice and showing a preference for her voice over others (Locke, 1994).

In the final trimester of pregnancy, the fetus is able to hear its mother's voice within the womb more audibly than the voices of other people, so it is not surprising that the brain becomes attuned to it. It is possible that this prenatal exposure also engenders a preference for the mother's language as well as her voice. Studies by Jacques Mehler and his colleagues at the Laboratoire de Sciences Cognitives et Psycholinguistique found that, as early as 4 days of age, babies born of French-speaking women prefer the sound of French to Russian (Mehler & Christophe, 1994).

Upon the birth of a child, one might wonder if there are critical time-sensitive periods during which emerging cognitive development must occur. There may be. However, scientists have generally not studied cognition linked to timing inputs, as they have for development of the five senses. We know that development of the visual system, for example, depends on stimuli from the child's environment following birth. At birth an infant sees a relatively dark world of movement through a long narrow tunnel centered on a line of sight. According to authors Schwartz and Begley (2003) visual resolution for the child at birth is one-fortieth that of a normal adult, only about eight inches out into space. From being able to focus on a human face, when held, the infant's brain rapidly adjusts to environmental stimuli and can see almost as well as an adult by the first birthday. Without stimuli, neurons predetermined to develop the visual system will atrophy or migrate to another area of the brain to "help out." There may be sensitive periods for cognitive development, as have been identified for the senses, but neuroscientists' tools have not identified them, if they do exist (National Research Council, Institute for Medicine, 2002).

> Without stimuli, neurons predetermined to develop the visual system will atrophy or migrate to another area of the brain to "help out."

Everyday interactions for most infants pose a world rich with opportunities to explore to stimulate cognitive growth. There are faces and voices to imitate, sights and sounds to remember, and problems to solve, such as "how do I get this big person to notice that I am hungry?" The language-related mechanism that allows the little one to develop sensitivity to **prosody**—the emotional qualities of speech, such as intonation and rhythm—occur discretely and rapidly. For the curious baby as well as for all people, meaning is captured from conversations by tracing the rhythm and intonations of spoken language. In fact, these prosodic cues are probably more important to meaning than the actual words. The phrase, "that's great," for example, can be either positive or negative. We determine the meaning by reading facial cues and the intonation of the speaker. Infants develop the ability to recognize these cues as young as 3 months (Jusczyk, 1999).

The language and accompanying emotional emphasis used by parents and caregivers as they talk to infants is often called *Motherese* or *Parentese*. This language, with its elongated vowels, repetitions, and over pronounced syllables, appears to be just what the baby needs to develop language skills. It models the prosody and sound structure—the phonology, syntax, and lexicon—of the mother tongue. Parentese has also been found to be more grammatically correct (99.44 percent pure, according to one estimate) than normal speech (Pinker, 1997). The parent is, in a sense, telling the baby how language is structured and to what uses it can be put. It is interesting that Parentese is apparently innate, appearing in every culture and used automatically by anyone who speaks to a baby (Eliot, 1999; Pence & Justice, 2008). In *The Scientist in the Crib*, Gopnik and colleagues (2000) tell us science proves that nature has designed adults to teach babies, just as infants develop to be able to learn from adults.

> The language and accompanying emotional emphasis used by parents and caregivers as they talk to infants is often called *Motherese* or *Parentese*.

The springboard for the development of language in infants is probably the social interaction between parent and child. When parents talk and coo to their babies, their speech, as well as their faces, is filled with expression. This encourages and sustains attachment and bonding that is obviously pleasurable for the infant. The baby, in turn, begins to smile, coo, and mimic the parent. Researchers have found that babies as young as 42 minutes old will copy adults who stick out their tongues (Meltzoff & Moore, 1977). Infants, who are not mobile, are increasingly sensitive to actions and movements around them. As they observe, they begin to form expectations for rational actions. "If I cry, I will be picked up," is a young child's way of

> The springboard for the development of language in infants is probably the social interaction between parent and child.

showing an understanding of intention of actions. Very young children can be observed to intently communicate through actions as they reach, point, gesture, and eventually use language as a form of communication. Language in infants appears to be a medium for social and emotional interaction between the babies and those who are important in their environment.

So how do parents start their infants off on the right track to become a child who reads? Not with any formal program, but by following their natural inclination to talk to their infants, smile at them, and express their positive affection. Parental intuition has been scientifically reinforced. The young child's mastery of language, as we shall see, would never proceed normally without the steady dialogic support from parents and other involved adults and siblings.

THE BEGINNINGS OF LANGUAGE

Around 2 to 3 months, the areas of the motor cortex that control the larynx and vocal cords have matured sufficiently to allow babies to begin to vocalize in what we call babbling. In babbling, babies appear to be experimenting with various ways of making sounds. Even when there are no listeners, they babble to themselves. (Deaf babies also go through a brief stage of babbling, although they give it up after a few months. These babies do, however, begin "babbling" with their fingers to begin organization of speech sounds around 6 or 7 months of age if they're exposed to sign language; Eliot, 1999.) While they make many different sounds, babies seem to show a preference for the sounds they experience repeatedly. Peter Jusczyk (1999), a psychologist at the State University of New York, and his colleagues found that 8½-month-olds who heard a simple recorded story several consecutive times listened much longer to words such as *ant* and *jungle* that had been repeatedly mentioned in the story.

The repetition of particular sounds begins to strengthen connections for these sounds in the brain. In the book *The Scientist in the Crib*, Patricia Kuhl reports on her findings that babies under the age of 10 months—who have normal hearing—babble in the phonemes of their own language (Gopnik et al., 2000). The baby is beginning to develop a preference for some sounds over others. In a series of experiments, Paul Luce (2002), of the State University of New York at Buffalo, found that 9-month-old babies listened longer to words containing sound segments that occur frequently in speech than they did to those containing segments that they rarely heard. This preference reflects changes that are taking place in the neural connections in the brain. For example, a 6-month-old Japanese infant can still detect the English *l* and *r* sounds. But if exposed only to Japanese in the next six months, this baby will lose the ability to hear the difference, and the two phonemes will sound the same. Potential for certain connections among the brain's neurons have been pruned to adapt the child's brain to the language it hears repeatedly (Deacon, 1997).

Repetition and reinforcement appear to play a critical role in the determination of which connections are made and which are pruned. As developmental psychologist Penelope Leach (1997) explains it, babies do not intentionally say words parents want to hear, like "mama" or "papa." These recognized sounds create a big reaction. According to Leach, the baby has said many other experimental combinations of sounds, and no one paid a bit of attention.

> Repetition and reinforcement appear to play a critical role in the determination of which connections are made and which are pruned.

Baby Signs

Infants comprehend words and phrases long before they are able to say much of anything. In the second 6 months, even though their first words are still months off, they are beginning to communicate. Infants quickly learn that they can get reactions to multiple forms of pointing, for example. Pointing to an object, *imperative pointing*, signifies a object to be retrieved, while a social interchange between an adult and the child may result in *declarative pointing* to identify a spoken object (Pence & Justice, 2008). Linda Acredelo, a professor of psychology at the University of California at Davis, noticed that her own daughter, Katie, had devised her own "baby sign" for the word *flower* by crinkling her nose as if smelling its fragrance. It occurred to Acredelo that, even though Katie could not speak, she was trying to become a partner in conversation. She taught her daughter several other signs and was fascinated with the results. Her daughter could now communicate her understanding of words and concepts through signing.

This led Acredelo and coresearcher Susan Goodwyn, of California State University at Stanislaus, to study 140 babies starting at 11 months and continuing until the children turned 4. One-third of the families were encouraged to use baby signs, whereas the other two-thirds were not. Acredelo and Goodwyn (2000) collected and analyzed nearly 1,000 videotapes of the toddlers in action. The results confirmed what they had hypothesized: The baby sign babies scored higher on an intelligence test, understood more words, had larger vocabularies, and engaged in more sophisticated play. Parents were enthusiastic about the increased communication, decreased frustration, and enriched parent-infant bond.

The work of Acredelo and Goodwyn and numerous others verify that prior to year one babies spend all waking hours exploring their environment, listening to conversations, and taking in sights and sounds around them. At this very early age, the child is building a brain that is able to categorize and retain meaningful units of information, as is evidenced by a spontaneous sorting of toys and blocks (National Research Council, Institute of Medicine, 2002). Perceptual categorization allows the child's brain to recognize what something looks like, while conceptual categorization helps to identify what the object is (Pence & Justice, 2008). We will see in Chapter 5 how cognitive development, even under 1 year of age, is preparing the child with a brain that is able to organize and connect meaningful units of understanding. As teachers of reading, we know word organization and recall is vital for reading with understanding.

> Perceptual categorization allows the child's brain to recognize what something looks like, while conceptual categorization helps to identify what the object is (Pence & Justice, 2008).

THE LANGUAGE EXPLOSION: 1 TO 2 YEARS

Around 1 year of age, children begin to speak their first words. Although they are beginning to produce speech, they do not yet appear to understand the linguistic rules. They are essentially parroting what others say. However, by 18 months, language comprehension has developed so the toddler can understand many statements, such as "Let's put your shoes on," or "It is time to get in the car." This progression of receptive language is due to maturation in the left hemisphere; the previously active temporal lobe develops neural connections with the parietal lobe and extends into the frontal lobe (Eliot, 1999). Simultaneously, vocabulary explodes with children adding a new word to their vocabulary at the astounding rate of one word every 2 hours or so (Koralek & Collins, 1997), even though the pronunciations may be only 25 percent intelligible (Pence & Justice, 2008). This period of rapidly expanding language development coincides with the time when synapse formation and metabolic activity are at their highest in the cortex (Eliot, 1999).

> Although they are beginning to produce speech, they do not yet appear to understand the linguistic rules.

Language Development Between 2 and 3 Years

By age 2, nearly all children have between 100 and 200 words in their vocabulary and have begun to combine words to form simple phrases. These phrases are usually word sequences they hear frequently in the speech of others, but spoken in what is called "telegraphic speech"—short phrases containing basic information such as "All gone" or "Daddy play ball." Children's neural pathways for language develop rapidly, and, between 24 and 30 months, their sentences become longer and more complete. The child's brain is not only going through a language explosion but through a grammar explosion as well. Children are now beginning to analyze the longer patterns of words that they hear and are experimenting with some rules. For example, they will figure out that you add an *s* for plurals and *ed* for past tense. Parents and other adults are advised not to correct children's language use during this time, as children are very good at "rooting out their own errors and matching their language to the model of those around them" (Eliot, 1999, p. 389).

While language advances result from a language-rich preschool program, the advantages can be lost when children from poverty areas enter poor schools (Eliot, 1999). Betty Hart, a professor at the University of Kansas, and Todd Risley, a professor at the University of Alaska at Anchorage, addressing this topic, were discouraged with the poor long-term results of a program to teach preschool 3- and 4-year-olds new vocabulary. They decided to study younger children. Hart and Risley (2003) spent two and a half years observing 42 families for an hour each month. They wanted to see what typically goes on in the homes with 1- and 2-year-old children who are just learning to talk. They discovered that the children turned out to be like their parents. Approximately 86 percent to 98 percent of the words recorded in each child's vocabulary consisted of words also recorded in their parents' vocabularies. More surprising was the size of the children's vocabularies. The range of words recorded went from 168 for children whose parents were on welfare to 1,116 for children of professional parents. Perhaps not as surprising, a follow-up study showed that the rate of vocabulary growth at age 3 was strongly associated with later performance in school.

The way children learn language, any language, is very predictable, and this shows how deeply rooted language is in our biological makeup. As we have emphasized repeatedly, children are born with a brain programmed for language learning. As neuroscientist Lise Eliot (1999) states in her book *What's Going On in There?* "Human language is an instinct, a behavior as innate and inevitable as sleeping or eating. Humans can't help but talk; it is our fundamental means of social interaction" (pp. 351–352). This is why it is so important for parents and caregivers to understand the role environment plays.

Parental and Family Influences on Emergent Literacy

Adults who live and interact regularly with children have a profound influence not only on the size of the children's vocabularies but also on the quality and quantity of their literacy experiences. While it might appear that there is not much parents can do with a child from birth to age 3 that will influence later reading ability, quite the contrary is true. Parental beliefs and attitudes about reading and literacy, as well as their behaviors, have a large effect on the emerging literacy of the young child (Snow, Burns, & Griffin, 1998). Early language development information is so critical and widespread, the U.S. Department of Education provides no-cost copies of publications for parents: *Shining Stars: Preschoolers Get Ready to Read: How parents Can Help Their Preschoolers Get Ready to Read; Dad's Playbook: Coaching Kids to Read;* and *Big Dreams: A Family Book About Reading: Preschool Through Grade Three*, for example (see edpubls@inet.ed.gov and http://www.edpubs.org).

> Adults who live and interact regularly with children have a profound influence not only on the size of the children's vocabularies but also on the quality and quantity of their literacy experiences.

Elements of a Literacy-Nurturing Environment

If we could become silent observers in a home during the first three years of a child's life, what would we see that would assure us that this child was being provided the best start possible on the road to reading? Research has given us a better understanding of how language develops in the brain and how language provides the foundation for reading. Studying the neurological aspects of language development allows us to understand the behavioral aspects from the studies. Some basic parent responses to children inherently help them develop language.

Talk, Talk, Talk

Talkative mothers have been vindicated! Providing a rich language culture is just what the developing language pathways in the brain need. Janellen Huttenlocher, a psychologist at the University of Chicago, and her colleagues (Huttenlocher, Haight, Bryk, Seltzer, & Lyons, 1991) report on a study they conducted that found that children of the most talkative mothers had 33 more words in their vocabulary at 16 months than did the children of mothers who were the least talkative. At 20 months, the difference was 131 words, and at 24 months, 295. She states that the differences probably reflect the number of opportunities children had to hear a word and then try it on their own.

Nearly all children can learn to use nouns and verbs correctly, but the critical period for learning to speak with correct grammar (the use of articles, conjunctions, and prepositions) appears to wane around age 3. Helen Neville (1995), a cognitive neuroscientist at the University of Oregon, notes that if language learning is left until too late, these systems for grammar will not develop normally. Expectations for expressive language at 24 months include (a) using 10 to 15 words meaningfully, (b) using two-word sentences

> Nearly all children can learn to use nouns and verbs correctly, but the critical period for learning to speak with correct grammar (the use of articles, conjunctions, and prepositions) appears to wane around age 3.

meaningfully, and (c) speech that is at least 50 percent intelligible. The expectations increase during the second and third year to (a) producing sentences of three to five words, (b) talking about past and future events, (c) asking questions using *what, who,* and *where,* and (d) having a vocabulary of 100 to 200 words with 75 percent intelligibility for caregivers (Rossetti, 1996). These communication guidelines were developed to alert adults to possible language delays; the early years are so critical to oral language development, and equally to reading ability in the school years.

The Most Important Interventions

The research is clear—children who are read to from an early age are more successful at learning to read. Dickinson and Smith (1994) confirm the positive long-term effects of story reading on children's vocabulary and story comprehension. Reading to children produces such distinct benefits for several reasons. First, it increases their vocabulary and helps them become familiar with language patterns. Repetition increases the strength of neural connections. Reading the same book to children repeatedly— which they love—serves to reinforce familiar words. Children often become so familiar with the vocabulary of a favorite story they can "read" it with an adult or pretend to read it to a sibling or to one of their dolls or stuffed animals.

What is happening neurologically while an adult and a child converse through story reading? During this activity, the adult reading pathway includes the brain structures identified in Chapter 2, Figure 2.4a. As the adult reads, an instantaneous process begins as the visual cortex automatically identifies shapes and patterns for words and stimulates the angular gyrus to identify sounds for the letters viewed. A quick pass through Wernicke's area makes certain the words have meaning in the sentences as they are revealed. Broca's area, aided in the case of oral reading by the motor cortex, pitches in to allow the words to be spoken as they are read with inflections and prosody. This review of the reading pathway gives insight into the effect reading has for a youngster. Activation in the primary auditory cortex would indicate a child's involvement with fine-tuning the sounds of words and their relationships to sounds of language heard every day.

> This review of the reading pathway gives insight into the effect reading has for a youngster.

Wernicke's area is activated as a youngster hears new and familiar words and makes connections to neural networks where the pathways to stored vocabulary become stimulated and more accessible. A young, future reader responds by using the motor cortex and Broca's area to clarify, repeat, and reinforce new ideas, words, concepts, and sounds (Restak, 2001). Through a review of the neurological processes involved when an adult reads to a child, it is evident why the following adult/child activities reinforce oral language development in very young children.

Reading to children encourages familiarity with the reading process. The prereading child has much to learn about print—how the book is turned when it is "right side up;" that the print is read, not the pictures; that you start at the beginning of the page and after finishing that page, turn to the next. Children learn about reading by observing others read to them. The benefit of reading to a child is further enhanced when the reader involves the child by asking him or her to point to or name pictures of persons or objects; points out objects in the story that are present in the child's own environment; explores common, everyday objects and events; encourages the child to retell the story; or otherwise involves the child in some type of discussion. These practice and rehearsal activities stimulate the child's working memory and draw on background knowledge to reinforce learning that can relate to other places and other times.

The "Nursery Rhyme Effect"

Pat-a-cake, pat-a-cake, baker's man.

Bake me a cake as fast as you can.

Roll it and pat it and mark it with a "B,"

And pop it in the oven for baby and me.

Why have we included a nursery rhyme in a book on reading? When two sounds are similar, they excite the same cells and their connections. As these sounds are heard repeatedly, the neural connections become stronger and the sounds become more easily recognized or familiar. In this way, the brain also begins to distinguish between sounds that are alike and those that are different. This is a process essential to phonemic awareness and, as we will explore in Chapter 6, relates to the realm of phonological processing for rapid word identification. Researchers have found that early knowledge of nursery rhymes is strongly and specifically related to the development of more abstract word processing skills and future reading ability (Maclean, Bryant, & Bradley, 1978). Moreover, it takes little searching to find support and resources to vindicate nursery rhymes for their enjoyment, repetitions, differences and similarities in sounds, and rhythm (Woolfolk, 2008). All these attributes appeal to the way the human brain learns and learns well.

> As these sounds are heard repeatedly, the neural connections become stronger and the sounds become more easily recognized or familiar.

PRECURSORS TO WRITING IN THE FIRST 3 YEARS

Reading and writing skills develop together. While children generally do not start writing letters and words until around age 4, there are many opportunities for parents and caregivers to encourage writing behaviors much earlier. Starting around the end of the first year, children can be provided with resources for drawing or coloring and be encouraged to experiment with making marks. Children can be offered a wide range of media as they express interest in drawing. Crayons, finger paints, clay, and Play-Doh are all good materials to use indoors, while "painting" with water or drawing with chalk on sidewalks are ways to experiment outdoors. Parents also have opportunities to model or demonstrate the uses of writing by signing the child's name to a birthday card, writing an item a child wants on a grocery list, writing the date a book is due at the library on a calendar, or writing a letter to a grandparent as the child dictates.

Children pass through several stages as they develop their skills in writing. The first stage could be called *early scribbling*, where the child makes random marks on paper. Children at this stage are probably more interested in the physical experience than in what is being marked on the paper. As children's motor skills develop, the marks become more controlled, with efforts to draw a straight line or a circle. This stage could be labeled *controlled scribbling*. At this stage, some children begin to distinguish between drawing and writing. With vertical lines under a picture, the child may ask, "What did I write?" or "How do you write 'Daddy'?" The third stage might be called the *pictorial stage*, where the marks and forms begin to be distinguishable and where the child understands that pictures and words are different symbols. In the final stage, which could be labeled the *letter stage*, young children begin to write letters to represent words and syllables and often can write their own names (adapted from MacDonal, 1997).

> The third stage might be called the *pictorial stage*, where the marks and forms begin to be distinguishable and where the child understands that pictures and words are different symbols.

As a final summary of language and literacy development in the young child, we present the following overview of the developmental accomplishments of the child from birth to age 3. This list is taken from the National Research Council's publication *Preventing Reading Difficulties in Young Children* (Snow et al., 1998, p. 61).

- recognizes specific books by cover
- pretends to read books
- understands that books are handled in particular ways
- enters into a book-sharing routine with primary caregivers
- vocalization play in crib gives way to enjoyment of rhyming language, nonsense word play, etc.
- labels objects in books
- comments on characters in books
- looks at picture in book and realizes it is a symbol for real object
- listens to stories

- requests/commands adult to read or write
- may begin attending to specific print such as letters in names
- uses increasingly purposive scribbling
- occasionally seems to distinguish between drawing and writing
- produces some letter-like forms and scribbles with some features of English writing

Learning to talk is probably one of the greatest accomplishments of an individual's life. Even though the structures for language appear to be hardwired in the brain and nearly all children learn to speak, we are obviously not born speaking. In this chapter, we have seen that the first three years of life are a cognitively critical period for developing children's language capacity, vocabulary, and writing skills. The environmental aspects of children's lives, their experiences, whether they are read and talked to, the opportunities they have to experiment with writing, all play an important role in building their brains with a strong foundation through connections for later reading success. Maryanne Wolf (2007) in her book, *Proust and the Squid: The Story and Science of the Reading Brain,* writes, "To acquire this unnatural process, children need instructional environments that support all the circuit parts that need bolting for the brain to read" (p. 19). In the following chapter, we'll take a look at the next years before formal schooling begins to see how the brain continues its rapid development for learning and language.

REFLECTIVE QUESTIONS

1. Explain the statement, "In a sense, learning to read begins at birth."

2. Assume that you have been asked to give a presentation to parents of young children. What suggestions would you make that will increase the probability of their children's future reading success?

3. If you are reading this book as part of a study group, ask someone to prepare a short presentation on the brain's benefits of reading aloud to young children.

4. Define the "nursery rhyme effect" and explain its importance in helping to develop a reading brain.

5. Suppose you have parents who believe that watching *Sesame Street* or other children's television programs will best prepare their toddler-aged children to become future readers. What would you say to these parents?

4

Emerging Literacy During the Preschool Years

I t is amazing to realize that during the preschool years the child's brain is actually constructing itself into a thinking, problem-solving, information-receiving brain. Neuroplasticity, the ability of the human brain to respond to environmental input, allows it to grow connections, develop and formulate skills and procedures, and learn concepts. Neuroscientists have aided our understanding of how and why children learn so rapidly. Since they have no other obligations, children spend all their waking hours trying to figure out their world. They observe and imitate by using a powerful system of mirror neurons. This amazing system allows children to activate a neural set of connections as if they were actually doing what is being watched. Researchers feel this discovery can explain learning that begins literally at birth.

Somewhere near the age of 4, the oral language pathway is in place. Broca's area, which is responsible for producing speech, and Wernicke's area, the lexicon or dictionary of meaningful words, are functional to allow the literal snowball expansion of vocabulary. The average vocabulary for 3-year-olds is about 900 words, 5-year-olds know between 3,000 and 8,000 words, and one year later the number of words known, for the average 6-year-old, is around 13,000. It is no wonder that when a child moves beyond the toddler stage, linguistic ability moves to an entirely different level.

Given this knowledge, the authors do not advocate for moving down academic teaching prior to kindergarten. However, adults, who are aware of the marvelous manipulations the brain is undergoing, are able to provide activities in natural ways to encourage, support, and reinforce language learning. Guidelines presented in this chapter include natural, child-initiated or -focused conversation, adult attention, gentle grammar corrections, rephrasing and extending thoughts and ideas, modeling creative language, asking for descriptive language, and posing curiosity questions.

Story time also has expanded purposes as children gain skills for comprehension. They form mental images of stories, increase general knowledge and background information, and listen for inferences during story time. During these years, children begin to pretend to read and become aware of print actually relating to the spoken words. When the environment is filled with print, children quickly learn to identify common words. They want to reproduce words they know and enjoy opportunities to write, for example, a grocery list, a birthday card, or labeling a toy shelf.

Learning the alphabet is more than singing the letters in one large, linguistic chunk to the tune of "Twinkle, Twinkle, Little Star." It also means being able to identify and say the names of the letters in the variety of forms they are represented. For reasons that will be clear in succeeding chapters, the sounds of the letters are not taught at this time—a child is simply asked to recognize and name the letters. Sounds for individual and combined letters can be learned later through an efficient, structured teaching program.

Phonemic awareness begins at this preschool time of brain development. We know that identifying phonemes as the smallest sounds in words is a critical precursor for reading decoding. So during children's preschool years, wise adults provide children with activities that include rhyming, alliterations (Happy Hippo), words with sound patterns (*him, slim, Jim*), oddity tasks (e.g., Which does not belong? *fun, run, sing, sun*), and engaging phoneme sounds through music. Children begin to experiment with writing symbols, some of which are recognized and common. Another structure of the brain, the cerebellum, begins to be trained for writing and other learning tasks. All this reinforcement to the child's brain of how oral sounds of words can be used, mixed, combined, or eliminated, and represented in print are done in a playful, often spontaneous manner.

During the preschool years, children's brains are undergoing a massive reorganization, building millions of new connections and at the same time pruning away ones that are unused. Which neural connections are kept and which ones are pruned depends largely on whether they are reinforced by experience. In a sense, the preschooler has a supercharged brain. Measurements made by Harry Chugani (1998) at Children's Hospital in Detroit show that 3- and 4-year-olds' brain cells are burning glucose at twice the rate of adult brain cells. This is not to say children are learning twice as much as an adult; rather, the youngsters are recording massive amounts of information by making connections in some helpful and also inappropriate ways. Adults, at their stage of brain development, have a brain already organized for learning. Adults are unconsciously more cautious about what information they are willing to hold in working memory and purposeful in what they commit to conscious memory. Toddlers attempt to learn and connect meaning to everything.

Why do children's young brains demand so much energy? What is the brain doing during this period of rapid growth? The brain is literally building itself. One of the human brain's most amazing capacities is its ability to sculpt itself based on what it experiences. This process is called **neuroplasticity**. Almost nowhere is this explosive neural activity as evident as in the young brain's ability to learn and store the language or languages it hears repeatedly. Brain wave measurements (electroencephalograms [EEGs]) show a dramatic upsurge of activity in both Broca's area and Wernicke's area,

> One of the human brain's most amazing capacities is its ability to sculpt itself based on what it experiences.

which is reflected in the preschooler's snowballing vocabulary (Diamond & Hopson, 1998). The preschooler's brain has reached a level of maturation to allow it to make great strides in language acquisition. Until around the age of 4, the language pathway of the brain is not fully functional. However, with maturation, which is identified through the process of myelination of the neurons' axons, Broca's area and Wernicke's area are fully developed and ready to speed language learning to a new level (Eliot, 1999).

MIRROR NEURONS DRIVE LEARNING

A relatively new discovery, a special type of neurons, has captured the interest of neuroscientists. The realization that mirror neurons exist was discovered quite unexpectedly. Neuroscientists Rizzolatti, Fogassi, and Gallese (2006), of the University of Parma in Italy, were experimenting with monkeys and their behavior. The monkeys were wired with electrodes for a PET, positron-emission tomography, scanning session. Inadvertently, and outside the research task, one scientist reached to pick up a raisin, and happened to observe the image of a monkey's neural activity. As the monkey watched the researcher pick up a raisin to eat, the primate's premotor neurons responded as if it had picked up the raisin itself. The astonished researchers repeated the actions and discovered a framework to help explain a host of previously puzzling questions. How do humans acquire skills to respond to social situations, use tools, and develop language? All of these abilities are necessary for humans to survive in a culture of close human contact (Dobbs, 2006).

As we advance our understanding of how youngsters acquire language, mirror neurons provide the needed driver for human progress. The neurons appear to be scattered throughout the premotor cortex, the parietal cortices, and key areas identified for language (Dobbs, 2006; Rizzolatti et al., 2006). The neurons fire when a person does an activity or as a person watches someone else perform the activity. Mirror neurons help explain how a child can within their capabilities imitate and replicate an activity performed and modeled by another. According to activity in the human brain, it is as if the person is actually performing the action by merely watching.

Mirror neurons' role in the most sophisticated of human skills, language, is being addressed by researchers. They have identified the mirror neuron system in Broca's area, which we have identified as a center for speech production. Additionally, they believe that language began with a combination of facial and hand gestures, which continue to be used for humans to communicate on a variety of social,

> Mirror neurons' role in the most sophisticated of human skills, language, is being addressed by researchers.

emotional, and conversational levels (Dobbs, 2006; Pence & Justice, 2008; Rizzolatti et al., 2006). For our study of language development in the preschool years, the role of mirror neurons is a critical part of how children are able to learn. They learn quickly and explosively, as figuring out their worlds and being able to express their needs is their only role in life.

ORAL LANGUAGE AND VOCABULARY

Between the ages of 3 and 5, children make tremendous strides in their mastery of language. Their average vocabulary at age 3 is about 900 words (Bee & Mitchell, 1980). Vocabulary acquisition grows at a rapid pace thereafter. By age 5, children will have a well of between 3,000 and 8,000 words on which to draw, and it is estimated that an average 6-year-old commands about 13,000 words (Pinker, 1997). At this age, children speak in more complex and complicated sentences, and are using language to meet their personal and social needs. They enjoy listening to and talking about the stories that are read to them, are beginning to identify familiar signs and labels, participate in rhyming games, and probably understand that print carries a message.

Preschool children also show growth in the speech fluency they need to express ideas. Most children are now ready to explore what it means to be a reader and a writer.* Whether their time is spent in a preschool or at home with parents or caregivers, these young children have reached a milestone in their literacy development.

The preschool years are a prime time to build increased *linguistic awareness* of the language foundation set down in the brain during the first three years. Research studies have shown that the language and literacy activities of the preschool years can have a significant impact on children's ability to read during the formal years of school (Dickinson, Cote, & Smith, 1993; Dickinson & Smith, 1994).

Developmentally Appropriate Oral Language Activities

While the preschool years are a prime time for developing the emergent reader's literacy skills, we need to emphasize that we are not advocating "pushing down" the kindergarten or first-grade curriculum. The idea that

---

*It is important to emphasize that while the information and activities in this chapter are designed for the preschool-aged child, there is tremendous variance in children's background experiences, their rates of maturation, and their readiness to engage in prereading activities. Some of the guidelines and suggested activities in this chapter will be appropriate for 3-year-olds. Other children's brains will be a bit slower to develop, and they may not be ready for the activities until perhaps age 5. The term *preschool* as used in this chapter refers to an age range (3½–5) rather than to children enrolled in a formal preschool program.

"earlier is better" is based on a lack of understanding of the reading process, of children's brain development, and of the types of activities that are best suited for different ages.

Linguistic awareness is best developed within the context of the child's world through play. The environment, whether at home or in preschool, should provide many opportunities to hear and play with language. These opportunities should, whenever possible, be a part of the child's natural experiences (Eliot, 1999; Herschkowitz & Herschkowitz, 2002). The preschool child's environment has potential to be rich with opportunities to develop language and emergent literacy skills. Shopping for groceries, visiting a park, going to the library, sorting clothes for washing, or preparing a meal all offer opportunities to build vocabulary and increase the child's understanding of concepts. Reading poems and stories, engaging in dramatic play, seeing classroom charts and other print in use, and singing rhymes are additional activities that are appropriate at this stage of development. Given the caveat that earlier is not necessarily better, next we will take a look at some of the appropriate linguistic awareness activities that best prepare the young child for more formal literacy instruction.

> Shopping for groceries, visiting a park, going to the library, sorting clothes for washing, or preparing a meal all offer opportunities to build vocabulary and increase the child's understanding of concepts.

Guidelines for Building Oral Language Skills

Many of the activities that nurture literacy and language development suggested in the previous chapter for younger children continue to be appropriate for 4-year-olds, but at a somewhat more advanced level. As we noted at the beginning of this chapter, children at 4 have experienced a relatively large jump in brain development during the previous year. Their brains are now approximately 90 percent of their final adult size and weight. They have not, of course, reached the same level of cognitive functioning as an adult. These young, yet sophisticated, learners continue to enjoy many of the language activities they engaged in at 2 and 3, but with their newly developed language and cognitive skills, they can now be expected to be more active participants.

The quality of adult-child discourse and the amount of time allotted to these interactions appear to be critical factors. Conversations need to be cognitively challenging and vocabulary rich for literacy learning to occur (Dickinson et al., 1993). Every parent is more than familiar with the ubiquitous "Why?" of 3- and 4-year-olds. Sometimes, adults spend time carefully answering their children's questions and miss an opportunity to *engage children in a discussion* of what they think the answer might be. This practice leads to conversing about a child-initiated or child-focused question. Although it is a natural adult tendency to "absent-mindedly" respond to the barrage of questions, a well-intentioned adult or care provider can make the most of this language enhancing opportunity by paying attention. Asking the child to rephrase a question or a statement encourages extensions of thoughts and ideas. Ask additional questions that provoke the child's curiosity, such as "Why do you think . . ." or "How do you suppose . . ." and "Do you wonder where . . ." Responding in this way allows the adult to discover and correct misconceptions prior to them being reinforced in the memory's recall system. An example of a misconception could be a child learning that a moving vehicle is called "a car." The brain sets up a memory system to identify moving vehicles as cars. The child sees a truck and identifies it as a car. Hence the opportunity arises to explore many different types of moving vehicles. Remember, these are conversations, not lessons. They are effective when they are *natural, unobtrusive, and not dominated by the adult* (adapted from Hall & Moats, 1999).

> Sometimes, adults spend time carefully answering their children's questions and miss an opportunity to engage children in a discussion of what they think the answer might be.

During this natural interplay of conversation, parents and care providers are cautioned to be gentle on corrections to sentence structure and grammar. Modeling or rephrasing can continue the flow of the child's language in a safe manner. Children need to know they can experiment with words and ideas without being criticized.

Comprehension and Vocabulary Building Through Story Time

In recent years, we have seen increasing awareness of the importance of parents and caregivers reading to children (Armbruster, Lehy, & Osborn, 2006; Bus, Van Ijzendoorn, & Pellegrini, 1995). One of the major advantages of reading aloud to children is that it develops a sense of story—beginning, middle, end—a key skill for future reading and comprehension of text.

> One of the major advantages of reading aloud to children is that it develops a sense of story—beginning, middle, end—a key skill for future reading and comprehension of text.

Being read to from many different kinds of books develops children's background knowledge about a variety of topics, especially those that are not a part of their present experience. One successful technique to help children understand what they are hearing is to ask them to "make a picture in your mind" (Bell, 1991). Further explore understanding by asking clarifying and descriptive questions. Encourage the youngster to imagine beyond what they have seen in the illustration from the story, a practice to keep information and words in working memory for rehearsal.

Reading aloud to children is enjoying the book together, reflecting on the story, asking open-ended questions, inviting discussions of the meanings of words, and supporting children's curiosity about print. It creates opportunities to introduce children to new words that represent concepts with which they are unfamiliar. Talking together about new words allows children to begin to store an inventory of mental images so that the words have meaning. Additionally, questions of "if–then" and "What else do you think..." or "How could it be..." help the child make inferences, a demand to recall and accumulate information from different places in the brain. Extended questioning and the resulting responses are the beginning of what teachers know all too well as higher-level thinking skills. The caveat is from research. Studies tell us when parents are taught to engage in these activities as they read to their children, the children ultimately score significantly higher on tests of verbal expression and vocabulary than children of parents who read stories straight through without the activities (Whitehurst et al., 1988). At this point, activities have focused on conversation: talking and listening. Before we adventure into letters and print, let's look at the aspects of phonemic awareness, individual sounds that make up the words we hear.

Phonemic Awareness

A considerable amount of research has been conducted on the importance of phonemic awareness for future reading success. A growing consensus exists that an understanding that speech is composed of individual sounds, phonemes, is essential for learning to read. What is generally known at this time and has been validated extensively by research is the finding that students with reading disabilities often lack the ability to hear and manipulate phonemes (Shaywitz, 2003; Stanovich, 1988). G. Reid Lyon (2002), of the National Institute of Child Health and Human Development (NICHD), points out that the typical disabled reader cannot distinguish phonemes and states that this deficit may be one of the causes of dyslexia among children who have average or above average intelligence.

> A growing consensus exists that an understanding that speech is composed of individual sounds, phonemes, is essential for learning to read.

Children learn best through active involvement and exploration of their environment. However, research confirms that many preschool children benefit from age-appropriate, explicit instruction in some areas of phonemic awareness and phonological awareness (Snow, Burns, & Griffin, 1998).

A distinction exists between the terms *phonemic awareness* and *phonological awareness*. As we have stated, phonemic awareness is the understanding that spoken language is made up of identifiable units or sounds. Phonological awareness is a broader umbrella term that includes phonemic awareness and more complex awareness, such as counting the number of phonemes in a word, blending phonemes, or distinguishing parts of syllables called onsets and rimes. Moats (2000) refers to phonological awareness as including perception, recall, and production of all levels of the speech sound system.

How do we determine whether children have phonemic or phonological awareness, and if they do not, how do we teach it to them?

How do we determine whether children have phonemic or phonological awareness, and if they do not, how do we teach it to them? Interestingly, similar activities often serve both purposes.

Developmental Levels of Phonemic Awareness

In her book *Beginning to Read,* Marilyn Jager Adams (1990) describes five levels of phonemic awareness, two of which will be discussed in the following section, while additional activities are identified in Chapter 5, as they are appropriate for school-age students.

According to Adams (1990), the simplest or most primitive level of phonemic awareness, beginnings and endings, involves not much more than being able to hear and recognize the sounds of words. For this level, it is **alliteration** to identify common beginning sounds and **rhyming** to find words that end with the same sounds. Alliteration activities are effective strategies to increase a child's attention to sounds from words. Playing with their friends' names—Happy Henry or Merry Megan—or tongue twisters, such as Peter Piper picked a peck of pickled peppers, are fun ways to introduce preschoolers to alliteration and increase their ability to distinguish between similar beginning phonemes.

As was pointed out in Chapter 3, teaching nursery rhymes is one of the easiest and most effective ways to increase a child's ability to hear the similar sounds of rhyming words (Adams, 1990). Recall also that the pattern of words in a rhyme or song appear to be stored in implicit or unconscious memory, and are easily brought to conscious memory as a whole thought or chunk. Think about the endings to the phrases, "'i' before 'e' except _____," or "When two vowels go walking, _____." The unconscious part of the brain remembers the rest of the phrases without conscious processing.

One natural and spontaneous way to work with children on alliteration and rhymes is to find literature that deals playfully with speech sounds through rhymes such as the Dr. Seuss book *There's a Wocket in My Pocket* (Seuss, 1974) or *Moses Supposes His Toeses Are Roses* (Patz, 1983). Yopp (1985) provides guidelines for using these books with children: (a) read and reread the stories; (b) comment on the use of language; (c) encourage predictions of sound and word patterns; (d) comment on or elicit specific aspects of sound patterns (e.g., "What sound do you hear at the beginning of all those words?"); and (e) be creative in inventing new versions of the language patterns utilized in the stories. Adding music to the mix often enhances the effectiveness of rhyming and alliteration. Young children have an amazing capacity to remember not only the musical tunes but also words of songs and nursery rhymes they've been taught.

A second level of phonemic awareness, **oddity tasks**, requires young children to compare the sounds, determining whether they are the same or different. In a fun and informal way, children are verbally presented with two or three words that rhyme and one that doesn't; the adult asks them to tell which one doesn't belong (*cat, mouse, bat*). Or the child may be presented with two or three words that begin the same and one that begins with a different sound (*pig, hat, pie*). Other more difficult oddity tasks ask children to make their decision based on the ending sound (*dog, hill, pill*) or the middle sound in a word (*man, fun, bun*). These oddity tasks have proved especially usable with prereaders, as they do not require children to decompose a syllable into a string of individual phonemes or blend sounds (Adams, 1990). Cognitively, these very actions are forcing the child's brain to stray from the typical oral language pathway and begin a route that can be designed for decoding words.

Word and Syllable Counting

Activities in addition to those for phonemic awareness connect whole words with their phonemic or sound parts. Syllables can be thought of as the bridge between words and phonemes, words being easiest to hear and phonemes being more difficult than syllables. Knowing words and syllables are easier to hear than phonemes, it makes sense, then, that counting syllables might be strongly related to reading acquisition. Indeed, it is stronger than the ability to count words in sentences. An ability to detect syllables in speech has been shown to predict future reading, correlates with the reading progress of beginners, and differentiates older dyslexic readers from normal first-grade readers (Lundberg, Olofsson, & Wall, 1980; Morais, Bertelson, Cary, & Alegria, 1986). For the preschool child, counting syllables in words can be a game if children are asked to clap hands or march in place for each syllable. The adult can start with a child's name (John-ny or A-lex-an-dra), objects in the environment (win-dow), or a feeling (un-hap-py), and when the child is successful with these, advance to more difficult multisyllabic words.

> Syllables can be thought of as the bridge between words and phonemes, words being easiest to hear and phonemes being more difficult than syllables.

PRINT AWARENESS AND ALPHABET

Print is everywhere. From cereal boxes to McDonald's signs, children are surrounded by letters combined in a myriad of ways to form thousands of words. At some point, it is essential for children to understand the many qualities of print as a code translation process through which meaning is understood (Moats, 2000). Adams (1990) outlines qualities of print as being available many places, for many reasons, produced in various forms, and in all instances symbolizing communication through language.

Developmentally Appropriate Principles of Print

Metalinguistically, we can put what children need to learn about print into developmental milestones. **Print interest** is attained when the child shows that print is stimulating and worthy of attention. Next, the child develops recognition that print provides meaning; there is a **print function**. The organization of print, **print conventions**, follows its function, as the child recognizes that there is an organizational scheme of left to right, and ways unique to a variety of genres. There are letter groupings for words, story titles, or even for words that are names of people they know. Closely associated with conventions of print is **print form**. Here, the child realizes that print units, letters, and words have names and are organized in specific ways. The last stage is **print part-to-whole relationships**. Now the child sees that letters can be combined to make words and words are grouped together to create larger meaningful units (Pence & Justice, 2008). This hierarchy develops naturally in a print-rich environment and does not need to be taught. It is, however, useful to teachers working with older children, possibly English learners, who have not been exposed to written language.

> Metalinguistically, we can put what children need to learn about print into developmental milestones.

Activities for Print Awareness

What children need to know about print and its relevance to reading can be summed up in four basic principles: (1) Words are read, pictures are viewed; (2) words appear and are read in English from left to right across the page; (3) letters placed next to each other form words; and (4) letters each have a large and small version and can be printed in various forms. Parents and others train children's brains to automatically respond to these principles by pointing to words as they read, making signs and labels for items in the children's world (such as their names on the doors of their rooms), and by pointing to different letter forms from the children's world (e.g., letters on the cereal box that differ from the way they are represented in the book just read; Hall & Moats, 1999). One last point is that children's performance on tests designed to measure print awareness predicts future reading achievement (Tunmer, Herriman, & Nesdale, 1988).

Teaching the Alphabet and Letter Naming

In the 1960s, several research studies reported the best predictor of beginning reading achievement to be a child's knowledge of letter names (Bond & Dykstra, 1967; Chall, 1983). (Please note that we advocate helping preschool-aged children to be able to identify the names of the letters of the alphabet, *not their sounds*.) This research was greeted with much enthusiasm, as it appeared to be a simple way to give children an advantage in learning to read. However, further research found that prereaders' knowledge of letter names, while a good predictor of future reading success, is not enough (Adams, 1990). Researchers verified the value of identifying letters accurately, but it is the fluency or ease with which they do so that gives them an advantage (Walsh, Price, & Gillingham, 1988; Wolf, 2007).

Why are the brain's processing speed and accuracy for naming such critical factors? The discussion in earlier chapters regarding automaticity makes it clear. Children who do not visually process quickly may not automatically see letters grouped into words as wholes, and they will have to invest a great deal of conscious effort in order to decipher each letter. This cumbersome process leaves little "space" in working memory for remembering. The ability to name most of the letters automatically will make it easier for the child to recognize patterns of letters—a key to reading words. Rapid, automatic naming is identified in Chapter 9 for its relationship to reading fluency.

> Children who do not visually process quickly may not automatically see letters grouped into words as wholes.

DEVELOPING WRITING SKILLS

Children not only need to be immersed in a print- and language-enriched environment; they also need to have opportunities to begin to express themselves through writing. As preschool children's fine motor control increases, interesting developments occur in the **motor strip**, the **frontal lobes**, and the **cerebellum** (refer to Figure 4.1). Planning, timing, and execution of hand movements are involved through activation of the motor cortex. The frontal lobe is activated to coordinate and orchestrate the movements (Berninger & Richards, 2002). As the child continues to experiment with various writing forms and different writing instruments for different reasons, the cerebellum becomes stimulated. The cerebellum is the relatively small, but cognitively powerful, structure located in the lower back of the cerebral cortex. This two-hemisphere mass is connected to the rest of the brain as a super support system for automatic movement, balance, and various other cognitive functions (Sylwester, 2005). It is as if the cerebellum needs to be trained through practice, practice, and more practice. At some stage of practice, which is different for each, the child's concentrated effort is reduced and the cerebellum takes over with seemingly effortless fluidity for many tasks.

> At some stage of practice, which is different for each, the child's concentrated effort is reduced and the cerebellum takes over with seemingly effortless fluidity for many tasks.

Figure 4.1   Complex neural involvement required for a child to write or copy words.

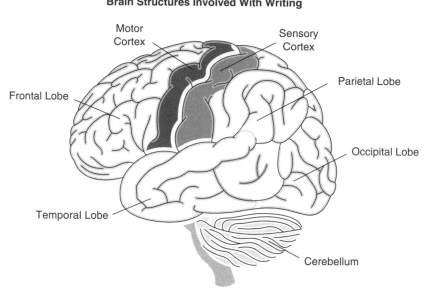

Brain Structures Involved With Writing

1. Planning, timing, execution of hand and finger movements are initiated by the motor cortex.
2. Orchestration is controlled by the frontal cortex.
3. The cerebellum coordinates unconscious, precise hand movements for marks on the paper (Berninger & Richards, 2002).
4. With practice, neural circuits wire, and writing actions become automatic.
5. Writing engages additional parts of the brain and expands the potential for learning during reading.
6. Writing provides practice to increase the ability of a student to store information about words in neural networks for retrieval.

Although we are examining the cerebellum's role in writing, its involvement in reading activities and all aspects of human learning are known. The cerebellum is involved as we unconsciously take care of things (brush our teeth, tie our shoes, read words while thinking about meaning, or write an e-mail message by thinking about what to write, not how to type). More information about this exciting and definitely interesting development in the brain is presented as we examine reading fluency in Chapter 9.

Developmentally Appropriate Activities for Early Writing

Scribbling is one of the earliest forms of writing engagement. In homes or schools where children observe adults writing for different purposes, children will mimic adults by making marks on a paper and then asking adults what their "writing" says. Adults should not expect a representational product. These attempts at writing are an exploration of print (Bredekamp, 1987). This response occurs more readily when children have tools for writing and various opportunities to write. Many preschool classrooms have a writing center, a post office, a restaurant with order pads, or a doctor's office with prescription pads where children can engage in pretend writing. Providing scribes to help children preserve their ideas or describe their artwork is another common practice.

As preschool children begin to write, they often use their tacit knowledge of word sounds, called *"invented spelling"* (or phonic spelling). Beginning writers may use the symbols they associate with the sounds of the letters they want to write (e.g., "lk" for *like*, or "bcz" for *because*).

Some educators and parents have worried that invented spelling promotes poor spelling habits. The research indicates quite the contrary. Studies suggest that *temporary* invented spelling may contribute to better reading and that children benefit from using invented spelling compared to having a preschool teacher provide correct spellings (Clarke, 1988).

Realizing how the human brain is built through its experience helps us to understand the role that parents and caregivers have to enhance children's language skills. No matter what their genetic potential, all children can benefit from a positive language environment, which may suggest less sedentary time with, for example, TV, and more reading, writing, and conversation (Eliot, 1999).

REFLECTIVE QUESTIONS

1. What is the benefit of holding conversations with preschool children, and what are some of the guidelines for these conversations?

2. Prepare an outline for a presentation to parents about how they can make story time a more productive experience for their children.

3. Explain what print awareness is and its role in emerging literacy.

4. If you are reading this book as part of a study group, be ready to discuss phonemic awareness, why it is important, how it develops and what educators need to do to help parents understand their role in developing it in their children.

5. Explain why early experiences with writing tools are beneficial and how the brain develops to allow writing experiences at this early age.

5

Beginning to Read

Ages 5 and 6

Priming skills—attention, concentration, memory, and organization—are often assumed to be "ready for action" in school-age children. However, for many children in the early grades, and some in later grades, these skills are not fully developed. Yet the attributes of priming skills are critical to the brainwork required for reading. **Attention** to a reading task requires most incoming sensory signals, not related to the reading task, to be blocked or ignored. **Concentration** on reading activities means children must maintain sustained, directed, thoughtful focus on specific visual or verbal cues. Frequently, concentration is maintained as the teacher directs students to rehearse, practice, or subvocalize instructional material. Of similar difficulty is the series of consciously stimulated activities needed for a child's brain to unconsciously move information from working to **long-term memory** for prompt recall. This complex memory task requires directed rehearsal and practice, which young children are not self-motivated to do. The final priming skill, **organization**, is viewed for both the child's physical work environment and the uniquely designed organization of each child's brain. Teachers and parents who are aware of the importance organization plays on the developing brain and for school success provide many opportunities to structure thinking and to make an environment that is effective and efficient for learning activities.

The skills necessary to do this complex brainwork are often assumed to be intact for young children. However, teachers easily identify children in the primary grades who are lacking in one or more of these identified developmental areas, which predicate ease with the reading process. Plain and obvious student behaviors tell the story of underdeveloped skills. Brain plasticity for young children makes these skills, as precursors to reading, highly teachable. Skill development for priming skills is already taught in direct, observable ways during every day in every classroom. This chapter challenges the reader to look outside the traditional classroom into the real world to reach intense levels of learning through episodic memory and real experiences. Identifying strategies supportive of building strong, essential priming skills for young early readers or developing them for older struggling readers is helpful for teachers as they make instructional decisions during reading instruction.

Kindergarten marks the beginning of a core transition in the life of young learners. Children arrive at kindergarten with tremendous variation in their maturity and prereading foundation. Despite a range of exposure to print, variation in vocabulary, understanding of story structure, and other foundation prereading skills, all children are expected to transition from prereaders to readers during their first two years in a formal, structured classroom.

What happens in the brains of these 5- and 6-year-old children during the years they are learning to read? Neuroscientists have shown that different structures of the brain are activated as children learn and practice the new skills that they will need in a literate world. Although a great deal of brain development occurs in the preschool years, neurons (nerve cells) in the brain continue the process of making connections and forming networks to store and assimilate information and concepts that the child is learning in primary school. Teachers who are aware of these changes can provide activities to help structure this neural development.

ထ ၈၁

INSTRUCTION ESSENTIALS FOR EMERGING READERS

In recent years, states and the federal government have worked to define curriculum standards that will promote success in reading. Research-based guidelines and standards for reading and language arts identify specific information, concepts, and skills for children to master at each grade level. Reading First is the portion of the federal government's No Child Left Behind Act that specifically identifies five components for effective reading. These components are phonemic awareness, phonics, reading fluency, vocabulary development, and reading comprehension. Another look at foundational elements for English language arts development is found in a document developed by a county superintendents' association designed for a systemwide literacy plan. Nine elements, based on relevant research, are selected for the technical skills of reading, which are specifically taught from kindergarten through third grade. They are listed in a manner that is linguistically logical and systematic: phonemic awareness, phonological awareness, phonics, decoding and word attack skills, oral reading fluency, spelling, vocabulary, comprehension skills, and literary responses and analysis (Curriculum & Instruction Steering Committee and

California County Superintendents Educational Services Association, 2007, pp. 110, 111). We discuss all identified elements in this book, but we have modified the elements by adding one new component and combining several in these chapters. In this and subsequent chapters, we address the following areas, along with their supporting elements: priming skills (a new component), decoding (phonemic awareness, phonological awareness, phonics, word attack skills and spelling), reading comprehension (vocabulary, comprehension skills, literary responses and analysis), and reading fluency (oral reading fluency).

Chapter 5 will explore priming skills and establish the accompanying brain development as a precursor to reading development. Two elements considered to be priming skills, attention and memory, were previously introduced in Chapter 2. These elements are basic to the other three priming skills of motivation, concentration, and organization. Teachers can assess these skill areas as they observe their students' work behaviors and concentrate on the quality of answers children provide. Because attention and memory are such vital skills for the developing reader, teachers need to clearly understand the brain processes associated with these factors and how they can support their development.

Neurons and Brain Function

We have referred to neurons in previous chapters, such as mirror neurons, the building blocks for learning (Chapter 4). However, an understanding of neurons and their function cannot be assumed. Certainly, neurons are the foundation of all connections and development of communication patterns and pathways in the human brain. These infinitely tiny nerve cells are the core of neuroplasticity, the brain's capacity to build itself during and following childhood for lifelong learning potential. A neuron is composed of three main parts. The cell body, called the soma, is where metabolizing and synthesizing proteins and general cell managing

> These infinitely tiny nerve cells are the core of neuroplasticity, the brain's capacity to build itself during and following childhood for lifelong learning potential.

and housekeeping take place. Within the cell body's nucleus are the DNA materials (genes and chromosomes). From the body extend numerous, branchlike tentacles called dendrites, which sprout in all directions. Dendrites seek input from other neurons. If the signal is strong enough, it can cause an electrical imbalance within the cell body. The result of this imbalance sends a charge through the neuron's only axon. The tail-like axon appendage shivers with the charge and spews out chemicals into a minimally sized gap, the synapse, between itself and a dendrite of a nearby neuron. The uptake of chemicals engages the next neuron in the amazing, stellar activation process (Greenfield, 2000; Pence & Justice, 2008; Schwartz & Begley, 2003).

Motivational Factors Lead to Student Attention and Learning

Instructional strategies teachers use can make reading a richly rewarding experience. And as a result, the children develop strong, responsive neural capacity. Teachers cannot make students learn. Students must be engaged with information through conscious focus for this unconscious neuron activation process to occur. As students focus and force neurons to build connections, reinforce connections, and speed the processes of the neural firing along the route, the demand on the circuits eventually becomes minimized (Schwartz & Begley, 2003). A chemical process called long-term potentiation (LTP) is the neural foundation for memory (Whitlock, Heyman, Shuler, & Bear, 2006). As a child makes a conscious decision to focus on a task, brain function is chemically affected. Neuroscientists report that blood flow activity in the particular brain circuits, which are automatically selected for the task, is amplified (Schwartz & Begley, 2003). Willingness on the child's part to sustain attention ultimately leads, through a chemical change within neurons, to effortless automaticity in the brain areas required to do the reading task.

> As a child makes a conscious decision to focus on a task, brain function is chemically affected.

Research Support for Learning Potential

Researchers working with rats identified a protein called PKM-zeta as the potential LTP chemical. The rodents were trained to avoid a certain area of their cages for fear of potential mild shock. Neuroimages identified the area of learning potential to be the hippocampus, an area found in the brain's interior for working memory. When the LTP protein was eliminated through chemical injection, amnesia and a loss of learned behavior occurred, and scientists observed that the animals would return to the area where they would receive a shock. The elimination treatment did not preclude all synaptic activity, nor did it have long-term effects. Scientists gained important evidence of the LTP protein's affect on formation of memories and learning (Whitlock et al., 2006).

Learning to Pay Attention

Many parts of the brain must work together for children to become fluent readers. However, the ability to pay sustained attention underlies the accomplishment of all reading tasks. Berninger and Richards (2002), professors of neuropsychology and neuroscience, respectively, at the University of Washington, describe the maintenance of attention as a job for the frontal lobes, as the reader seeks to interpret and identify meaningful words. How is a child able to attend during the complex process of interpreting print when the task is complicated and there are so many distractions in the classroom? In an intriguing study conducted at the Berlin NeuroImaging Center, Blankenburg and a team of researchers (Blankenburg et al., 2003) used functional magnetic resonance imaging (fMRI) to monitor brain activities.

Researchers intentionally produced unimportant, irrelevant stimulation, and then looked at images to determine what the brain did to inhibit the unnecessary signals. According to Blankenburg and his colleagues (2003), certain brain cells are called *inhibitory neurons.* The task for these neurons is to screen out many of the unimportant sensory signals when they reach the brain's thalamus, a structure in the primitive part of the brain for relaying sensory input. This study found that the majority of the signals were not only detained but also dropped from memory as if the input were never received. This process appears to free the cerebral cortex to focus attention on the specific sensory information that is the most relevant to the individual task at hand. During instruction, teachers observe this inhibitory process as children focus on classroom work, look at the teacher as though listening, or follow print on a page.

> The majority of the signals were not only detained but also dropped from memory as if the input were never received.

Although children's brains appear to automatically filter incoming stimuli, they may need prompts to attend specifically to a reading task. The reading brain is challenged to perceive visual symbols, interpret them, and determine if they are identifiable with words that are already known. Psychologist Franklin Manis (cited in Ackerman, 2003), of the University of Southern California, refers to a focused, complex process that occurs in the brains of successful readers as they process letter distinctions fast enough to maintain the flow and fluency of the text (Ackerman, 2003). If the perceived letters or string of words is unfamiliar or appears to have no meaning, the process slows down or stalls. It is then the job of the brain's frontal lobes to help determine if the visual input is important enough for the child to maintain attention (Berninger & Richards, 2002). The complexities of maintaining attention to identify and learn sounds don't happen for most children without practice.

> Although children's brains appear to automatically filter incoming stimuli, they may need prompts to attend specifically to a reading task.

Attending to Tasks

In school, children receive a multitude of sensory input from the classroom environment, and some 5- and 6-year-olds need help to develop the kind of selective attention that school demands. There are external noises— children moving, papers shuffling, a cough, a truck driving by outside— and there are internal signals from the child's own body indicating hunger, thirst, or a feeling of being too hot or cold. Learning to read demands that attention be paid to specific sensory input, such as a teacher's signal or a written prompt, while ignoring irrelevant sensory information. Teachers need to provide various prompts for young learners to develop the habit of focusing on the relevant instructional stimuli.

Students' attention to a task needs to be broken by practice aimed to shift activities among instructional formats, move from teacher input to hands-on activities, assign students to individual seatwork, or engage them at learning centers. Varying amounts of time can be devoted to different activities, depending on the difficulty of the task or the amount of motivation that the task requires from the children.

Sustained focus to a lesson on sound-symbol relationships might last a tightly focused 10 to 20 minutes. Highly motivating, hands-on activities of writing letters in a tray of sand or using colored markers on wipe-off boards may sustain children's focus longer. In addition to varying the length of instructional periods, kindergarten and first-grade teachers may schedule "brain breaks" with quiet time, large motor activities, songs, or games to rejuvenate mental energy (Levine, 2003).

Teachers know that giving breaks during instructional times pays the benefit of increased learning. But do we understand why? During times when children pay intense attention and concentrate, the neural systems employed work hard and demand brain fuel (oxygen and glucose) in huge quantities. Eventually, increased blood flow and the neuron firing systems get fatigued. We might say the LTP for learning has been diminished. A child will disengage when the work gets too tough. Indeed, mind wandering is so commonly acknowledged that a number of researchers have decided to study it. Numerous reports on the wandering attributes of the adult brain indicate wandering thoughts occur 30 to 40 percent of the time and focus on life's problems or things that need to be done (Ritter, 2007). While we do not have this kind of information for children, an instructional plan to change activities with regularity is a smart plan. Not only do student behaviors indicate a need to refocus, but the added caveat is that neural connections quiet down so learning can be consolidated. It is more likely that what has been practiced will be remembered (Schwartz & Begley, 2003).

> A child will disengage when the work gets too tough.

Getting Set to Listen and Attend

Effective teachers use varying attention-focusing strategies for classroom management to help children develop the habit of following directions. Prompts may be specific directions, such as "Stop what you are doing," "Put down whatever is in your hands," "Look at me," or "Return to your desks." In each case, a finite amount of time is allowed for children to transition from an active task to focused attention and to then be ready to listen. A signal, such as the teacher raising five fingers one at a time with the expectation that children will give full attention by the time all five fingers are visible, reinforces required behaviors.

Teachers who prepare children for transition activities—to get ready to work, to listen, to go outside, or to clean up—model expectations and help the brain to disengage from one activity and prepare for the next. In the same way, teachers can prepare students to pay attention to peers when they expect them to show attending behavior for listening. In the class-room, the key points for active listening can be identified, practiced, and posted. The rules (adapted from Hamaguchi, 2000) might look like this:

One person talks at a time.

Look at the person who is talking.

Wait to raise your hand until the other person is finished talking.

Candice Goldsworthy (1996), professor and department vice chairper-son at California State University at Sacramento, suggests prompting children through "vigilance, focused listening and looking" (p. 135) with a variety of teacher-directed activities. Children who are easily distracted may need to be alerted or refocused with "Ready?" or "Get ready!" Most teachers automatically use prompts that demand attention from their class.

Concentration Requires Focused Attention

Concentration is an extended period of attention in which the child focuses on and is engaged with incoming stimuli. The child enters a state of consideration, understanding, or remembering. Teaching may be the very act of directing concentration and can set the stage for student learning through nontraditional strategies:

> Teaching may be the very act of directing concentration and can set the stage for student learning through nontraditional strategies.

Strengthen sensory stimuli with vivid pictures, colorful labels, soft or loud verbal input, rhythm, or rhyme.

Add novelty, such as curiosity through problem solving, uncovering a secret, giving an unusual set of directions, search for answers, follow clues, solve a puzzle, or use of technology.

Build associations through access to real-life experiences, personal background experiences, or positive feelings or emotions.

Construct a task with a purpose so the student sees how the task will be personally rewarding.

Establish a possible level of difficulty so the student has a sense that success is possible.

> Some children have particular problems concentrating long enough to maintain the names of objects or words in working memory.

Some children have particular problems concentrating long enough to maintain the names of objects or words in working memory. Liberman and her research colleagues (Liberman, Shankweiler, & Liberman, 1999) report that this type of deficit is generally associated with linguistic objects. The impairment for recall, which is noticeable in some, but not all, children who are poor readers, is specific to reading attributes.

It does not appear to be an all-embracing memory problem, since the same reading-challenged children showed no deficit in remembering nonsense shapes or unfamiliar faces (Liberman et al., 1999). When teachers determine a child is not able to remember objects, letters, or words, a teaching response is to have the child concentrate on identifiable attributes of the items to be remembered. The following section describes how this brain discrepancy can be remediated by instructional practices.

Teachers can help all children extend the length of time they are able to concentrate on a task. During reading instruction exercises, which require "wait-to-respond" time, such as "Remember the words I am saying and give them back to your study partner," or "Think of three words that end like 'bear.' When I give the signal, Partner A will tell the words to Partner B." This type of direction requires the child to formulate an answer, but the child is not allowed to immediately respond. During the wait-to-respond time, students must rehearse the answer and hold it in working memory. Notice children are not asked to write the responses. Adding the requirement to write will demand additional brain resources, including the motor cortex, and add to the complexity of the task. Retrieval from working memory for initial concentration improvement requires a *verbal response*.

A more advanced level of concentration-extending activities occurs within normal classroom routines, such as when the teacher gives directions and then pauses before the children execute the command. An example is, "When I say 'ready,' you can number your paper from 1 to 10." Or the teacher might say, "Pass your paper to the front of the room when I hold up both hands." The prompt is given, "Hold these words in your mind until I say go; then write them down in the same order." This direction in its simplest form provides word clusters, such as four hamburger toppings, *ketchup, relish, mustard, tomatoes;* or zoo animals, *tiger, elephant, giraffe, anteater;* or weather, *rainy, sunny, cold, warm.* The strategy increases in intensity when the words do not cluster or chunk together around a common theme, such as *recess, bananas, shoes,* and *dog.* And as would be anticipated, increasing the number of words, items, directions, or numbers will increase the level of practice and rehearsal needed to hold the items in conscious memory.

> Classroom environments with large and small group activities, learning centers, and individual work areas help children learn to concentrate on tasks assigned to them as individuals.

Purposeful simulations of distracting conditions also provide powerful cognitive preparation for classroom environments during the early school years and beyond. Classroom environments with large and small group activities, learning centers, and individual work areas help children learn to concentrate on tasks assigned to them as individuals.

THE BRAIN'S MEMORY SYSTEMS

Learning to pay attention and extending attention to focused concentration are skills that support the next priming process. This process is the development of permanent, automatically accessible memory storage for information, concepts, and skills necessary for competent readers. Functional memory accesses three systems: sensory memory, working memory, and long-term memory (see Figure 2.5). First, let us review the brain's memory systems as they work for the reading process.

From Sensory Memory to Working Memory

The five senses are always receiving information, and as discussed earlier in this chapter, we know that an extremely small amount of the massive information being transmitted by all of the senses is selected as important for the task of reading. Pertinent input from sensory memory is moved into working memory.

Once in working memory, the information will remain available for up to 18 seconds (McGee & Wilson, 1984) or, according to Woolfolk (2008), 5 to 20 seconds. To maintain information for a longer period, the brain uses an articulatory loop as it holds information in working memory for rehearsal. Rehearsal or practice of this type engages the brain in subvocalization, a conscious process of holding the string of words or other information to be repeated over and over. Thus, the 18-second limit can be extended for the targeted material. During this activity, other information stored in long-term memory is enlisted as the memory system for new information expands its capacity (Figure 5.1). Relatively new thinking includes an association loop extension, as the child seeks background knowledge in visual or auditory centers. Some consider the activity of association as elaborative rehearsal (Wolf, 2007; Woolfolk, 2008). Thinking that involves the elaborative, associative loop would sound like, "I already know about hurricanes. My family was delayed when we were traveling in our car because of bad weather caused by a hurricane (long-term memory). Hurricanes, spelled h-u-r-r-i-c-a-n-e-s, are violent storms causing winds over 70 miles per hour" (new information being rehearsed through a working memory task). Making the association with previously stored information creates a "hook" and increases the possibility that new, associated information will be remembered (Pence & Justice 2008; Wolf, 2007).

Figure 5.1 Diagram of information processing model with association loop.

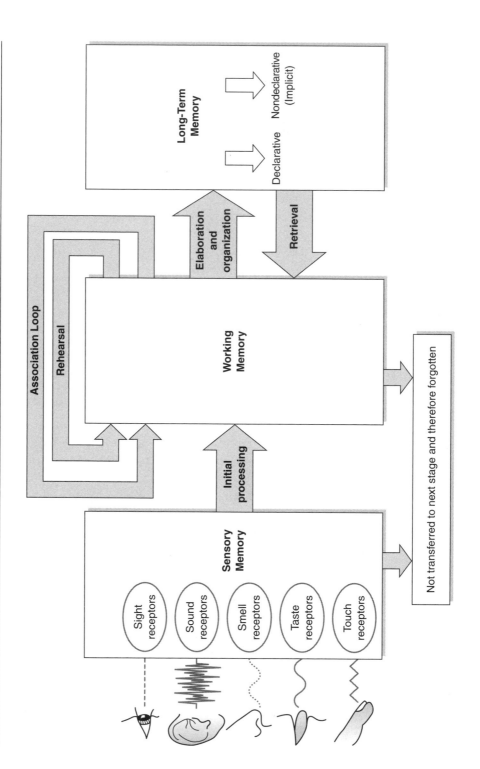

Figure 5.2   Working memory guidelines to gauge instructional planning for student practice and rehearsal.

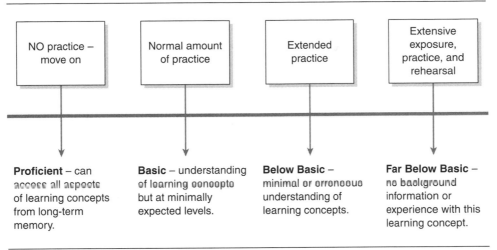

With enough practice, the information, concept, or skill becomes available for recall or demonstration from long-term memory (Figure 5.1). One important aspect of carefully controlled reading instruction and practice activities is to help students to hold relevant sensory input in working memory to practice and associate that material until it can be recalled automatically from long-term memory. Varying amounts of practice are needed for children based on preassessment of what they already know. Children who are proficient with the information need to move on with new information. Students who are far below expected levels of understanding need extensive exposure to the information and continual repetitions at various times during different activities within the school day. Yet teachers frequently provide the same amount of rehearsal and practice activities for the entire class and wonder why some children "do not get it." Teachers are encouraged to continue preassessment practices to determine student background knowledge for previous information, concepts, and skills and then use the continuum (see Figure 5.2) to determine an instructional plan to support learning for all students.

Teachers can design classroom activities to help children consciously practice and manipulate information essential to success in reading. For example, children practice and manipulate material in working memory whenever the teacher has them work with specific letters. Consonant blends such as /pl/ are used as first-grade children become proficient in working

> Teachers frequently provide the same amount of rehearsal and practice activities for the entire class and wonder why some children "do not get it."

> Teachers can design classroom activities to help children consciously practice and manipulate information essential to success in reading.

with sound identification. Children are first asked to say the blend, then to say words that have this sound. Seeking and discovering other words from long term memory with this sound, using the words in spoken or written sentences, and seeing words with /pl/ on their spelling list are other typical classroom activities that reinforce the selected consonant blend as it is practiced in working memory and cemented into long term in memory.

Rehearsal of information is a function of working memory, and as we have seen, it appears to reside in multiple areas of the brain, depending on the task the reader is attempting. For written language, children store the same item in multiple ways. It may be practiced in memory with codes for its orthographic word form (the letter sequence and their shapes), phonological properties, semantics (meaning based upon experience), and morphological structure (how words are ordered to have meaning), as identified by Berninger and Richards (2002). Regardless of the storage location, neuroscientists using fMRI techniques have noted that as tasks become more complex, they are likely to be managed and finalized through activity in the frontal lobes (Wolfe, 2001).

Long-Term Memory Systems

The ultimate goal of rehearsing and manipulating information in working memory is to move it into long-term memory so the child can recall and use it at will. To plan instruction that matches the brain's memory functions, teachers must understand two different long-term memory systems. We focus next on the two functional systems that the brain uses to store long-term memories for reading development: declarative (explicit) and nondeclarative (implicit) memory.

Declarative (Explicit) Memory

Declarative memory allows children to store information in an organized format to subsequently recall it by speaking or writing. To access declarative memory, most likely the child thinks consciously about the subject; has a quick, internal mental discussion about its attributes; and makes an overt response. Memories stored in the brain's declarative long-term system are statements of fact, labeling, and location types of memories that are recalled through a conscious effort. The brain calls on the *hippocampus,* a pair of structures under the temporal lobes where working memory holds and drops information, to identify a category for the stored information, while other areas of the cortex, particularly the temporal lobes, provide the collection of stored information (Sylwester, 1995). Information stored in long-term declarative memory uses two very distinct memory processes: semantic and episodic.

> To access declarative memory, most likely the child thinks consciously about the subject; has a quick, internal mental discussion about its attributes; and makes an overt response.

Table 5.1   Declarative Semantic Memory Strategies

Process	Teacher Directions	Student Response
Practice	Put your spelling words on flash cards to self-check.	Writes, spells, and sorts words.
Rehearsal	Say the rules and match three words for each.	Reviews rules and shows understanding.
Prompting	It begins like *bubble*.	Selects word from a list.
Organizing	Put your words in groups that begin with the same sound.	Makes a chart that organizes words into groups with the same beginning sound.
Reciting	Look at the word and say the rule.	Reviews the word list for orthographic rules.
Writing	Write the words as I say them.	Listens to sounds and attaches graphemes.
Sequencing	Put these words for the days of the week in order.	Sorts and orders word cards.

Semantic Memory

Words, phrases, sentences, or other forms of text recalled and articulated through speech or writing, which are reflective of the individual's background information and experience, are from what experts have identified as the semantic memory system. When children practice spelling words, they are working to get the information into semantic long-term memory. When they complete worksheets that match definitions with words, they are reinforcing learning for semantic memory. Likewise, using blocks or letters to represent sounds in words during phonemic manipulation provides practice for this type of memory. Some reading concepts that competent readers hold in semantic memory include phonological rules, syntax and semantics for language, spelling patterns, and word meanings. In each case, the child can declare or use written means to tell what is known from memory.

Classroom activities are designed so children can master information or concepts and store them in long-term semantic memory. Teachers may be surprised at the variety of ways they support their students in learning materials that ultimately will reside in semantic long-term memory. To identify those activities, think about reading tasks designed for practice, rehearsal, prompting, organizing, reciting, writing, and sequencing (Table 5.1). As children sort a list of words into categories with phoneme labels, what is the memory goal? They are developing organizational patterns of sounds to be stored in declarative semantic memory.

Episodic Memory

> While lessons are strategically planned for children to practice and manipulate information for semantic memory, experiences recorded in episodic memory generally happen with careful planning at school or by chance in the real world.

> Long-term declarative memory, source memory, of a happening or occurrence is accompanied by strongly felt emotions or active engagement and becomes a part of an episodic memory system.

While lessons are strategically planned for children to practice and manipulate information for semantic memory, experiences recorded in episodic memory generally happen with careful planning at school or by chance in the real world. Long-term declarative memory, **source memory**, of a happening or occurrence is accompanied by strongly felt emotions or active engagement and becomes a part of an episodic memory system.

A child who witnesses the family dog giving birth to puppies, a fire, or an emergency happening at school will have strong memories about that unique experience. The event and the child's opportunity to experience it were not necessarily planned. However, such experiences, due to their extreme emotional nature, allow the brain to effortlessly move details of the event into long-term episodic memory. Accessing long-term memory for needed reading skill development using episodic experiences is powerful but challenging. Teachers help children access prior experiences with broad prompts or questions about locale or the core experience from a reading selection, such as "Think about a time when you went to an exciting place you'd never been before." Teachers need to be careful, however, about asking questions that may tap traumatic experiences, such as "Were you ever bullied?" or "Think of a time when you were afraid." Because of the uncertainty of what children may remember, accessing prior knowledge or providing new experience through episodic memory is less likely to be a part of the school experience. It takes more time and planning for children to attend a field trip, engage in elaboration activities, act out a story, role play an incident, or give a demonstration (Table 5.2). What children remember from an episodic activity depends on each child's needs and interests and on what the teacher emphasizes after the activity is complete. Teachers are encouraged to plan high-impact activities as part of instructional planning for reading to take advantage of the emotional aspects of the brain and the "fast route" to long-term memory.

An episodic experience is a quick, active way to get information into long-term memory, but it is not always accurate. Experience tells us that as

Table 5.2   Declarative Episodic Memory Strategies

Strategy	Learning Event	Student Involvement
Experience	Taking a field trip.	Firsthand sensory stimuli.
Elaboration	Describing an incident from the story with words beyond what the author told.	Expanding conceptual understanding by picturing and identifying new details.
Story play	Reading out loud or acting out a story.	Active engagement or active attention to peers.
Role playing	Pretending to be the character or person named on a card.	Active engagement from another's perception.
Demonstration	Showing a story or details from informative text through a PowerPoint presentation, with props or realia, on a flannel board or chart.	Heightened attention due to novelty of presentation.

an experience is retold, it is enhanced or fabricated with plot and detail additions and omissions. The details become less clear and often become distorted with each recall. We experience this phenomenon when adults retell a joke or silly story. Each time the humorous situation is repeated the details become less like the original version.

Likewise, children form their own individual long-term memories of an episodic experience. If they talk about the experience at home, chances are strong that they will each have a unique way of describing what they remember and what seemed most interesting to them.

If, however, the teacher structures discussion or emphasizes concepts from lesson objectives following a source, or episodic experience, children focus less on the action of the story and more on abstract concepts (Sylwester, 1995). For example, the teacher may ask, "What words can you think of that describe how the foolish man must have felt?" Alternatively, children may develop what they see as an applicable truth from the story, such as the need to plan ahead or to avoid making friends with troublemakers. Pairs of students could work together to use vocabulary from narrative or informational text in new ways. Activities of this type help children to move an episodic, long-term memory experience into the declarative memory system to allow them to talk about and declare what they learned.

Nondeclarative (Implicit) Memory with Rote and Procedural Skills

While semantic and episodic declarative memory stores the "what" part of memories, "how" something is done accesses nondeclarative or implicit memory. Nondeclarative memory consists of habits and skills that have been practiced to the point that they can be performed automatically without conscious thought (procedural) or with a prompt (priming). As applied to reading, an example of *rote* nondeclarative memory is the rapid, automatic decoding of words. Fluent readers decode words almost effortlessly below the level of conscious thought, allowing the reading brain to consciously focus on their meaning. An example of *procedural* nondeclarative memory is the ability of the child's eyes to rapidly race across a line of print, seeing every letter but stopping for none. Other examples of procedural nondeclarative memory for reading-type tasks include talking and writing in sentences, using correct syntax, turning the pages of a book, or typing on a computer keyboard.

> Nondeclarative memory consists of habits and skills that have been practiced to the point that they can be performed automatically without conscious thought.

Children do not begin reading complete sentences with automatic fluency and comprehension. Some of the skills they must master before arriving at reading sentences include concepts of print, alphabetic awareness, word concept awareness, phonemic processing, word attack skills, rapid processing, skilled eye movements, understanding of written vocabulary, phrase understanding, and world knowledge or experience. Classroom activities to turn the individual reading attributes of decoding, comprehending, and reading with fluency into an automatic procedure include rereading stories, practicing sight words, rapid identification of new or nonsense words, and other rehearsal type strategies. Children use an articulatory loop to practice information and associate it with previous learning, so it will eventually become an automatic response from procedural memory. The ultimate reading goal for third graders to is to become fluent, competent readers. Skills are mastered in declarative memory so that reading can be performed with automaticity from procedural memory. As a child reads narrative or expository text automatically with unconsciously fluent word recall, the cognitive load is reduced, as discussed in Chapter 2, and the focus can be on meaning and understanding.

Teachers who understand what children must do to move skills for reading into automatic, implicit long-term memory can design instructional strategies to help their students become skilled readers. Instructional strategies to prepare children to read with implicit automaticity are repetition, practice, priming, experience, and demonstration (see Table 5.3).

It is not necessary for teachers to identify specific memory categories, such as semantic or episodic declarative memory. However, an understanding of the functions of sensory memory, working memory, and long-term memory are a helpful guide for teachers to structure classroom activities. Teachers who understand that learning is measured by what children can retrieve from long-term memory are more likely to select instructional practices that engage children in memory-enhancing activities.

Table 5.3   Nondeclarative Memory Strategies

Strategy	Learning Event	Student Involvement
Repetition	Passage rereading.	Students read and then record time and accuracy.
Practice	Read along.	Teacher reads, teacher and students read together, students read silently, and students read out loud.
Priming	Teacher presents and discusses new words before students encounter them in text.	Students read text consistently without interruptions for new words.
Experience	Students listen to and have conversation about a story read in its entirety.	Students converse about story contents and then read the story on their own.
Demonstration	Teacher reads a passage with expression.	Children practice various passages for reading with expression.

BREAKING AWAY FROM STATIC TEACHING TRADITION

Current research exemplifies how important learning and remembering are to the human position. Creative practices are being researched to engage learners in highly motivating, nontraditional ways. Educators are challenged to go beyond the classroom structures created at administrative levels that direct teachers to deal with the academic world only. The current widely accepted instructional design is witnessed through lesson objectives, direct instruction, focused student learning, and accountability for students' adequate measured learning progress. There is a real world and why doesn't school look more like the world? Many studies and programs presently being watched connect the real world to children's learning in exciting, enticing, and joyful ways. A consortium of researchers from multiple universities lament upon the purpose of educating the whole child to the fullest potential. If that premise is embraced, it cannot be accomplished by providing an educational system focused on traditional, hard-academic content (Patoine, 2008).

> There is a real world and why doesn't school look more like the world?

Beyond the Traditional Classroom

Research targeting the arts—visual arts, music, dance, and drama/theatre—for their impact on reading achievement has revealed a correlation between music and reading. A brain-imaging technique called diffusion tensor imaging (DTI) was used to measure the white matter (axons) in the brain. Studies revealed a remarkable amount of axon connections associated in areas observed for phonemic awareness (Patoine, 2008). Future studies may reveal that early stimulation to the oral language system from the sounds of musical notes can be correlated with an increased sensitivity for the sounds of language.

Another study searches for a systematic relationship between outdoor curricula surrounded by green space and learning (Faber Taylor & Kuo, 2006). These researchers cite four studies, which included longitudinal measures extending from six weeks to several years later. Participants reported beneficial outcomes from their nature experience. The premise is that if participants are engaged and pleased with their experience, they are more likely to learn from it and remember the information, concepts, and skills at a later time. We acknowledge that episodic memory experiences are more likely to be remembered and are remembered vividly. Additionally, researchers claim children deal better with daily challenges when they are surrounded by scenic natural settings (the brain is built to experience the world, not a desk, chair, pencil, and whiteboard). The educational world watches research of this type with interest but takes little action, because the studies are limited by the reliance on self-reported measures, not statistical, test-proving data. Of equal interest are programs linking the visual or performing arts to learning and content curricula.

Actions to Stimulate Memory and Remembering

Many educators remember when recitations from poetry had its place in our classes. Through this task, the brain's declarative memory participates to understand what is being communicated and to practice and recite the piece with exactness. When the poem is learned as one complete chunk of language, long-term rote memory has been tapped for action. Likewise, remembering lines from a play or lyrics to a song place a load on nondeclarative memory once the lines have been memorized. Consider the important aspects of learning and recall that are available to us through rote memory. It helps us to recover information with automaticity and no conscious thought. How would we ever read and comprehend without this capable aspect of the brain's memory system?

> Consider the important aspects of learning and recall that are available to us through rote memory.

Beyond stimulation for the procedural and rote aspects of our brain's remembering systems, participation in the performing arts acts on the emotional aspects of learning (Table 5.2). As discussed in Pat Sherman's (2007) article, Merryl Goldberg, college professor in San Marcos, California, and founder of Center Artes, decided to incorporate the arts into curricula for students who are preparing to become teachers. History, language arts, science, and math projects are developed for students who were at risk of academic failure. Goldberg's future teachers incorporated puppet shows for fifth graders to learn about the digestive system, for example. Puppets, drama, poetry, and other expressions of art are designed to present content curricula topics expressed through art. The program is hailed by teachers for improving academic outcomes for their at-risk students (Sherman, 2007). So while recitation stimulates rote memory, acting, drawing, and creating music through rap, rock, or rock and roll stimulate working memory systems that form semantic, episodic, and procedural long-term memory experiences.

MORE PRIMING SKILLS FOR 5- AND 6-YEAR-OLDS

We view the attainment of priming skills as essential support for the child's developing language-to-literacy transition. These priming skills are not to be confused with readiness skills that were a topic for educators during the 1980s. The late Dr. Jeanne Chall (1983) provided discussion of readiness in her classic book, *Learning to Read: The Great Debate.* At that time, some educators advocated readiness activities for children who were not ready for direct reading instruction, while others argued for all children to begin reading instruction immediately upon starting school.

> We view the attainment of priming skills as essential support for the child's developing language-to-literacy transition.

In this book, we look at instruction that is most appropriate to what is needed for children's brains to organize, categorize, and store information needed for reading. The skills we refer to as priming skills—the ability to pay attention, focus, and concentrate, to access memory to recall previous learning, to set the instructional stage for student motivation, to engage learners in concentration, and to think in organized, meaningful clusters of words—are all brain-related developments that can be integrated within the context of beginning reading instruction.

Motivation and Energy for Learning to Read

Many school-age children have already developed motivation to read by the time they arrive at school. Still, teachers find that some children may not be equipped with necessary motivation to do the hard brainwork that is required. It takes great amounts of energy for a child to concentrate on reading preparation tasks, even in the best of circumstances. When we consider the amount of mental energy that is required to decode and read, some children may be energy challenged. In fact, although the brain is only about 5 percent of the young child's total body weight, it often uses 20 percent to 25 percent of all the energy available to the body (Wolfe, 2001). Teachers should be alert to the amount of mental effort required when children are asked to perform activities that are difficult or not particularly interesting. A child with a normal amount of energy can focus on a task, even if it is considered boring. A child who is tired or has a low glucose (blood sugar) level—possibly from beginning the school day without break-fast—may lack motivation to do a task or may be unable to maintain attention and concentrate sufficiently to complete the work. Recognizing that children have different levels of interest in reading and varying amounts of energy that they can devote to a reading task, teachers can plan lessons that capture the students' interest and sustain and direct their energy toward the reading activity. Additionally, they can structure instruction and practice activities in appropriate time blocks to match the energy levels of their students.

> A child who is tired or has a low glucose (blood sugar) level—possibly from beginning the school day without breakfast—may lack motivation to do a task or may be unable to maintain attention and concentrate sufficiently to complete the work.

Organization

Often, children need prompts to organize their thinking. The priming skill of organization prepares emergent readers to structure thinking into big ideas, categorizes information into meaningful networks, and provides connections to previously stored information.

At school, teachers can use mind-mapping strategies that reflect the way the brain sorts information into categories (represented by neural networks) that will ultimately help students manipulate and recall the information. For example, if students are studying arachnids, they might start with spiders as one type of arachnid. To use a mind-mapping strategy, the teacher writes "spider" in the middle of the chalkboard. Students provide information from previous experience with spiders. If the teacher perceives student experience with the topic is limited, actual spiders or pictures of spiders can be introduced to establish an initial knowledge base. Another activity teachers frequently use to learn what children know is to ask what they know about spiders and record their responses. This information is organized under the heading "What We Know." Then children are asked what questions they have about spiders. The teacher records their responses under a heading such as "What We Want to Know" (Ogle, 1986). This technique strengthens existing neural networks and develops new connections to be used for storage of information about spiders. Teachers check for students' previous knowledge and experience, and they correct misconceptions, such as a belief that spiders are

> Through experiences such as mind mapping, children put conscious effort toward ordered thinking and develop self-assurance for success with the next reading task.

insects. It also provides direction for the continued study of spiders and other arachnids. Through experiences such as mind mapping, children put conscious effort toward ordered thinking and develop self-assurance for success with the next reading task.

In addition to needing structured prompts to help organize their thinking, children often need help to organize their materials and physical workspace. At home, parents can encourage students to take an initial look *through an entire school assignment* before they begin to work. This allows them to collect the materials they need and ask questions before they begin to work. Children often find it easier to be organized when they have a special place to work. Families who plan a work area that has good light, contains materials to complete school work, and is relatively quiet help their children to develop a positive, "can-do" approach to school work.

> In addition to needing structured prompts to help organize their thinking, children often need help to organize their materials and physical workspace.

Children also need to know before they start their work at school or at home how they will know that they are finished and what to do when the task is done. Self-prompted questions might be "What will my work look like when I am finished?" "Where do I put the completed work?" "What happens for clean up?" or "Where are school materials kept when they are not being used?" Students can learn, even at an early age, to have an internal dialogue to organize their task, assess what materials are necessary, direct their thinking toward a work strategy, and be clear about what to do when they complete the assignment.

Teacher's and Student's Work

Sue Bredekamp and Teresa Rosegrant (1992) describe a cycle of learning and teaching. What teachers do—*create, provide, describe, help, and guide*—and what children do—*become aware, engage, explore, inquire, and utilize*—define teaching and learning activities that surround each new learning task. Children apply skills of attention, concentration, and engagement when they are exposed to a rich variety of reading and language arts activities. They draw on long-term memory to recall facts, details, and concepts. In first grade, for example, a folktale can be expanded with instructional activities that go far beyond vocabulary and reading, to include phonics, spelling, writing, social sciences, and art. Broad thematic exposure through integrated-subject teaching is brain-compatible teaching that corrals students' attention, motivates them as learners, and provides real-life experiences, such as exploratory walks in nature, moving the classroom outside its four walls, interacting with community resources, expressing learning through performances, or creating a work of art to link the mentally stimulated child to active remembering.

How Much Time?

Learning to read is so important in the primary grades and beyond that a significant portion of the school day needs to be available for reading instruction and language arts. Richard Allington (2001) suggests that more time for reading instruction be reclaimed from noninstructional duties in a schoolwide plan for reading:

> All teachers must understand the enormous benefits from a large volume of reading instruction. In such a plan long blocks of uninterrupted time for reading and writing are scheduled. Reading and writing would be integrated across all subject areas and a curriculum that featured wide reading and writing of informational texts, as well as narratives, would frame the lessons and activities. (p. 43)

Time for activities is secured by having other content areas, such as social studies, science, and at times, math, embedded within the language arts schedule.

In the primary grades, schools are encouraged to allocate as much as two and a half hours of protected time for reading-based activities. Devoting a major portion of the school day for early literacy development is a recommended practice and is responsive to the rigorous demands of most state-based guidelines. More important, the brain is prompted to sort, combine, and organize information for recall from several overlapping content areas.

> More important, the brain is prompted to sort, combine, and organize information for recall from several overlapping content areas.

Parents' Work

During the early years of formal schooling, parents continue to play a vital role in supporting the development of literacy. It is of primary importance for parents to support reading development during elementary school by continuing to have conversations with their children, share language play, make library trips, tell stories, and enjoy active, playful reading together. Reading books with their children in the primary language of the home and making it a pleasurable experience is the best help parents can give to support the development of their children as readers.

As they collaborate with the school, parents can also support these important skills:

Concentration: by giving children a quiet place without distractions to read and do school papers.

Organization: by establishing family routines that provide sufficient time for reading and other school-related tasks. Children can be encouraged to sort and place their school-type tools, toys, and clothes in places where they are easily found.

Motivation: by showing interest in their child's classroom progress and school activities. Posting notes from school, "refrigerator art," and "papers to-be-proud-of" encourages and supports children to maintain a positive school attitude.

Consistency: by becoming familiar with classroom learning games and teacher expectations and incorporating similar activities at home.

Attention: by helping children to remember to listen and respond to parents when they talk with them or give directions. Parents can provide prompts at home to support the habit of focusing attention.

It is clear that children are expected to learn to read in the early grades. By the end of first grade, teachers and parents already know if a child is on the way to becoming a fluent, competent reader or if there will be struggles in the years to come.

REFLECTIVE QUESTIONS

1. Attention and concentration are identified as skills students need to become readers. Describe some brain-compatible classroom prompts and activities to strengthen attending and concentration abilities. Parents, describe how home activities can encourage children to "pay attention."

2. If you are reading this book as part of a study group, as a group make a practical list of strategies teachers or parents can use to help children organize information and concepts into memory networks.

3. Declarative memory has two parts: semantic and episodic. How are they different?

4. Children practice skills for reading through declarative memory activities and rehearsal strategies. Once learned, these skills are accessed unconsciously to allow a child to read with fluency, automaticy, and understanding. Explain why practicing skills and learning concepts can lead to fluent, competent reading. How are working memory and long-term memory involved?

5. When teachers understand the energy requirements that reading places on emergent readers, they can structure classroom activities with children's needs in mind. Give an example of a reading task from the early grades, explain what is requested of the students, tell how much time you anticipate the activity will take, and what responses you would expect from the students.

6

Breaking the Reading Code

Learning to Read Through Instruction

Learning to read is so much more than learning phonemes, phonics, vocabulary building, comprehending text, or reading fluently. It is navigating various parts of the human brain through neural systems, igniting strings of neurons and allowing others to disengage. Reading requires the young reader to consciously focus and think about print and known words while the child's brain miraculously activates a complex series of electrical and chemical connections to develop a reading pathway. Teacher-led specific, direct, sequenced instruction with oral practice and rehearsal activities help a primary-school child's brain to build reading superhighways for fluent, accurate reading with understanding.

In the early primary grades, most reading instruction focuses on phonological processes, and include phonemic manipulation, phonics, and print processing until recognizing words becomes a procedural, automatic process. Research supports instructional activities for encoding (constructing words) as a precursor to decoding (reading words). Additionally, teaching sight words through rote practice activities allows students to read decodable text independently. Other instructional activities for storytelling, listening to stories, play or puppet acting, answering questions, having conversations, writing simple sentences, and learning to spell words augment teaching encoding and decoding and prepare the student for more complex reading skills in subsequent grades.

> The road to building a reading brain for decoding words and achieving reading fluency is not a uniform, one-size-fits-all pathway.

The road to building a reading brain for decoding words and achieving reading fluency is not a uniform, one-size-fits-all pathway. Every teacher knows that children in each kindergarten and first-grade classroom exhibit a wide range of reading potential. Some children have already developed skills that put them in good stead to learn. They are motivated, attentive, can concentrate, and are relatively well organized. Many, but not all, of these children are on their way to becoming competent readers by the end of first grade. In the real-life classroom, teachers must be prepared to meet the needs of all children regardless of their level of preparedness.

There is an achievement gap. It is not as though teachers are unaware of this situation; they simply are not certain what to do about it. According to researcher and CEO of the Center for Performance Assessment Douglas Reeves, who spoke to California educators in November, 2007, "The good news is that there are no new ideas about effective instruction; we already know what to do. The bad news is that effective instruction isn't going to make a difference unless 90 percent of the [faculty] are doing it" (Reeves, 2008, p. 3). "Doing it and doing it right" is the challenge for kindergarten and first-grade teachers as they lay the foundation for reading. Teachers can follow the framework standards set by the state offices of education, can explicitly follow lessons and extended practice activities from textbooks and materials from the state adopted list, can assign worksheets for independent practice, and use enrichment activities—and still not "do it right." It is the premise of these authors that "doing it right" means following the standards, using strong, replicated research to direct the use of best practices; engaging students in learning through novel, innovative, exciting ways; *and* understanding how the learner's unique and individually organized brain puts it all together to learn to read.

READING AND LANGUAGE ARTS GUIDELINES FOR KINDERGARTEN AND FIRST GRADE

Because education in the United States is decentralized, each state's department of education sets forth educational guidelines and curricula. A review of reading and language arts standards across the nation reveals a consistent focus on reading and literacy during the primary years. A summary of generally accepted skills for mastery in kindergarten and first grade includes the following:

Word analysis with phonemic awareness, phonological processing, and skills for decoding

Fluency or speed of processing through skills ranging from identifying letter names to producing letter sounds to reading controlled text

Systematic vocabulary development, including learning specific words and word-recognition strategies

Reading comprehension, including the ability to predict what will happen, compare information from different sources, and answer essential questions, such as *who, what, why,* and *what if*

Literary response and analysis that progresses from character focus, setting, and recognizing important events in kindergarten, to plot and story design in the first grade

Writing strategies and applications, beginning with upper- and lower-case letters and knowledge of letter sounds in kindergarten and moving to word and sentence production during first grade

Curriculum plans and frameworks for reading skills include specific student objectives and frequently provide examples of expected student responses. With regard to decoding and word recognition, for example, a child may be expected to blend sounds to be able to read one-syllable decodable words during the kindergarten year. For comparison, a first grader may be expected to use knowledge of vowel digraphs and *r*-controlled letter-sound associations to read words. In this case, a vowel digraph /ea/ would be recognized for its variance in *bear* and *seat*. The expectations are clear. The public education system expects kindergarten students to work with individual sounds. First-grade students are expected to develop an awareness of words and their relationship to speech and conventions of print, and to expand their reading word base.

STRUCTURING THE BRAIN FOR DECODING

A young child's brain is hardwired for speech, not reading. As we discussed in Chapter 2, the initial pathway for oral language begins when a sound is perceived. The pathway for reading, however, begins with visual input. To read, the brain must interpret signals that are received from the visual cortex and co-opt parts of an existing system for listening and speaking to

> Building a reading brain does not happen with naturally designated neural mechanisms for reading; the reading system must be developed.

create a new pathway that processes print for meaning. A child's propensity for building a reading brain does not happen with naturally designated neural mechanisms for reading; the reading system must be developed.

Structured teaching of phonological processes systematically leads the emerging reader's brain to facilitate links between the areas of the brain that need to be connected for reading. This allows words stored in implicit long-term memory for speaking or listening to be reconsidered and manipulated when they appear as printed symbols. Children become aware of phonemes by working with sounds they already know. They blend sounds, segment words into sounds, replace sounds, add sounds, and delete sounds through structured phonemic play. Each time sounds and combinations of sounds are introduced in another way, the child is engaged with brainwork through practice and coarticulation. The automatic process for phoneme manipulation then becomes a part of long-term memory as an initial skill fundamental to the entire reading process. With practice, children ultimately associate visual patterns with words that they hear and speak.

Mastering Decoding With Phonological Processes

We use phonological processes as an umbrella term to identify children's conscious mental operations, perception, interpretation, recall, and production around the sound structure of oral language when they learn to decode successfully (Moats, 2000; Torgesen, Wagner, & Rashotte, 1994). Phonological processing requires a child to be able to segment and blend phonemes, pronounce words, identify words and syllables, detect syllable stress, and remember names and lists (Moats, 2000). It turns out that neither the ability to hear the difference between two phonemes nor the ability to produce them is as important to effective decoding as a conceptual awareness that individual sounds exist, can be manipulated, and can be stored in long-term memory for ordered recall (Adams, 1990). A child needs many concepts and skills in order to become comfortable with abstract symbols and their manipulations for successful decoding of text. This section describes print awareness and alphabetic principle through phonics, while vocabulary development, processing speed, spelling, and writing are addressed later as skills that develop in tandem with the decoding processes.

Phonemic Awareness

Phonemic awareness is a conscious understanding that words are made of individual sounds (phonemes) from speech, and the ultimate awareness that these sounds represent letters of the alphabet. As we gain new insight into the reading brain and the reading process, a vast array of common research tells us most children need focused teaching to become skilled in phonemic awareness. Many reading experts identify a lack of phonemic awareness as a major cause of reading difficulties in children and adults who are poor readers (Adams, Foorman, Lundberg, & Beeler, 1998a; Liberman, Shankweiler, & Liberman, 1999; Lyon & Fletcher, 2001). The case for auditory, sound production, engagement is taken a step further by the work of Linnea Ehri (cited in Herron, 2007). Her research indicates the sight of a word sets off a signal to pronounce the word, as it is the sounds for pronunciation that have been stored in memory. Speech memory, according to Ehri, is the brain's system for recall, not strings of letters seen visually. Certainly, this conclusion supports our understanding that the oral language system develops first and would be more likely to provide the massive storage system for remembering our spoken language and the articulation of written language.

For adults who already know how to read, it seems quite logical that sounds heard in speech are paired with the letters on the printed page. However, Marilyn Jager Adams and her colleagues (1998a) identify "that without direct instructional support, phonemic awareness eludes roughly 25 percent of middle-class first graders and substantially more of those who come from less literacy-rich backgrounds" (p. 19). To address the serious reading problems children have when they cannot hear, identify, or understand the concept of phonemes, these professors have developed a classroom curriculum specifically for phonemic awareness (see the Instructional Resources). Phonemic awareness can be taught through planned activities for rhyming, alliteration, oddity tasks, phoneme segmentation, phoneme blending, phoneme manipulation, and syllable splitting. Activities designed to develop specific skills for reading may appear to be child's play, however, this work is not the same as the random, spontaneous activities that children engaged in during their infancy and preschool years to develop oral language.

In Chapter 4, we discussed developing phonemic awareness through rhyming and oddity activities that are addressed during the preschool years. Now, we look at more advanced phonological processing skills of phoneme segmentation, phoneme blending, phoneme manipulation, and syllable splitting.

Phoneme segmentation requires children to break words into the smallest possible sounds they can distinguish. In the case of *hand*, this would be *h-a-n-d*, with children providing sounds for each letter rather than identifying letter names. The opposite of phonemic segmentation is phoneme blending. To blend, the teacher pronounces sounds with an exaggerated, slow pronunciation *h—a—n—d*, then asks the children to put the sounds together and to say them quickly as a meaningful word.

In phoneme manipulation, children are asked to change the sound they hear at the beginning or end of a word to another sound and, consequently, to another word. Note that the results may be a real or nonsense word. For example, children are given the word *fox*, and the teacher asks that the beginning sound be changed to the /b/ sound. The response is *box*. If children are asked to change the middle sound to /a/, they generally laugh as they realize that *bax* is not a real word. Phoneme manipulation places extended demands on oral language structures, as this sensory input is meant for deciphering individual sounds from words that are familiar in their entirety.

> Phoneme manipulation places extended demands on oral language structures, as this sensory input is meant for deciphering individual sounds from words that are familiar in their entirety.

When children are asked to engage in phoneme syllable splitting, the teacher gives a word such as *dog,* and the children are asked to give the beginning sound in isolation. When asked for the beginning sound, they would respond, "d-d-d-d." Or if asked to give the rest of the word without the beginning sound, they would say, "og." For these tasks of phonemic awareness, the brain begins the tedious and awesome task of unconsciously reshaping pathways that are a part of the oral language process. The neural pathways children use for reading begin with those used for oral language interpretation. These are then co-opted to connect and to make sense out of sound and letter relationships.

> For these tasks of phonemic awareness, the brain begins the tedious and awesome task of unconsciously reshaping pathways that are a part of the oral language process.

Print Awareness

Awareness that print represents sounds and words provides a foundation for the child's brain that is under construction for reading. Although this awareness happens gradually, when a child's brain has scored this point and stored it in long-term memory, it is a monumental building block in the reading process. Print awareness develops in most children through interaction with their environment prior to school attendance. Experiences with pictures, colors, shapes, and symbols bring the concepts of print to the young child's attention.

Children may recognize the logo for McDonald's or Kmart or the title of a Dr. Seuss book. Gradually, they begin to recognize a word such as *zoo* for its unique appearance. Susan Hall and Louisa Moats (1999) refer to this type of prealphabetic learning as *logographic reading*. Letter recognition, phoneme processing and maneuvering, learning sounds with attached letters or letter strings, and predicting relationships between letters and sounds are all dependent on the abstract concept that sounds and words are represented by patterns of written symbols.

Reading depends on an awareness of how alphabetic letters are represented through their phonological structure as words. During the transitional phase of putting letters to sounds, children must recognize that phonemes may overlap or run together in speech, but the phonemes as letters are represented distinctly in print. For example, *next door* becomes coarticulated in speech and may be interpreted to sound like *nex store* or *an animal* may appear to be *an nanimal*. Production of individual sounds in words, such as strings of consonants, consonant blends, or vowels, can be vocalized at a rate of about 8 to 10 per second.

Because speaking sounds occurs so rapidly, Liberman and colleagues (1999) maintain it may be difficult for some children to determine how a spoken word or letter string is spelled. As children become familiar with phonemes, their sounds, and their letter representations, they become adept at automatically reconciling these inconsistencies between sounds and the letters that represent them.

Alphabetic Principle Through Phonics

Phonics is a system to identify symbols used in alphabetic writing that represent sounds. Phonics is used by Moats (2000) to describe sound-symbol reading instruction, which may also be referred to as a phonics approach to teaching reading (p. 234). Almost all beginning reading programs include phonics instruction, but there are many different approaches among the existing programs. The National Institute for Literacy's document *Put Reading First: The Research Building Blocks for Teaching Children to Read* (Center for the Improvement of Early Reading Achievement, 2001) identifies six distinct methods for phonics instruction (p. 13):

- Synthetic phonics converts letters or combinations of letters into sounds, then blends sounds for recognizable words.
- Analytic phonics scrutinizes the letter-sound relationships in words that are already known, but does not pronounce isolated sounds. Analogy-based phonics identifies unknown words by word families.
- Phonics through spelling segments words into phonemes, then develops new words using the phonemes that have been learned.
- Embedded phonics exposes children to phonics as examples become available through text.
- Onset-rime phonics identifies sounds before the first vowel (the onset), then addresses the remainder of the word (the rime).

Children learn that letters represent the sounds of spoken language and not that the letters of the alphabet each have a sound. Consider the elusive /k/ sound, which is represented by the words *cup, kettle, deck, school,* and *oblique.* Children can easily learn the sound and then anchor the sound to a letter or letter sequence (a grapheme). In addition to mimicking the way alphabetic writing was invented, this sequence gives the brain a logical way for ordering and storing the sounds and their accompanying letters for retrieval.

> Children learn that letters represent the sounds of spoken language and not that the letters of the alphabet each have a sound.

An effective phonics program has instructional components that

- give teachers support for systematic instruction;
- build understanding for students about relationships between sounds and letters, and provide practice for what is learned with words, sentences, text, and writing;

- are modifiable based on student assessment; and
- include related learning for alphabetic knowledge, phonemic awareness, vocabulary development, and text reading. (Center for the
Improvement of Early Reading Achievement, 2001)

Data from the National Institute of Child Health and Human
Development (NICHD) do not support any particular approach to teaching phonics (Fletcher & Lyon, 1998). Likewise, there is no specific sequence
for sound introduction, number of sounds, or set of rules that identify the
ideal phonics program. We strongly emphasize that, to read, children must
understand the sound-letter relationships that are studied through the
teaching of systematic phonics. However, programs specifically designed
to use a variety of phonics techniques have been successful for students. A
sound-to-symbol relationship fits the needs of first-grade children at this
stage of reading development.

Brain-Compatible Phonics Instruction

Phonics instruction is a major component in any reading program.
Children need simultaneous instruction to develop vocabulary; build
understanding and comprehension; acquire
listening skills; express ideas through spoken
language; practice letter, word, and sentence
writing; and develop a repertoire of words
that can be spelled correctly (Center for the
Improvement of Early Reading Achievement,
2001; Fletcher & Lyon, 1998). Phonics instruc-
tion using brain-compatible guidelines is one element of a complete plan
for teaching reading.

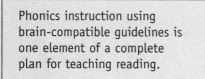
Phonics instruction using brain-compatible guidelines is one element of a complete plan for teaching reading.

Sounds to Letters, Not Letters to Sounds

Programs to introduce the 26 letters of the alphabet and then attach
sounds to the letters not only appear to be ineffective, but they can cause confusion for students (Liberman et al., 1999; Moats, 1998). A teaching program
that presents print-to-sound teaches only part of the code. This approach,
which is found in some conventional phonics programs, leaves gaps for
sounds that have to be added on to the sound recognition system that the
child has constructed. Of approximately 40 phonemes, 12 remain unex-
pressed when phonics is taught according to the 26 letters of the alphabet.

Since the initial publication of this book, significant information has
become available from brain research to support the sound-to-letter
instructional approach. Skilled readers, according to Linnea Ehri (cited
in Herron, 2007), look at thousands of words and instantly recognize
their meanings. To do this from their visual appearance alone (pattern

recognition) is not possible. According to Ehri's studies, it is the pronunciation of words that glues them to memory and recall.

Additionally, common sense tells us in a letter-to-sound approach, some letters have no uniquely defined job. For example, the letter /c/ shares sounds with /k/ and /s/. Some letter names bear little relationship to the sounds of the letter they represent. For example, the letter /x/ is named "eks" and sounds like /ks/ or /z/. Children may confuse these sounds during spelling and attempt to spell a word such as *box*, as *boks* or *boz*. Reading expert Louisa Moats (1998) encourages explicit teaching to distinguish each sound first and then to attach a letter or letters to the sound. Children may be asked to identify the sounds in words such as *mat*, *sad*, *pan*, *pale*, or *made*. If children know the rules that govern short and long vowels, they can apply the rules to these predictable words.

Primary Word Walls

Word walls used in some primary classrooms can be effective when they are designed to reinforce vocabulary development. Word walls for phonics, however, can be illogical, complex, and confusing if they are based solely on the alphabet. An illogical word wall list for /Aa/ might include *and*, *away*, *all*, *are*. A first-grade child who tries to make decoding sense out of this list containing irregular sounds for the letter /a/ may become confused about letters and sound relationships. A list that is compatible with the way children learn would list a phonic sound, such as /ā/ for wait, /ǎ/ for hat, and /aw/ for bought.

Orthographic Rules

Almost all words are completely regular by orthographic rule, but words use patterns that are somewhat obscure and do not exist peacefully with other decoding rules. An example would be a rule that states all words ending with a /v/ must have an /e/ at the end. The words *shove*, *live*, and *leave* all have the required /e/ after the /v/. But the final /e/ rule that says the preceding vowel should make a long sound is in conflict.

Teachers identify these inconsistencies through a systematic and explicit approach to teaching phonics with orthographic rules. Children, then, can make sense out of letters, sounds, and words and develop the cognitive capacity to deal with the inconsistencies of English.

Identification of Common Letter Blends and Word Families

Children may be confused when they are asked to use a word attack strategy that requires them to sound out words letter by letter. Much of the predictability of English comes not from individual letters but from letter spelling units where two or more letters together make a sound. A better approach, one firmly based on phonics instruction, is to identify the following when approaching the traditional "sounding out" process for unknown words:

> Much of the predictability of English comes not from individual letters but from letter spelling units where two or more letters together make a sound.

common consonant blends (e.g., /bl/, /br/, /pr/, /shr/, /thr/, /tw/)

vowel graphemes (e.g., /ai/, /eigh/, /ie/, /ough/, /ou/, /augh/)

word families (e.g., a base word, such as *care*, identified in *careful, caring,* and *uncaring*)

A letter-to-sound strategy, primary word walls based on the alphabet, incomplete orthographic rules, or sounding out individual letters in words are some of the teaching practices that can lead to confusion for a child's brain as it seeks order and patterns that are meaningful. Teachers who understand the child's brain with its pattern-seeking nature are likely to provide clear, logical word recognition strategies for children to use.

WORD RECOGNITION GAINS SOPHISTICATION

As children move through the primary grades, they gain more sophisticated ways of learning new words. They progress, for example, from sounding out all of the letters to recognizing letter patterns and phonemes, then to decoding words by syllables and identifying morphological components. Using the word *uncomfortable,* first-grade instruction would sound out the phonemes, u/n/c/o/m/f/or/t/a/b/le. Second-grade students would look at syllables, un/com/for/ta/ble. This allows them to extend letter combinations, seek larger orthographic units, and look for predictable beginnings and endings. By the third grade, students' advanced abilities allow them to look at larger and more complex orthographic units. Third graders would approach this sample word as un/comfort/able.

Effective instruction follows a progression of word recognition strategies during the early elementary years. This instructional design allows children to build meaningful units of morphemes, words, word origins, and understanding through a core knowledge base when they are in fourth grade and beyond (Moats, Furry, & Brownell, 1998).

Brain-Compatible Teaching
Programs for Phonological Processing

Effective teachers respond to children's word attack needs with classroom strategies that are designed to captivate young potential readers, particularly children who appear to lag behind in their understanding of phonological processes. One response for students who struggle with reading is a phonics and spelling supplement developed by Cunningham, Hall, and Heggie (1994). During a 10- to 15-minute whole-class teaching block, children work with an individual pocket chart and selected letters. Children initially develop two-letter words and progress to making bigger and bigger words. Discovering a mystery word using all of the letters is the climax of each lesson. Children are delighted with the suspense created by the mystery word, particularly as words become more complex. Each child's brain is primed during this group lesson with neural hooks to build connections and categories for sound-letter correspondences and word families.

Another supplemental program gives repeated exposure to spoken language during beginning reading phonological processing. By using oral language exposure, Goldsworthy's (1998) *Sourcebook of Phonological Awareness Activities: Children's Classic Literature* encourages children to form phonics bins, clusters of sounds with properties in common, such as /a/ in *cat, sat,* and *bat,* or the beginning sound of /b/ in *bear, box,* or *balloon.* Children can use these theoretical bins to accumulate sound categories that they recognize as speech sounds. Exposure to phonological processing, representation, and deviations, as Goldsworthy refers to them, strengthens the sound categories that children develop. Activities in this program include classic stories that provide complex, but naturally familiar, words. Stories are read and discussed at least three times. The stories may be accompanied by focused attention enticers: a flannel board presentation, hand puppets, or role-play. Parents support the process at home by reading and talking about the stories and particularly discussing the vocabulary. In this way, the vocabulary becomes familiar to the children before classroom activities, which require work with phonological processes.

Using "Goldilocks and the Three Bears" as a target story, activities may include simple word-counting procedures, such as "How many words do you hear in 'The bears went for a walk'?" More complex activities ask students to change the first two sounds in a pair of words. In this case, *middle sized* becomes *siddle mized,* and *big voice* becomes *vig boice.* Children enjoy the novelty of this kind of activity. The author emphasizes that activities move from sounds to letters, which, as we have seen, leads to logical, confusion-free phonological development for children (Goldsworthy, 1998).

To summarize, students achieve intended outcomes for phonological processing when they are motivated to read and when they are exposed to a logical sequence of instruction. The NICHD reported on studies that were conducted at 36 different sites to check reading development. The studies included 34,501 children with normal reading development and children whose reading development was impaired. Interventions that produced successful readers went beyond explicit teaching of phonics.

Successful readers were encouraged to read and write for enjoyment and were stimulated to do so with practices, such as those described in the two previous examples, which fostered positive attitudes toward reading (Fletcher & Lyon, 1998). Thinking once again about the message from Douglas Reeves (2008), presented at the opening to this chapter, the achievement gap is highly retractable; what is needed is "deep implementation" of the known key concepts and skills needed to produce successful readers. A deep understanding of phonemes and phonological concepts that incorporates a child's naturally available oral language system makes perfect sense.

TEACHING ENCODING: SPELLING AND WRITING

Learning to spell should occur simultaneously with learning to assign letters to sounds for decoding (Adams et al., 1998a; Fletcher & Lyon, 1998; Liberman et al., 1999). Even more than being suggested, Herron (2007) insists **decoding**, print to speech, must absolutely be taught with **encoding**, speech to print, for brain-efficient teaching. While decoding is reading words, encoding is constructing words. Writing becomes an effective road to early reading as it efficiently activates memory for sounds and left hemisphere structures for word processing (Ehri, cited in Herron, 2007). Children learn the same new patterns of language across the domains of listening, spelling, writing, and ultimately reading, thus strengthening the networks of neural connections as the child's brain categorizes words first for how they are articulated, then for what they mean, and finally for how they are represented by letters. Words are learned with efficiency and with greater likelihood for retention and retrieval when they are practiced at different times in different ways through phonological processing instruction designed to pair spelling and writing with learning to decode.

Spelling

Spelling instruction can be based on a number of premises, such as sound-symbol correspondences, syllable patterns, orthographic rules, word meanings, word derivation, or word origin. We know, however, instruction is most compatible with the reading structures of a child's brain when spelling words are meaningfully organized into groups with common word patterns and coherently sequenced grade by grade. Moats (2000, p. 153) suggests a spelling program linked to phoneme awareness in kindergarten, consonant and vowel correspondence for first grade, more complex spelling patterns for second grade, and syllabication, compounds, and word endings for third grade.

A spelling list of 10 to 12 words per week may contain words children are using in their reading or writing that exemplify orthographic patterns from a sequenced word study program. Teachers frequently include additional words that students find confusing and that need to be clarified. Ideally, the study of orthography, the spelling of words, in the early school years is closely matched with words that occur in reading texts with high frequency, but spelling lists also contain some commonly misspelled words in the mix.

Systematic instruction for phoneme-to-grapheme spelling is emphasized through the second grade and beyond. As children become more sophisticated with their ability to decipher new words, selection of words for spelling study takes a vocabulary-building emphasis. Intense spelling instruction for letter and word patterns in the early school years secures an understanding of words and their parts that allows older children to employ self-initiated analysis techniques with new vocabulary they encounter as they read.

> Intense spelling instruction for letter and word patterns in the early school years secures an understanding of words and their parts that allows older children to employ self-initiated analysis techniques with new vocabulary they encounter as they read.

Storytelling and Writing

Children in kindergarten and first grade are capable of developing complex thoughts far in advance of their ability to express these thoughts in writing. When they are expected to write independently, the difference between what they know about words and what they are physically capable of recording on paper becomes apparent. Recognizing this disparity, teachers can take an active role during their students' early writing efforts by allowing students to dictate their ideas and stories. This intensive one-to-one interaction can be handled by parent volunteers or older student helpers who write for the children, or the whole class can become involved in story development as the teacher writes on an overhead projector or large chart. Writing, as a developmental skill, is a natural and necessary companion to the process of learning to read.

Although writing is a natural partner to a reading program, it does not happen easily. Writing places a new set of demands on the developing brain by calling on the motor cortex to respond in new ways. Picture a child who is beginning to experiment with writing. The youngster concentrates on holding a pencil between the thumb, pointer finger, and middle finger. At first, this feels and looks awkward, and the child must concentrate on gripping the pencil with the appropriate amount of tension and really think about touching the lead of the pencil to the paper. As the fingers press and move the pencil, the child consciously thinks about the shapes that are being made, staying within the lines, and manipulating the pencil.

While this struggle is visible, what is going on in the brain is not (refer to Figure 4.1). Planning, timing, and execution of finger, hand, and arm movements, initiated in the premotor and motor cortex, are ultimately orchestrated by the frontal lobes. The cerebellum, located at the lower back of the brain, unconsciously coordinates the precise hand movements when a child puts marks on the paper (Berninger & Richards, 2002).

With practice, the neural circuits used for writing eventually function automatically and the child no longer needs to be conscious of this very complex process. Teachers can provide other classroom activities, often thought of as art or craft projects, such as stenciling, tracing, coloring within small spaces, cutting, and pasting, that act as developmental activities for the mechanics of writing. In a well-designed program, writing and spelling work in tandem with reading, so that children have an outlet to expand complex thinking skills and express complex thoughts and ideas.

READING BEYOND ENCODING AND DECODING

Reading is a developmental process that involves being able to identify words in text, understand what the words mean, seek connections for word meanings, and do all this with speed and fluency. In kindergarten and first grade, reading instruction designed to build the reading (decoding) pathway moves beyond phonological processing skills to include comprehension skills, speed of processing (fluency), and development of sight vocabulary. Researcher Guinevere Eden (2004), from the Center for the Study of Learning, studies the neurological basis of reading through pediatric brain imaging. A team of researchers looked at the brain's structures while a child was involved with reading a story. They found areas of the brain in addition to those initially identified. While these topics are explored individually in Chapters 8 and 9, it is imperative to recognize we do not address reading skill development in a sequence of skills in which one must be proficient before we teach the next skill. The human brain develops in all ways at the same time. So while the primary emphasis in the first two years of schooling may be to break the alphabetic code, other information, skills, and concepts are developing as well.

Building Vocabulary for Comprehending Text

Comprehension depends greatly on the words a child knows and can call on automatically. Educators are encouraged to provide a wide variety of listening and print exposure experiences during the first two years of school, including books based on the alphabet, informational stories, classic and contemporary literature, children's magazines and newspapers, dictionaries, and reference materials. Teachers can initiate questioning and discussion before, during, and after reading these materials to help students comprehend and draw meaning from them as well as develop new vocabulary.

It is interesting that children attending preschools are not given a learning advantage for vocabulary development when the curriculum is based upon early decoding and prealphabetic skills at the expense of language development activities (Biemiller, 2003b). Consider also that some kindergarten teachers spend as much as 40 percent of their language arts instructional time on sound-letter instruction and decoding unfamiliar words that children have not previously seen and cannot define (Bucuvalao & Juel, 2002). Emphasis on vocabulary building must happen concurrently with phonological processing and decoding instruction during the early school years.

Vocabulary development initially occurs through talking. Teachers who discuss the meaning of words with children and provide opportunities for children to engage in conversations about words enhance their spoken language and expand the ways children store language and vocabulary in accessible long-term memory for retrieval. For example, share time in kindergarten and first grade helps children learn how to express their ideas or experiences in complete, coherent, syntactically correct sentences.

When a teacher also provides opportunities for students to respond to the vocabulary used by their peers, the experience takes on an additional level of learning sophistication (Beck, McKeown, & Kucan, 2003). A teacher may ask another student, "What does it mean when Sheri said that she was confused by the picture?" or, "How did Manuel act to make us understand that he was embarrassed?" Providing many experiences for oral language comprehension, as addressed in Chapter 8, makes sense because how well children are able to comprehend during listening has been confirmed to be an excellent predictor for future success with reading comprehension (Aaron, 1995).

Processing Written Symbols, Orthography

Orthography, as addressed earlier, is the visual pattern for written language with features of graphemes, phonology, and semantics. At what speed does the brain process the orthography of print? Children develop processing speed as they learn more words at an automatic level. In terms of the human brain, processing speed engages neural circuits that are required to fire and connect again and again (Schwartz and Begley, 2003). As a child focuses attention on the written symbols, the representative circuits become hardwired and are accessed automatically. When kindergarten and first-grade children develop a repository of words stored in long-term memory and decode at an automatic level, they are able to move seemingly effortlessly along each written line, seeing each letter and each word, but being detained by none.

> When kindergarten and first-grade children develop a repository of words stored in long-term memory and decode at an automatic level, they are able to move seemingly effortlessly along each written line, seeing each letter and each word, but being detained by none.

Many areas of the brain are involved with the reading of even an individual word, and if words are not known by the child at an automatic level, the process can stall at any juncture. If the child is not able to process words rapidly and automatically, comprehension suffers. Reading with fluency begins to develop in the early years, but it may take several years before these skills are comfortably in place. Chapter 9 will discuss fluency in depth.

Teaching Sight Words

Teaching sight words is not an either/or proposition. An emergent reader who is building strong decoding skills can simultaneously learn, and will automatically add, common sight words to an ever-expanding sight vocabulary in long-term memory.

Words known by sight are taught using rote memory techniques through frequent exposure. Once learned at the automatic recall level, the words reside in long-term memory within neural networks of similar words and experiences. Words such as *and, from, the, of, to, that, for, was, are, with,* and *you* should be recognized by sight, as they are often not included with sound-to-print instruction that prepares students to read decodable text. In addition, as children learn sight words, more interesting stories are accessible for children to read.

There are limitations to teaching sight vocabulary. Some children with excellent memory skills learn to easily store new words in long-term memory, rather than going through the hard work of learning the orthographic rules for encoding and decoding. Remedial work with students who are identified as unsuccessful decoders indicates that some of these children have excellent memory skills for sight words. They are generally successful readers until the middle or end of second grade, as long as they read relatively short words. However, when they are faced with text that has longer multisyllabic words, words that look similar, and words with many letter sequence deviations they begin to show

> Remedial work with students who are identified as unsuccessful decoders indicates that some of these children have excellent memory skills for sight words.

signs of reading difficulties. Instruction that encourages students to learn too many sight words during the early years can give readers a false sense of reading success, when actually they are taxing memory capabilities in place of developing decoding strategies.

Children progress from being ready to read—to encoding and decoding and from developing vocabulary and understanding—to the ability to read with fluency and accuracy. In tandem, they begin to learn spelling patterns and start to record their own ideas in writing. Not all children develop these skills at the same rate. The next chapter addresses important reasons to catch children before they are unsuccessful with any aspect of their reading development.

REFLECTIVE QUESTIONS

1. The brain has structures that are hardwired to attend to and produce speech. What is different about the demands that are placed on the brain to respond to input for reading?

2. If you are reading this book as part of a study group, ask three people to prepare a short lesson that plays with sounds using phoneme awareness activities. Have the group define concepts children are learning when they practice sounds through these exercises.

3. Prepare an outline or concept map for a short faculty presentation to trace how pronunciation and articulation of sounds to letters, not letters to sounds, efficiently direct a child's brain to remember words. Consider a discussion about how phonics instruction is taught at your school.

4. Writing is a natural accompaniment to a reading program. In what ways do teachers prime their students and their brains for the physical process of writing?

5. Comment on some of the advantages and disadvantages of teaching sight words.

7

Assessing and Responding to Readers at Risk

S tudents in the elementary years are privileged to have high-powered, quick thinking brains. It is estimated their neurons fire up to 225 times faster than the average adult brain during a similar thinking task (Kotulak, 1997). Teachers use this information to provide instruction that is meaningful, information laden, and logical. Children are constructing, not brain structures themselves but, rather, organized connections and superhighways among existing structures for memory and recall.

There are several reasons for some children to be unsuccessful with the reading development process. Many have a genetic tendency to avoid brain structures that would allow them to build a reading pathway that is efficient. Some children lack early oral language stimulation. Others have infrequent school attendance and do not receive sequential instruction for the development of all the skills necessary to become proficient readers. Whatever the cause, we know through the study of neurology that when children struggle with any aspect of the reading process their brains demand huge amounts of brain sugar—glucose. This need for energy in the neural cortex remains high anytime the child attempts to do a reading task. These children get tired of reading quicker than their peers who access the decoding reading pathway to read with ease.

Teachers can identify readers who struggle by their behaviors, as well as by how they perform at their reading tasks. They frequently act in ways that are disruptive or unacceptable in the regular classroom environment. When children tell us by their work or their behavior that reading is not progressing normally, school programs for assessment and intervention must be in place to provide the support they deserve. Programs within the regular classroom, such as supplemental instruction in tandem with a core reading program or a replacement reading program, provide instruction that is tailored for struggling readers—to catch them up with their grade-alike peers.

CR ЄO

THE CASE FOR EARLY ASSESSMENT

Teachers find that some children enter school already reading, some are ready to read, and others lack basic print awareness. The National Association for the Education of Young Children (NAEYC, 1998) warned that "most children learn to read at age six or seven, a few learn at four, some learn at five, and others need intensive individualized support to learn to read at eight or nine" (p. 30). This means that, as early as kindergarten, there may be a two-year variation in reading ability in a single classroom that expands by third grade. A range of potential abilities, coupled with differences in background experiences, interests, personality, and temperament, challenges teachers who are expected to produce academic results for every child in a predetermined time frame based on grade-level standards (NAEYC, 1998). With a large variation in language abilities even among 5- and 6-year-olds, teachers find they must identify children who are at risk for academic failure early in the first year of school.

This chapter approaches formal reading instruction with the belief that all children are ready for reading instruction when they enter school and then discusses assessments for successful and struggling emergent readers. Specific programs will be identified to meet the varying needs of children who are at risk of reading failure and for those who stumble along the way. Children who enter school with good oral language skills in English and are ready to read but subsequently fail to make adequate progress must be identified. Likewise, those who have insufficient oral language development need assessment, for neither group of children learns to read at expected levels without instructional interventions (Lyon & Fletcher, 2001).

No Waiting Allowed

Neuroscientists using positron emission tomography (PET) scans have identified critical developments in the brain between the ages of 4 and 12. During this time, learning appears to surge. Imaging technology follows the brain's consumption of glucose, the fuel nerve cells use when they are active and making new connections among themselves.

Prize-winning science writer Ronald Kotulak (1997) describes this energy spurt as a time "when the brain seemed to glow like a nuclear reactor, pulsating at levels 225 percent higher than adult brains" (p. 36). Kotulak speculates that this is a time that the brain determines to keep regularly traveled neural pathways or prune connections from deserted routes, as it eagerly responds to stimuli from the senses.

The years from birth through age 8 are furthermore considered to be critical for literacy development. In terms of cognition, during the primary years, children are extremely responsive to instruction with malleable, plastic brains that are more open to new learning than at any other time during their formal education. Educators' responsibility to every child, particularly during this period of rapid brain development, is to make learning accessible and challenging for every student and to provide appropriate interventions for those who do not keep up. All children must have their learning needs met, even if the necessary intervention programs are time and personnel intensive and more costly for children who are not progressing as expected.

> In terms of cognition, during the primary years, children are extremely responsive to instruction with malleable, plastic brains that are more open to new learning than at any other time during their formal education.

Educators know that while children arrive at school with a wide range of backgrounds for reading, they all are expected to meet state and federal performance standards. The obstacles to be overcome by both teachers and students sometimes look formidable. Consider a study conducted by Susan B. Neuman (2001), Assistant Secretary for Elementary and Secondary Education, U.S. Department of Education, and her colleagues. The study took place in four neighborhoods of Philadelphia that represented two middle-class and two low-income areas. In each instance, the researchers determined how many children were in the area, how many places were available to purchase children's books, and the number of different book titles that were available within the geographic area. Additionally, logographic signs were identified and child care center libraries were scrutinized. The researchers found that in the best situation, the neighborhood potential for books to be purchased provided approximately 12 book titles for each child. Researchers deemed this number as a significant choice of books. In the neighborhood with the least print availability, there were 33 book titles in total—all of which were coloring books—available for approximately 1,000 children.

The researchers identify three educational ramifications from this study that focused on book availability in neighborhoods. First, they refer to the "Matthew effects" in which children with more opportunity for book exposure grow in academic achievement, while those with less print availability become weaker in their ability to break the code for reading text. An environmental opportunity hypothesis identified earlier by Keith Stanovich (1986) speaks to the fact that children who have limited exposure to print are less likely to be able to hear the phonology associated with print, some-thing we know is essential for learning to read. Second, Neuman (2001) refers to a familiarity hypothesis: Children who are familiar with books and stories develop mental models that go with reading different kinds of text. With familiarity comes comfort with reading.

The third hypothesis the researchers identify is the most powerful—the knowledge gap. Individuals learn, really learn with a depth of under-standing, what they are able to access through print. The good news reported by Neuman (2001) is that something can be done about the knowledge gap. Teachers can provide carefully constructed educational environments that are rich with exposure not only to direct instruction but also to large numbers of books to captivate young minds.

Important studies such as this one help educators to understand the differences that potentially could be represented among schoolchildren from different socioeconomic groups. Realize, also, that information reported in this study only represents the environmental impact on children from English-speaking families. Teachers are faced with another set of considerations when children learn English as a second language.

ENGLISH LANGUAGE LEARNERS

In an ideal educational environment, students whose first language is not English are assessed for English language skills immediately on entering the school system. In the 1999–2000 school year, an estimated 9.3 percent, or 4.4 million, American students were English learners (ELs). Of these, 77 percent were native Spanish speakers (Antunez, 2002). Each student who is not proficient in English needs a reading program that is tailored to that student's specific needs. While assessments that determine the level of competence a student possesses in both English and the child's primary language are needed, some additional questions can add meaningful information to help the classroom teacher to make instructional decisions:

- Does the child's primary language have a Roman alphabet? A written form?
- Does it contain phonemes, and how do the phonemes compare to English sounds?
- Can the student fluently speak, read, and write the primary language?
- How well does the student speak English?
- How old is the student?
- What staff, programs, and resources are available to teach this student? (Antunez, 2002)

The student's fluency in English, along with an assessment of available school resources, is used to determine the language of initial reading instruction. For students who are not proficient in English, answers to the previous questions prompt decisions about the type of program—primary language, English only, or bilingual (integrated primary language and English)—that will be appropriate when these choices are available. Unfortunately, many districts and states do not offer a range of appropriate choices, and many students do not receive the support they need to succeed with written and spoken English.

Children who lack exposure to adequate oral language preparation in their native language, who live or have lived in an unsafe environment, who lack a family that provides loving care, or who have had little formal schooling are best served in a bilingual program (Linquanti, 1999). A bilingual program can help develop oral language for ELs in both their native language and in English. Language development in one language tends to nurture development in the other when schools provide an environment that allows children to learn in both languages (Cummins, 2000).

Children who come into the formal education system already speaking and reading well in their native language are often placed in a regular classroom that provides an English-only program. The background information about language that they already possess provides a foundation for instruction in an English-only program. These programs are particularly successful when they have instruction provided in a varied format that actively engages students in speaking, reading, and writing. And research validates the advantages of bilingualism developed at an early age.

Judy Foreman (2002) reported on intellectual advantages for children who grow up in bilingual homes. Since they deal with language abstractions early in life, they develop strategies to resolve differences. Abstract tasks—one study involved building with LEGOs and another larger-sized block—do not create a problem for 4-year-old children who speak dual languages. It is as if they are able to ignore obvious visual tasks that are incongruent. A monolingual child is generally not able to complete this task satisfactorily until one year later. Children with dual languages are also able to switch back and forth between different rules and codes between the two languages they are learning. This ability is most likely due to the discovery by neuroscientists that both languages operate from the same language pathway, involving Broca's area. However, brain scans reveal that when a person learns the second language later, after puberty, two separate parts of Broca's area register activity (Foreman, 2002). An additional caveat for bilingualism is reported by Dahlberg (2007): A team of Canadian researchers treating patients for dementia found that patients who spoke two or more languages developed dementia on the average four years later than their single-language peers. Older, dual-language individuals continued to be better at paying attention even when distractions were present.

During the time English language is developing, the issues for learners are diverse. Although their needs for decoding are similar to those of their English-speaking peers, ELs may need additional practice and modified instruction through the regular education program. One difficulty ELs experience is that the sounds of English phonemes are often different from those in their native language. For example, Spanish-speaking children are familiar with similar sounds for the consonants *b, c, d, f, l, m, n, p, q, s,* and *t* in their primary language. However, the vowels are named differently. There are challenges to teaching decoding skills, phonemic awareness, and phonics for children who are learning English. However, teachers can effectively teach skills necessary for reading competence if they have adequate knowledge about their students and about their native language (Antunez, 2002). Teachers who lack background in the primary language of their students frequently benefit from receiving expert consultation from another educator. Realistically, with the many languages children bring, this is often not possible.

> Although their needs for decoding are similar to those of their English-speaking peers, ELs may need additional practice and modified instruction through the regular education program.

Often, school districts have an inadequate number of appropriate assessment instruments and trained personnel to determine if a child has English language acquisition needs and if those needs occur in tandem with a learning disability. Special education programs in certain districts show an overrepresentation of ELs. To counteract overrepresentation of non-English speakers who receive special education services, schools are urged to identify children with limited or no English ability early and to create school environments with instructional strategies that have proven to be successful for these students at risk (Ortiz, 2001). What Works Clearinghouse (2007) offers insights into what works for reading, mathematics, and English language development: peer tutoring and response groups. Peer tutoring assigns partners (a tutor and a tutee) who read together and complete assignments. Peer response groups give a group of four to five students shared responsibilities for completing an assignment. Both methods have high improvement indices for English language students and their classmates (WWC Intervention Report, 2007).

Two particular instances have been provided as environmental issues that block student success with reading: low socioeconomic status and lack of exposure to English. We also know that biological or neurological differences among children are a cause of disparities in reading achievement.

Understanding the need for assessment, having a plan for reading instruction that targets most children, and providing intervention for those students with special needs are appropriate expectations for our public school systems. First, we will look at reading assessment information and instructional responses for normally progressing readers, followed by assessments and intervention programs for students who need special consideration.

ASSESSMENT OF STUDENTS WITH REGULARLY DEVELOPING READING SKILLS

Children who progress normally in reading are for the most part assessed in the classroom through basal readers. The range of assessments that teachers use during the first two years of reading instruction covers concepts of print, phonemic awareness, phonics, fluency, oral reading, spelling, vocabulary, and comprehension. As students progress through the grades, teachers also assess students' ability related to organizational features of text and reference skills. Teachers also use district or state guidelines to direct their assessment practices.

Ongoing classroom assessment allows teachers to identify children who are not progressing in any skill area. Often, additional instruction time or skills practice will remediate the problem through ongoing regular classroom interventions.

Instructional Responses to Assessment

Teachers frequently use strategies of preteach, reteach, modify, model, and adjust as they respond to the diverse needs of their students. While there are many skill development designs that involve whole-class instruction, teachers also find it helpful to use flexible classroom grouping to meet the needs of their varied student population. Usually, teachers decide to assess and reconfigure their instructional groups many times, even during the kindergarten year. When teachers find they need to work with small groups, it is important that children are able to work independently. Teachers often spend a considerable amount of time—five weeks or more—at the beginning of the year to set up classroom procedures for students to work independently. As the rest of the class works at their desks or on projects at learning stations, the teacher is free to target instruction to meet the varying needs of children in a small-group setting.

> Usually, teachers decide to assess and reconfigure their instructional groups many times, even during the kindergarten year.

DIFFERENCES IN BRAIN DEVELOPMENT

The brains of children who cannot read easily may be working very hard, perhaps harder than the brains of those who have no difficulty. Neuroscientists have observed huge demands in the brain for glucose (energy) as poor readers struggle with reading tasks. But the students' hard work does not yield successful reading results. As you may recall from information discussed in Chapter 2, there may be a lack of connectedness in the reading system in some children's brains (Shaywitz, 2003). Good

Neuroscientists have observed huge demands in the brain for glucose (energy) as poor readers struggle with reading tasks.

readers have integrated, smoothly functioning connections among the structures of a well-defined decoding system for reading. In contrast, dyslexic readers use ancillary connections among structures and frequently do not activate areas in the brain that effective readers use. These alternate connections may allow struggling readers to accurately read words but do not permit them to attain and recall mental models for words that would allow fluent and automatic reading (Shaywitz & Shaywitz, 2001).

Digging Deeper Into Reading Disabilities

Dyslexia has been defined by Sally Shaywitz (2003), at Yale University, as a cognitive deficit relating to phonological processing, particularly the ability to decode and recognize words and to write and spell. According to Roxanne Hudson and her colleagues (Hudson, High, & Otaiba, 2007), identification of children who experience dyslexia is difficult. The term can be broken into two parts: *dys*, meaning difficult or not happening, and *lexia*, meaning involvement with words and language associated with reading. Based on her extensive research in the area of dyslexia, Shaywitz (2003) reports that brain-imaging studies revealed markedly different brain activation patterns in dyslexic readers compared to those in good readers. While Shaywitz and other medical personnel, researchers, and clinicians tend to identify all readers who are unsuccessful as dyslexic, other reading specialists use a variety of descriptions. Commonly used terminology includes "poor readers" (Moats, 2001), "children with special needs" (Vukelich, Christie, & Enz, 2002), "struggling readers" (Allington, 2001), or "disabled/impaired readers" (Fletcher & Lyon, 1998). Classroom teachers, too, would tell us that there is a range of children who struggle with reading. Some children have minimal skill deficits, while at the other end of the continuum are children who are identified with learning disabilities and who qualify for special education services. There is not agreement among experts on a single term that adequately defines the variety of readers who are unsuccessful or the intensity of reading problems children experience.

We do know that reading problems are neurobiological, meaning they result from problems located physically in the brain. It is not solely caused by speech or hearing impairments, a developmental delay, or being from a low socioeconomic background, although these characteristics may contribute to a higher risk for reading problems (Hudson et al., 2007). Based on the uniqueness of each child's brain, there is not a simple cause, nor is there a single instructional response to reading problems.

Regardless of terminology, many children who experience reading problems have been exposed to regular reading instruction and may exhibit strong abilities in higher-order reading skills of vocabulary, syntax, and reasoning discourse. Yet they lack the ability to decode and read rapidly.

The inability to discern and manipulate abstractions associated with phonemes has been identified as a significant cause of many reading failures. A relatively small number of emergent readers, however, do not respond to regular or extended classroom interventions for phonemic awareness and decoding deficits. If these children are given additional instruction and practice and they continue to fall further behind their classmates, they may have cognitive differences that block their ability to even think about phonemes and the variation of sounds they represent.

Other Causes of Reading Disabilities

In Chapter 5, we discussed cognitive priming skills that need to be in place for the emerging reader. These skills, particularly attention, concentration, memory, and organization, may not be identified through traditional classroom testing. Traditional assessment determines what a child is able or unable to do, not necessarily what cognitive skills may be providing interference with reading progress.

> These skills, particularly attention, concentration, memory, and organization, may not be identified through traditional classroom testing.

Traditional assessment does not provide information about how the brain is structured for reading when we look at students who are struggling with cognitive differences. P. G. Aaron (1995), professor of education and school psychology at Indiana State University, suggests a "deeper elusive problem with cognitive processes that underlie reading" (p. 345). An example of one such problem could be visual processing. In this instance, a child is unable to concentrate on or focus on tracking words or make the necessary conversions from the visual input to a sound or word output. Current work by neuroscientist Guinevere Eden, who is the director for Georgetown's Center for the Study of Learning, and colleagues (2007) studied a group of 80 students identified as dyslexic readers. In addition to the phonological awareness problem identified as critical to the learning-to-read cycle, Eden and her colleagues have uncovered that children with dyslexia may rely on visual perception more than children who progress to successfully recognize phonological cues for reading. At initial reading stages, visual cues are dominant for all prereaders; children who experience reading success switch emphasis to rely on left-brain tasks for deciphering sounds of language (Eden et al., 2007; Eden, Turkeltaub, Weisberg, Flowers, & Basu, 2004).

Much of the information we currently receive about aberrant brain function during attempts at reading come from studies neuroscientists are conducting that compare brain imaging of successful and nonsuccessful readers using functional magnetic resonance imaging (fMRI) scanning technology. Hudson and her colleagues (2007) reviewed studies on structural differences in the brains of children who are successful readers and those who are identified as reading disabled. Their report identifies the differences in white and gray matter. In the brain, gray matter is the nerve cells themselves, which are responsible for processing information. The counterparts in the brain, the white matter, represent axons coated with glial cells, which communicate with a myriad of dendrites. The white matter is located deeper in the brain and is responsible to pass information to all the various parts of the brain. Reports indicate that people with dyslexia have less gray and less white matter in the area of the brain identified earlier as the angular gyrus, the sound-to-letter area in the parietal/temporal lobe junction in the left hemisphere (Hudson et al., 2007). Hence the strategy of practice, practice, practice that is inherent to intervention programs may result in children developing new connections and pathways, increasing gray and white matter. While neurological research has identified this apparent deficit in white and gray matter for unsuccessful readers, it has not proven how reading instruction can improve the density of the matter. Until that type of sophisticated study is available, the neuroscience information simply infers appropriate instructional practice.

It is not possible, nor would we suggest, that a child having reading difficulties undergo a brain scan. The technology and the professionals and assistants required to run it are cost prohibitive for education. Additionally, reports of findings are based on group outcomes and are not deemed reliable for individual diagnosis. We do submit, however, that educators who are consumers of information from brain studies can increase the depth of their assessments and have a greater understanding of their observation methods. Understanding differences in the struggling reader's cognitive function leads educators toward a more informed course for remediation.

One example of intense assessment and observation in reading intervention is the program developed at the Lindamood-Bell Center. Pat Lindamood and her colleagues (Lindamood, Bell, & Lindamood, 1997) at the clinic identify and treat individual reading deficiencies through sensory-cognitive function. Assessments done by clinicians use standard tests of reading progress and additionally check a child's ability to manipulate phonemes. The Lindamood program, different from and more intense than most interventions, uses a tactile/sensory approach. Children learn to pay attention to sounds by feeling what is happening with their mouths and to identify how they form sounds with labels such as "lip poppers" or "tongue tappers." This methodology progresses from oral sounds to having the child represent sounds with colored blocks.

Ultimately, children progress to letters and words. This sequence of instruction appears to activate the child's brain for attending to sounds through a tactile approach and stimulate a pathway to the brain's language centers for sound identification. It represents a cognitive response to reading difficulty that goes beyond traditional approaches for poor readers.

ASSESSMENT AND READING STANDARDS

Reading First legislation requires support at the state and local levels for the selection and implementation of informal and formal assessments beginning in kindergarten and first grade. These assessments identify progress of both normally progressing readers and children who are failing. An assessment committee funded by the federal government reviewed and applied stringent criteria to commercially available assessment tests. A report summarizing the work of the committee, prepared by Edward J. Kame'enui (2002), professor at the Institute for the Development of Educational Achievement (IDEA) and the College of Education at the University of Oregon, is available to educators. The committee identified 24 formal assessment measures that have sufficient evidence to be used for screening, diagnosis, progress monitoring, and measuring Reading First outcomes. Assessments that met the criteria for the five reading components of Reading First legislation (phonemic awareness, phonics, reading fluency, vocabulary development, and reading comprehension) are listed on the University of Oregon Web site (see the Instructional Resources). These assessments can be used for normally progressing children and for children whose reading is impaired.

Children with cognitive functioning deficiencies challenge educators to look more closely at the way these students interpret sensory input the brain receives for reading. When children experience serious reading difficulties, assessments administered by a psychologist or language specialist provide in-depth information about the prerequisite cognitive functions required for reading.

Some examples of the many commercially available assessments include the Gray Oral Reading Test (Gort-3), the Phonological Awareness Test (PAT), and the Lindamood Auditory Conceptualization Test (LAC). Some assessments are directed toward one specific cognitive function, such as phonemic awareness; digit span; number, sentence, or word memory; short-term memory; auditory or verbal comprehension; or processing speed. Other assessments provide subtests for several of these cognitive functions. Combining assessment reports from a school psychologist or language speech pathologist with the teacher's classroom assessments and process observations provides a thorough picture of the struggling reader's strengths and needs. In this way, a complete battery of assessments can provide precise information to match deficit skills with an appropriate reading intervention program.

For educators, there is a strong message. The longer a child continues to struggle with an inefficient system for reading, the more urgent it becomes that we intervene. We observe this long-term effect, not by brain imaging, but by substantial research supported by the National Institute of Child Health and Human Development (NICHD). Without systematic, focused, and intensive intervention, the majority of children who enter school at risk for reading failure are rarely able to catch up with their peers who are nonimpaired readers (Lyon & Fletcher, 2001). It is our challenge and responsibility as educators to select reading intervention strategies and programs that will correct the weaknesses individual children experience in their language systems. Intensive reading programs appear to change the neural networks in a child's brain and activate the brain in different ways to create an effective pathway for word and sound recognition and ultimately for fluent reading.

RESPONSE TO INTERVENTION: READING MODELS

Estimates of the number of children with serious reading problems in our schools today could be as high as 15 percent to 20 percent. This means that as many as 10 million children across the United States could be struggling with reading failure (Sherman, 2002). Educational organizations serving the student population of disabled readers, such as the Haan Foundation (2007), provide an equally startling picture. They estimate the number of poor readers to be upwards of 20 million children or 38 percent of the U.S. school population. The criteria used for this statistic is a student who is unable to read at grade level. Although we know special education serves many children with learning and reading needs, it is stated that as many as 9 million children could experience severe reading failure (Haan, 2007). This means there could be millions of children who do not qualify for special education services but still need evidence-based early identification and intervention programs to reach successful reading levels.

Reading intervention programs have specific goals. They are designed to target children who are making inadequate reading progress, provide flexible instruction to remediate reading skills deficits, and attain positive results. Elements of an effective reading program for prevention/intervention are defined by Joseph K. Torgesen (1998), a research professor of psychology and education at Florida State University:

> Some of the word-level skills and knowledge these children will require instruction on include: phonemic awareness, letter-sound correspondences, blending skills, a small number of pronunciation conventions (i.e., silent e rule), use of context to help specify a word once it is partially or completely phonemically decoded, strategies for multisyllable words, and automatic recognition of high frequency "irregular" words. (p. 34)

Furthermore, Torgesen (1998) emphasizes that this instruction should be embedded with meaningful reading and writing opportunities (p. 34). Research, planning, and school staff

> Research, planning, and school staff commitment are essential to provide the type of intense remediation that accompanies a program designed for all children to achieve reading success.

commitment are essential to provide the type of intense remediation that accompanies a program designed for all children to achieve reading success.

Responsiveness to Reading Intervention

A model to successfully provide early identification of children who are at risk for reading problems and to promote success for students was designed by Professor Virginia Berninger and her colleagues (2002) from the University of Washington. A team of educators worked with 18 schools in the state of Washington in the late 1990s. The program, called the Student Responsive Delivery System, requires screening during its first tier. *Every* kindergarten through second-grade child is evaluated using research-based assessment measures that are brief, easy to administer, and accurately identify both reading and writing failure. Identified students receive Tier 1 instructional modifications and careful monitoring in the regular classroom. Teachers may preteach a lesson or reteach a difficult concept as they pay careful attention to the needs of their students at risk.

Tier 2 support is provided for children who do not make adequate progress even though they had Tier 1 special assistance. Teachers are prompted to identify children who do not make adequate progress in spite of the increased instructional attention. The intervention is intensified as a team of educators, usually consisting of teaching peers, scrutinizes classroom assessment data. At this stage, modifications are still provided at the regular classroom level. Rather than simple instructional modifications, the Tier 2 level provides intense interventions, which include supplementing the regular reading program with additional curriculum, changing how instruction is presented, using revised instructional materials, and providing extra skill practice.

If needed, Tier 3 moves beyond interventions within the general education classroom. The third level requires a multidisciplinary team to review all previous student assessment; add formal, standardized assessment; review student records; and possibly interview the student, teacher, and/or parents. An assessment and planning team at the third level most likely includes the school psychologist, a language speech specialist, reading teacher, special educator, and/or a general educator.

Students who have not been successful during the first two levels of intervention are generally in need of special education services. Responsible parties, including parents and educational support staff, come together to decide if the child meets special education criteria. If so, the child is identified as having a learning disorder that is affecting reading (Sherman, 2002). An individualized education program (IEP) is developed with a written plan designed to address the child's individual reading needs. This plan identifies the child's strengths for reading as well as areas of deficit. Included with a child's IEP are global reading goals, benchmarks for progress, and specific objectives that will pave the way for grade-level appropriate reading development.

The three-tiered system of support designed by Berninger for needy readers is aligned with current practices for regular classroom interventions and for processes required to identify children for special education with two differences. First, the tiered plan identifies children early in their formal education, ideally before they experience failure and develop feelings of self-doubt. Second, the tiered approach is an expansion of student support or study teams that are in place at many schools. However, the three-tiered process contains steps that are more specific, defined, and intense than those we find at most schools.

Impressive results were realized from the model during the 1998–1999 school year. The need for complete assessments in Tier 3 was cut by 73 percent from the previous program, where children were assessed for special education without Tier 1 and Tier 2 interventions. Of the 215 students with reading problems who were identified for the study, 138 needed no further support following a year of intervention. Only 28 students needed special education services through Tier 3 intervention (Sherman, 2002).

Not long after the results of the Berninger model and others with a similar goal and outcomes were publicized, the federal government approved Public Law 108–446 with language rendering a new response from the educational community at large. Responsiveness to intervention (RTI) demands a new approach to identify special education students. No longer is a child who needs reading intervention tested for a severe discrepancy between achievement and intellectual capacity, which previously was a precursor to receiving services from a special education program. Current law requires school programs to determine if a child will respond to a scientific, research-based intervention as a part of the evaluation process for children through the general education program (Kame'enui, 2007). The RTI concept is highly consistent with the accepted and expected practices of special education programs, including a continuous process of student evaluation.

SCHOOL INTERVENTIONS THAT WORK

> The first level of intervention, however, is always through teacher-initiated regular classroom modification.

There are no sure-fire recipes for schools to follow for reading intervention programs that will work with every child. Successful interventions depend on the needs of the individual children, the level of sophistication that teachers have for teaching reading, the resources that are available to the school, and accurate assessment of the reading deficit. The first level of intervention, however, is always through teacher-initiated regular classroom modification.

Classroom Modifications

Most students who are struggling to read are initially helped in their regular classroom. This is the type of student support that was provided in the Washington model through Tier 1 interventions. Reading instruction for students who are just slightly below expected reading levels may be enhanced as teachers identify specific difficulties and introduce instructional strategies to overcome them. Teachers may also select from value-added materials that provide additional practice with the same concepts that the whole class learns for students who are not making adequate progress. When supplemental materials are not built into reading programs, teachers need to develop additional activities for students to practice emerging skills. In this way, classroom modifications can change the amount of time spent on each skill, provide additional materials, or revise instructional methods. Interventions selected by the teacher that modify classroom instruction are generally appropriate for students who are ELs and for students who qualify for special education services.

Supplemental Instruction

Students with more severe reading problems need a direct-instruction reading program to supplement regular classroom instruction. This type of intervention must be based on careful evaluation of the child's individual reading deficiency. Deficiencies may occur in the areas of cognition, decoding, comprehension, or fluency. Because children can have deficit skills in more than one area, supplemental programs must be designed to correct all deficit areas if the child is to become a fluent reader. The classroom teacher, language speech pathologist, or reading specialist can provide supplemental regular reading instruction.

One study in Houston and Tallahassee (Mathes, 2003) focused on value-added direct reading instruction. It was designed to provide groups of three to five students with intensive "double dose" instruction. Each day, children received 45 minutes of instruction in addition to their regular classroom reading program. The daily lessons followed strands for decoding, fluency, and reading comprehension. All children made impressive gains. The researchers surmised that the method of instruction pales in importance when the instructional content is precisely defined, relates to the child's assessed needs, and is intensive, interactive, and consistent.

Match the Child and the Program

Educators need to know what interventions to use with which children at what grade level and for what purpose. Results of a study by Foorman and Connor (in press) found that when children enter first grade with high decoding skills, extensive time focused on direct instruction for decoding had little impact, while the results were positive for the children who had deficit decoding skills. Results from this type of study offer no surprise to educators. We need to make good use of the precious classroom time we have for advancing children's abilities for reading, not for reiterating skills already in place (see Figure 5.2, Chapter 5). The question is valid: When should intervention be provided? Teachers and parents do not need to be alarmed if a first-grade child is not reading with fluency. However, they do need to pay attention when a third grader reads haltingly. Likewise, it is unreasonable to expect all first graders to decode words, read, and demonstrate comprehension of text. Third-grade students need to read fluently and understand what they read. A second-grade child is expected to use phonics rules to write and to drop "invented spelling" that was accepted the year earlier.

Grade-level guidelines define reading skill expectations (see Table 7.1). When a child does not achieve at expected levels, there are three options:

- Provide additional instruction within the regular reading program.
- Supplement instruction in tandem with regular classroom reading instruction.
- Implement a stand-alone reading intervention program (a complete and intensive reading program, administered during an extended reading period).

The third option is appropriate for students who are ELs or students who have serious reading problems, are in fourth grade and above, and are two years or more behind their age-alike peers (California Department of Education, 2000b). Teachers serve students effectively when they base instructional decisions on assessment data and then match the strategies or program specifically to the individual needs of each student. Supplemental intervention programs are heavy-duty instructional programs. A child who is experiencing comprehension difficulties may be competent with decoding but may need a program designed for vocabulary development and strategies to comprehend and analyze appropriate grade-level text. Similarly, a child who reads slowly may know all the rules for decoding and be able to understand text but be unable to process text rapidly. Not all intervention programs are created for the same purpose. Children who do not develop reading skills to advance with their classmates need supplemental instruction that matches their needs.

> Not all intervention programs are created for the same purpose.

There are many reasons a child's brain may not be performing the tasks for reading at expected levels. The following nonexhaustive list of intervention programs has been reviewed for four reading deficit areas: cognitive function, decoding, comprehension, and processing speed.

Table 7.1   Expected Skill Attainment per Grade Level

	Kindergarten	*First*	*Second*	*Third*
Cognitive skills	X	X	X	X
Phonological processing		X	X	X
Comprehension			X	X
Fluency				X

Note: X indicates skills expected to be mastered and the grade children are most likely to show competent performance.

Contact information for the programs can be found in the Instructional Resources. It is highly recommended that educators review these or any other programs for their most current research information to determine positive student performance results from studies collected by individuals not sponsored by the publishing company.

Cognitive Function

Classroom interventions are listed in Chapter 5 and include teaching memory, attention, concentration, and organization skills. Although many games have activities that help improve cognitive function, no commercial programs were found that are designed exclusively to develop this area of reading development.

Decoding

For decoding, the following are helpful:

Earobics (Steps 1 and 2)

Fast ForWord

Lindamood Phonemic Sequencing (LiPS)

Phonemic Awareness in Young Children: A Classroom Curriculum

Reading Mastery (Levels I and II)

Teach Your Child to Read in 100 Lessons

Language Tune-Up

Alphabetic Phonics

Waterford Early Reading Decoding Program

Leapfrog Literacy Center

Interactive Phonics Readers

Road to Code: A Phonological Awareness Program for Young Children

Comprehension

The following focus on comprehension:

Visualizing and Verbalizing

Read Write & Type

Destination Reading

Little Planet Literacy Series

Reading Mastery (Level III)

Waterford Early Reading Comprehension Program

Alphabetic Phonics

Processing Speed

To provide practice for increased processing speed, consider Fast ForWord, Seeing Stars, Scholastic Fluency Formula, Read Naturally, Waterford Early Reading Fluency Program, read and reread as an informal classroom practice, and practice with Random Automatized Naming Charts (discussed in Chapter 9). Instructional programs, regardless of quality of the materials, cannot be implemented successfully without a knowledgeable, expert teacher in the classroom.

The reading challenge is to close the gap between what research tells us is needed for struggling readers and what is provided in our schools. Teachers want to be effective, but if they lack effective preparation to teach reading, do not understand how children's brains are built to read, have inadequate teaching materials, or lack school-level support they may be unable to help children who are challenged by reading demands. Professional development support for primary teachers, and for all teachers who provide reading instruction, is our best protection to prevent children from becoming *curriculum causalities.*

> The reading challenge is to close the gap between what research tells us is needed for struggling readers and what is provided in our schools.

REFLECTIVE QUESTIONS

1. Educators believe it is urgent that children at risk for reading failure be assessed and receive intervention promptly. What leads educators to take this stand?

2. Some children enter school with a small oral vocabulary. Why is oral language development so important to the reading process, and how can teachers respond to the needs of children with vocabulary weakness?

3. What are some important considerations for reading instruction for children who are ELs?

4. What are the advantages for children who learn a second language? How would you recommend our school system respond to research that supports learning a second language in the elementary years?

5. If you are reading this book as part of a study group, describe one or more interventions for a school to implement that are responsive to the needs of all children, particularly those who are unsuccessful readers or are ELs.

6. How would you decide whether to recommend a reading intervention for a second-grade child who can decode words and comprehend text but is not able to read fluently?

8

Comprehension and Vocabulary

Challenges for Second Grade

C hildren create connections among neural bunches as thoughts and concepts are expanded in novel and exciting ways. New understandings abound and an extensive vocabulary is created. Classroom activities, and other personal experiences, have a major impact on this process. In this chapter we explore materials and strategies that reflect brain-friendly learning to build vocabulary and comprehension.

The first two strategies deal with illustrations and the use of informational text. Teachers are reminded how enticing pictures are and cautioned that pictures may encourage some children to rely on the visual images rather than on the discrete symbol shapes and, more important, their sounds for reading words. Reading a story or book for the first time without pictures is one instructional technique to provide interesting conversation about illustrations, which are introduced later. Likewise, teachers are encouraged to use informational text in addition to traditionally used fictional stories in the primary grades. Children are inquisitive about local and worldly topics and benefit from increased vocabulary and meaningful information through expository text.

Why do adults, particularly parents, want their children to be exposed to hard reading materials for leisure reading? The success rate for independent reading was established in the 1940s and remains appropriate for today's readers: For children to read comfortably for fun or information they need to rapidly identify 95 percent to 97 percent of the words in the book or selection and experience a comprehension rate of 75 percent or more. Yet we frequently encourage students to read materials that are enticing but too hard, and in the process we run the risk of discouraging children from enjoying independent reading.

Building vocabulary cannot mean teaching all words—there are just too many. Basal readers contain excellent strategies for vocabulary development. But responding to how the brain learns through practice, engagement, and repeated exposure gives us even more ideas. Sample strategies use learning frames, retelling stories or re-creating information, responding to questions with no right or wrong answers, and self-checking during reading. Teachers who understand the curious qualities of the human brain can identify a larger repertoire of ideas than those presented in the book.

A visitor to any second-grade classroom will see many similarities to the first-grade classroom across the way. However, the urgency of learning how to decode text has settled into more specific objectives, such as learning spelling patterns, multiple-syllable words, and the more irregular features of English. The classroom speaks to the overriding objective for second grade—to learn to read fluently, accurately, and with comprehension.

> Think about the mind expansion that happens as children seek new understanding, build extensive life reflecting and academic vocabularies, and make more complex neural connections to expand memory chunks.

The frontal lobes in a child's brain are called on to coordinate thought processes that are progressively more expansive. Think about the mind expansion that happens as children seek new understanding, build extensive life reflecting and academic vocabularies, and make more complex neural connections to expand memory chunks. Through this complex yet automatic process they are able to expand connections between thoughts and concepts in novel and exciting ways.

⸙

READING AND LANGUAGE ARTS GUIDELINES FOR SECOND GRADE

In second grade, word-decoding guidelines require that children learn word patterns, decode multisyllable words, and learn about speech conventions. Teachers provide instructional activities that also include the following:

Writing and writing applications

Written and oral English language conventions

Listening and speaking strategies

Organization of oral communication

Speaking conventions

While decoding continues, the expectation for this year in school is that children will go beyond the mechanics of decoding as they expand all areas of the language arts curriculum and learn to comprehend the meaning of the text that they read for themselves.

In this chapter, we focus on reading comprehension; fluency is discussed in Chapter 9. What comes first in reading development, comprehension or fluency? Some argue that children must be fluent readers to comprehend what they are reading. The fluent reader's brain automatically processes the underlying connections among the reading structures and is free to devote full attention to the meaning associated with the words. Reading researchers generally agree that there is a strong correlation between how fast children read text and how well they are able to understand it (National Institute of Child Health and Human Development, 2000; Shaywitz, 2003).

Comprehension, the other part of this equation, is tied explicitly to vocabulary knowledge. Steven Stahl (1999) bases his support for the relationship between the difficulty level of vocabulary and the ability to understand text on evidence from correlational and experimental studies and readability research. The answer to the question of what comes first, comprehension through vocabulary development or speed of processing text—fluency—is neither. Both appear to be developed simultaneously as a child becomes a proficient reader; furthermore, these reading skills are dependent on each other.

> The answer to the question of what comes first, comprehension through vocabulary development or speed of processing text—fluency—is neither.

INSTRUCTION FOR VOCABULARY AND COMPREHENSION

Possibly, the easiest way to consider how vocabulary and comprehension can be developed would be to consider, once again, how the brain systems are connected for learning. In this instance, let's look at an input and output instructional model. First, we acknowledge that all we know, we know because we have received input from our environment through the five senses. And second, we show what we know by accessing what is stored in our memory systems. The process is simply input of information and responsive output to show understanding. Educators would be elated if the process were so simple: I teach; you learn. However, since the process is not that explicit, what is an instructional model that reflects the way the human brain is constructed to learn?

Table 8.1 represents the sensory input processes used during the time a child is engaged with learning and identifies the output potential production or products a child will use to draw on the brain's memory systems. The model shows reciprocal actions used in the learning process. Bold type indicates the most common instructional activities used in schools.

Table 8.1   Instruction Model for Memory Input and Output

Sensory Input	*Memory-Related Output*
Reading	**Writing**
Listening	**Speaking**
Observing	Modeling/acting
Examining	Making a product
	Following steps or a sequence

Referring to Table 8.1, take this challenge. (1) If a student receives information from reading, then what output options are appropriate to check for understanding? (2) If a child is asked to make a product to show what was learned, such as a model of a car for the future, what input could be consulted for information? The answers to both are any of the listed reciprocal activities from the model. In classrooms, we are most likely to pair the reciprocal aspects of reading and writing or listening and speaking. Creative teachers realize children are capable of learning from a variety of input options, as they occasionally incorporate unique and innovative strategies, such as modeling the steps to develop a persuasive essay; demonstrating on a large screen how to access an Internet site; acting out a vocabulary word, such as *bewildered* or *authoritarian;* or making a drawing of the British flag or an Alaskan igloo. Likewise, children can show what they have learned by writing or speaking or modeling or making a product. The human brain is constructed for input from all the senses and output from the memory systems in ways that involve a variety of motor responses.

WAYS TO TEACH THE CURIOUS BRAIN

Teachers have a large repertoire of information about how to teach vocabulary and to develop student comprehension. From the vast array of strategies and instructional techniques, the ones listed in this chapter are specific to the way a child's brain is coaxed to maximize instructional time and learning efforts.

The Illustration Trap

Why would second-grade teachers be cautioned about using material with colorful, descriptive pictures for read-aloud stories, textbooks, or other reading materials? In prereading and early reading experience, as we have seen, illustrations can lure and invite children into the world of text. However, as children become readers, teachers must also become sensitive to the possibility that illustrations take away from the students' ability to comprehend text. Children's brains are curious and impatient as they constantly try to make sense out of sensory experiences. When teachers read aloud to students and show pictures to augment the written words, children tend to pay more attention to the pictures because it is easier to interpret pictures than it is to concentrate on words and their meanings.

The brain usually responds to the sensory stimuli that are easiest to understand. When illustrations are vivid and inviting, children tend to ignore the linguistic content of the story and rely on pictures to provide responses to comprehension questions (Beck & McKeown, 2001). Text with pictures may inhibit the way children access background information from their own memory systems. Accessing stored information is essential for children to create their own internal, meaningful understanding. Teachers can encourage their students to self-reflect and visualize by withholding pictures until children have responded to questions about the text. Some publishers provide text without pictures for reading practice. These materials are useful to practice fluent reading and to engage the student in creating self-generated understanding. Another concern with illustrations occurs when pictures are not an accurate representation of the text content. When illustrations are used concurrently with children's reading assignments or listening activities, teachers can be careful to use stories or informational books with pictures that specifically represent text and are not in conflict with the story's content.

Lack of Informational Text

Some educators criticize basal readers in the first two grades for relying too heavily on fictional stories, claiming that young children need a far greater exposure to text that helps them to understand the world around them (Duke, Bennett-Armistead, & Roberts, 2003). Young readers are not so far removed from early childhood when the whole world was new. They are still eager learners about animals, airplanes, and stormy weather, to name a few of the broad range of topics that interest them. In addition, children, even in the early grades, may be expected to follow signs, read instructions, heed warnings, and use newspapers, magazines, and books that are available to the public in general. Exposure to informational texts beginning in first or second grade can pique children's interests and curiosities. Of equal importance, text based on information about the natural or social world prepares students for the demanding work of the later grades when grade-level expectations include understanding and using informational text.

We learn just how alarmingly scarce informational text is in the first grade from a study conducted by Nell K. Duke (2000) of Michigan State

University. First, we look at the terminology used by Duke for this study. *Informational* texts are generally those that intend to communicate information about the world, presumably from someone more knowledgeable than the reader, which contain factual content and technical vocabulary and have consistent repetitions of a topical theme. Indexes and diagrams or other graphical elements are frequently included in text that is informational in nature. The researcher also identifies two additional types of informational text. *Narrative informational* writing provides information about the natural or social world, yet is written with narrative features, such as books in the popular *Magic School Bus* series. When information about the natural or social world is conveyed through verse, it is *informational-poetic.*

In Duke's (2000) study, data from 20 first-grade classrooms in the Boston metropolitan area, representing both low and high socioeconomic groups, were collected throughout the school year. Each classroom was visited for four full days. Observers reported on the types of text evidenced on the walls and other classroom surfaces, in the class library, and in written language activities. The results of the study indicated that not only was there a relative absence of informational text in the classroom print environment but also that a mean of only 3.6 minutes per day was spent on informational text–type activities during classroom written language periods. The amount of time was generally more limited for children from classrooms in low socioeconomic areas.

> The rationale for using texts with information moves beyond the notion that children are interested and likely to pay attention.

Informational text expands background information and builds background knowledge networks. The rationale for using texts with information moves beyond the notion that children are interested and likely to pay attention. For vocabulary evolution and linguistic enhancement, teachers can explore factual information with their classes. Using factual, concrete vocabulary, children are able to classify, categorize, and define new vocabulary. For problem solving, contrasting, and comparisons, children can draw on facts, ideas, and concepts from nonnarrative text.

Academic Language Needs of All Children

One of the latest buzzwords among reading and language arts educators is *academic language,* which by its name suggests it is beyond the language used in everyday interactions. Rather, it is language used for cognitive academic interactions. Often reserved for teaching to English learners (ELs), this specific vocabulary is identified as both general and content-specific vocabulary, may be a part of complex grammatical structures, and may contain language with abstract meanings or functions, all of which are needed to acquire new knowledge and skills. Reciprocally, academic language skills and understandings allow students to interact with information they are learning, and even to pass their interpretation or understanding of the topic on to others (Bailey, 2007).

Research in 2005 by Robert Marzano (2006) studied the progress of 2,683 students who participated in a special program to build academic language. The results were positive for students' test scores in comprehension of reading material. Impressive gains of 8 percent to 16 percent above control group scores on multiple measures indicate the value of a focused attempt to teach language to unfurl the mysteries that surround academic requests, directions, and conversations during instruction.

Not surprisingly, the first step to teaching academic language is to identify the terms that may be confusing to students and to provide a definition and example of the new terms or phrases. All of the next steps request students to talk. They are engaged with a term by stating a description or giving an example in their own words. Using another memory output strategy, students next construct a graphic representation of the term or phrase. Finally, the teaching strategy insists students rehearse the term at a variety of times through discussion, games, and other activities requiring oral language involvement. The results of Marzano's study are cohesive with other studies, as they encourage oral language involvement and match with best practices for brain-friendly learning.

Building Knowledge Networks

Reading comprehension moves beyond the mechanics of learning to read. We are aware that children's brains make new neural connections as they store information from classroom instruction, their experiences, and the environment in which they live. As children are exposed to new information, they unconsciously search long-term memory systems to bring previous, similar experiences to working memory to consider, use, and connect to as they make sense of the new information.

Chunking

Children develop a base of knowledge when they learn new information and attach it to information previously stored in neural networks. To accomplish holding more and more related information in working memory, a child's brain generally tries to organize facts, concepts, and ideas into meaningful chunks of information. In Chapter 3, we discussed the concept of chunking and indicated that people can hold only a limited amount of unrelated information in working memory and then only for a short time. The number of information pieces we can retain is related to age. Young, school-age children may be able to hold only three or four pieces of information in working memory.

Chunking is the process of combining several pieces of information into a single item that occupies one slot in working memory. We previously discussed how children use chunking of letters to form a meaningful phonological pattern, or word, during decoding. Chunking a phrase or sentence allows the brain to conserve memory space and to develop higher-order conceptual thinking. To help a child organize information and ideas into conceptual chunks, teachers or parents can use strategies to tie new information to already acquired core knowledge. To capitalize on the brain's tendency to seek novelty, adults can add rhyme or rhythm to make information chunks firmly etched in working memory for practice and ultimately for automatic long-term storage and recall.

> Chunking accounts for some of the differences teachers find between children who give simple responses to comprehension questions and those who respond in detail using a wealth of available, previously stored background information.

Chunking accounts for some of the differences teachers find between children who give simple responses to comprehension questions and those who respond in detail using a wealth of available, previously stored background information. Children with an information-rich memory have developed the ability to make multiple connections from the words they read and to chunk information while they contemplate it in working memory (Hirsch, 2003).

Hard Reading Materials

Reading can be hard or easy depending on the relationship between the capabilities the child has to read the words, the knowledge or experience base required for the text to be understood, the level of commitment the child has to read the selection, and the complexity of the written style. Let's assume a child not only wants to read about dinosaurs but also has a strong desire for more information about these prehistoric beasts. The child is well versed in the topic from previous conversations with parents, television viewing, and previous book experiences. Also, this child is considered to be a strong reader by the classroom teacher. However, if the selected book or selection has a vocabulary load with too many new terms, a linguistic structure that is more common to scientific text, and organization of ideas that appear in a different discourse or style, the text can become too difficult, even to the child who is seemingly ready for more in-depth information.

Adults often prefer that children read challenging books that are full of important information not only for classroom instruction but also for leisure reading. Yet if we let adult preference for magazines be our guide, suggests Richard Allington (2001), professor of education at the University of Florida, it would appear that adults, even those with advanced degrees, do not choose leisure reading materials that are difficult or too challenging. Magazines such as *Scientific American* or *The Economist* simply do not have as large a readership as *Newsweek* or *People*. If adult magazine sales indicate that more people like to read publications that have a lesser vocabulary load, require less comprehensive background information, and do not pose complex linguistic styles to interpret, then why do educators and parents think that children will react any differently to advanced materials? Contrary to the wishes of many

> Adults often prefer that children read challenging books that are full of important information not only for classroom instruction but also for leisure reading.

adults, children have a higher level of reading success with greater learning and improved attitudes toward learning when they read materials that are relatively easy for recreational or leisure reading.

The issue of success rate for reading based on vocabulary loading was originally reported by E. A. Betts (1946) in the book *Foundations of Reading Instruction* and, subsequently, has been available to teachers for over 60 years. For children to read comfortably, their ability to recognize words in the reading selection needs to be at a rate that allows them to read 95 percent to 97 percent of the words accurately with a comprehension rate of 75 percent. Betts defined word accuracy below 95 percent and comprehension below 75 percent as frustration-level reading. Numerous studies and teacher observations validate that when reading tasks become too difficult, children lose their interest in reading, are less likely to feel good about their reading, achieve poorly, and ultimately give up on reading.

How can teachers measure the appropriateness of reading materials for their students and avoid books that are simply too hard for them to read and enjoy? Allington (2001) provides one quick and easy measure. Children select a book for leisure reading. Next, they read the first page or two, depending on the number of words per page. While they read, they hold up a finger for each word that they cannot read. If they have three fingers up before they finish the page or pages, then the book is most likely too hard, and they need to be encouraged to select another, unless the topic is very interesting or important to them. In that case, the teacher can closely monitor the reading process and support the reader as much as possible.

Accelerated Reader and Lexile Framework are two popular school programs that use research-based methods to determine the readability levels for a large variety of children's books. Both use computer-assisted management systems. Accelerated Reader gives a zone of proximal development for children to ensure that readers feel challenged without being frustrated with their reading selections. Lexile Framework characterizes each reader with a measure, called a Lexile, and forecasts the level of comprehension that the reader will be able to attain with a selected text. In each case, the programs are designed to align with state standards and often with basal readers. Books for leisure reading are also given a reading level. Equipped with this kind of detailed information, teachers and parents can help children to select books that match their individual reading skills.

BUILDING THE BRAIN FOR COMPREHENSION

The rest of this chapter centers on strategies for teachers to help their students build word and world knowledge, organize their thinking into meaningful information chunks, and experience different styles of writing and text, all of which are vital to comprehension. We visit vocabulary in many variations: speaking and listening vocabulary, and reading and writing vocabulary. Further, we discuss the purpose and extent of vocabulary instruction, and, finally, strategies are provided for teachers to use to direct students toward purposeful, strategic reading.

Vocabulary Instruction

Vocabulary grows through interactions with people, activities, and books that introduce new words, ideas, and concepts. This learning does not take place from students' own reading during the initial school years, since their reading content is not as advanced as their oral language levels. Reading vocabulary does not catch up to oral vocabulary until the seventh or eighth grade (Biemiller, 2003a). However, children are eventually able to read and write words that are more advanced than the ones they use in common conversation.

Classroom experiences that include read-alouds, specific vocabulary instruction, and other word and world knowledge pursuits immerse children in language arts activities that are imperative for oral and reading vocabulary comprehension and concept formation, which leads ultimately to fluent reading (Hirsch, 2003).

Speaking and Listening Vocabulary

Four distinct types of vocabulary—speaking, listening, reading, and writing—are accessed together and separately in the brain. For most children, the first two, speaking and listening, have an impressive start prior to school attendance. At school, teachers are faced with instructional considerations based on their students' broad variability in the development of speaking and listening vocabulary. Speaking and listening vocabulary development is initially dependent on childhood oral language experiences and conversations. As children advance in school, their classroom experiences and leisure reading activities expose them to more and more words, and their active vocabulary for speaking and listening greatly expands.

Vocabulary Development Through Story Reading

Many classroom schedules include a time for the teacher to read out loud to the class, particularly in the primary grades. Teachers are surprised to learn that this practice is not efficient use of classroom time, unless the activity is cognitively challenging (DeTemple & Snow, 2003). Mind-engaging techniques for story time include reading the selection more than one time, each time with a different incentive (to look for a storyline, topic development, or flow of information, and the next time to listen for new vocabulary). Another strategy is to develop understanding for vocabulary located in the reading through direct teaching. Adult/child discussions are suggested as the strategy changes from being "read to" to being "read with" and "talked with" through concentration-engaging questions that move beyond a traditional yes or no response. Sometimes, smaller groups of children, four or five in a group, can have a short but substantial talk directed by a prompt from the teacher.

Vocabulary development cannot be placed on hold until the reading vocabulary catches up with the speaking vocabulary, nor can vocabulary enrichment be effectively expanded from materials that young children are able to read for themselves (Beck & McKeown, 2001). With this knowledge, teachers should select materials to read to children that are several levels above the children's own reading levels. Selections as much as two years ahead of the grade level can be used by teachers to promote vocabulary growth (Walsh, 2003).

Researcher Isabel Beck, a senior scientist at the University of Pittsburgh, and her colleagues (Beck, McKeown, & Kucan, 2003) conducted a study with 80 trade books that could be read aloud to children. Three new words were selected from each story for children to learn, with children learning six targeted new words per week. Children were also exposed to many other words that they could individually select to remember.

The process Beck used to teach vocabulary is called Text Talk. The program incorporates a read, reread, and discuss strategy. New words are taught after the children hear the story. Vocabulary instruction follows this sequence:

Conceptualizing words from the story

Repeating words

Defining words

Using words in other contexts

Stimulating children's examples

Saying words repeatedly

New words are maintained during successive Text Talk lessons through frequent exposures. A word wall or vocabulary chart allows children to revisit new vocabulary frequently and continually during sub-sequent stories. For example, the teacher may say, "Remember the word *trouble*? How could you use that word to tell about something that happened in this story?" Children learn vocabulary development for listening and speaking concurrently with vocabulary development for reading and writing. Oral language development will advance quickly through activities such as read-alouds, but eventually, children's reading vocabularies will catch up with and advance beyond what they are able to understand through oral language activities.

> Eventually, children's reading vocabularies will catch up with and advance beyond what they are able to understand through oral language activities.

Vocabulary Development for English Learners

Earlier, we identified strategies for ELs to be able to decode text. Think about it this way: Phoneme awareness and phonics instruction are precise. They follow the structure of language and have rules. When a student is given systematic, explicit teaching and sufficient practice, decoding skills can be mastered. However, ELs may be able to read with phonetic correctness and yet not comprehend a word of what they have read unless they have the background or experiences to understand the vocabulary. No program can teach all the words a child needs to know at the first, third, or even at the 12th grade.

Vocabulary acquisition depends, as we have seen, on both direct vocabulary instruction and on learning how to identify and categorize new words. ELs acquire most of their vocabulary outside of planned instruction, as they have conversations with adults, listen to adults read, and read on their own (Antunez, 2002). The difficulty of vocabulary development for these children is compounded by the fact that important adults in their lives may not be English speakers. There is also a significant difference between proficiency for face-to-face communication, referred to as basic interpersonal communication skills (BICS), and proficiency needed to comprehend language in the educational setting, or cognitive academic language proficiency (CALP). Because of the difficulties that children who are ELs may experience, these students need every minute of vocabulary development that school can offer.

A proliferation of research centers around the needs of a nation steeped with accountability issues and a diverse student population that falls short in command of the English language among nonnative speakers. Most studies indicate ELs require instruction in basic vocabulary, academic language, and more sophisticated words (Collins, 2005). At the same time, ELs need the same instruction all students need—definitional, contextual, analytical, usage, and elaboration. They need more practice and engagement through opportunities to talk using new vocabulary, responding to questions, learning songs, and acting out word plays. More than regularly progressing native speakers, they must be prompted to speak, not simply to listen. Previously suggested strategies of partner talk and work, and small-group projects with native English speakers are highly engaging and provide needed social and academic interactions.

Reading Vocabulary

Ultimately, children gain the majority of their vocabulary growth through reading. From detailed vocabulary analysis provided by Cunningham and Stanovich (1998), we realize there are large differences between the opportunities for vocabulary growth between what children hear through speech and what they are exposed to from print. New word

> It seems likely that the varying amount of print that students read is responsible for major discrepancies that exist in school performance among students.

learning for competent readers happens more rapidly through exposure to print than through exposure to conversation. From this finding, it seems likely that the varying amount of print that students read is responsible for major discrepancies that exist in school performance among students.

As we noted earlier, good instruction for vocabulary building matches the way children's brains are organized. To teach vocabulary from reading, the teacher must draw the students' attention to the word or words to be learned. Students say the word, spell the word, and learn its meaning before they encounter the word during reading. The best practice is for them to be exposed to the word again in many ways and many places after reading it.

Explicit elaboration techniques can be used to hold a word in working memory. For the word *bumpy*, students can make a mental picture of candy with nuts in it, tree bark, a bed with someone under the covers, or something similar. They can describe the object, structure, or person by talking, writing, or drawing, thus using visual images to hold it in working memory for an extended time. Teachers can have their classes look for targeted words in other contexts, turning vocabulary acquisition into a game of word hunt that extends from the classroom to the neighborhood and beyond. Additional activities can use games, such as student-made crossword puzzles, student drawings of target words (*Pictionary*), or "I spy a word that means . . ." As children become actively engaged with the word through extended practice activities, they experience repeated word exposure and increase the likelihood that they will retain the word and its meaning in long-term memory.

Writing Vocabulary

Vocabulary for writing is primarily learned during the school years. Instruction that includes specific teaching of words during reading is fortified through reexposure to the words during writing exercises. What is described as "novice writing" in the preschool years and "invented spelling" in first grade quickly advances to independent writing as students develop larger vocabularies and expand their understanding of orthographic and syntactic patterns.

Teachers foster independent writing when they integrate reading and writing activities. We see early writing in first grade that reflects topics that have meaning to the students and represents some attempt at capitalization and punctuation. During second grade, students begin to understand that writing takes different forms, such as stories, poems, or expository writing. Specific instruction directs students to proofread for editing and revisions. Second graders begin to realize that the words they write follow orthographic patterns and rules for spelling. Third-grade students are expected to write in several different formats and to revise their writing. They produce final drafts of their work with appropriate and interesting vocabulary, and their finished product is free from spelling, grammar, and punctuation errors.

Neurologically, the writing process is very different from reading, but it relies on some of the same brain structures. During reading, the brain responds first to visual stimuli, which then are processed into thoughts with meaning. When older children compose and write, the brain is commanded to start with internal thoughts. Brain structures connect in a reverse direction from reading to select appropriate vocabulary and then produce the symbols for these words in written format. In writing, the frontal lobes direct the motor cortex to coordinate arm, hand, and finger movements rather than to activate the mouth, tongue, and jaw as it does for speaking. As a child's fine motor movements become less tedious and more automatic, the cerebellum learns the writing procedure, allowing the child to produce print without concentrating on making the letter shapes. This automaticity frees the child to concentrate on what is being written and communicated. This process is similar to learning to read with automaticity, for the child's working memory to be freed to concentrate on what is read. It is easy to see that there is a symbiotic relationship between

> Students read for pleasure and knowledge, and students write so they can have their thoughts and ideas read by others.

the reciprocal processes of reading and writing. Students read for pleasure and knowledge, and students write so they can have their thoughts and ideas read by others.

Not All Vocabulary Is Taught

Text has far too many words to teach each word that is unfamiliar to all or part of the class, and vocabulary instruction can take up a lot of class time. Teachers carefully make their own choice of 8 to 10 new words each week or use words selected by the textbook publisher. This number is insignificant compared to the number of words students are learning and need to learn to meet grade-level expectations.

Vocabulary development, then, must take on other, more efficient strategies. Children learn to strategically analyze unknown words on their own. Teachers explicitly teach the morphology of new words through identification of prefixes, suffixes, and roots that help students to identify words' meanings and pronunciations and to determine their parts of speech. Children learn to identify prefixes (the most common are *un-, re-, in-,* and *dis-*) and suffixes (some with heavy use are *-s, -ing, -ed,* and *-ly*). Words are then broken into parts—beginning, middle, and ending. Frequently, the middle part of the word is from a word family that children already know. The word *unfriendly,* although lengthy, becomes identifiable when it is viewed as *un-friend-ly.* Word families have the same base formation as seen with *time, timed, timetable,* or *untimely.* Children can expand vocabulary by chunking letters in long words into morphemes that hold meaning through self-applied analysis strategies without needing explicit instruction for each new word that they encounter.

The use of context clues for reading is most effective when tied to brain-compatible techniques. Approaches teachers use effectively with older students draw on students' prior knowledge and how words work together in sentences, or syntax. Readers are encouraged to use cognitive resources, what they know about phonics and morphology, and additionally to determine what makes sense for the unknown word in the particular sentence (Irvin, 2001). This expanded look at unknown words in text can be used with younger readers to draw on what they know rather than relying on limited clues provided by pictures or surrounding words.

> This expanded look at unknown words in text can be used with younger readers to draw on what they know rather than relying on limited clues provided by pictures or surrounding words.

Vocabulary and Memory

How do we know when a child owns a word and has it stored for automatic recall in long-term memory? First, it is helpful to define some terminology. *Unknown* indicates that the child has no previous experience with the word. *Acquainted* indicates having some understanding. And *established* means a student can identify the word and give its meaning consistently. An unknown word carries the risk of being dropped from working memory without repeated exposure. Acquainted words are available in working memory but have not yet received the "go ahead" to be associated with similar or connecting words in knowledge networks found in the long-term memory system. Established words are owned by students and are firmly attached to a network of words, ideas, and concepts that the brain can easily access.

A definition for a single word becomes more complex when the word is combined with a phrase or new concept. Each word can be stored in the brain in several ways, depending on exposure and experience with the word. The word *work,* for example, can have one meaning when the child is told to "Work this math problem." The meaning becomes more complex when it appears as a noun in the phrase "A mother's work is never done." A known root word can have an enriched meaning when it is used in different situations. For example, the root word *dash* could represent a written symbol, mean to move quickly, signify a small amount, or be expanded to related words, such as *dashing, dasher,* or *dashboard.*

Vocabulary development, as we have seen, can become an engaging part of reading instruction. Playing with words in whimsical ways through puns, exaggerations, metaphors, idioms, or cartoons captivates students (Stahl, 1999). Vocabulary development, whether it is vocabulary for speaking, listening, reading, or writing, when provided in ways that are appealing and exciting, helps the child's brain to hold on to words, practice identification of words, and to sort and connect words to neural networks for ease of capture and automatic recall.

How Many Exposures to Words?

The amount of exposure that a child needs to move a target word into long-term memory for automatic recall depends on whether previous neural networks are available or if they need to be developed to attach the word. Regardless of whether it is through conversation, reading, or writing, 4 exposures are not enough for children or most adults to remember or attach meaning to a new word (Stahl, 2003). While 12 exposures are enough for most readers, teachers find some children need to use a word 20 or more times before they are able to automatically recall it.

> The amount of exposure that a child needs to move a target word into long-term memory for automatic recall depends on whether previous neural networks are available or if they need to be developed to attach the word.

STRATEGIC READING WITH COMPREHENSION IN MIND

We know that if children are to hold a rich selection of words in automatic long-term memory, they must be exposed to and interact with new words. Students' comprehension and understanding can be enhanced with structured reading opportunities that activate prior knowledge, encourage visual imaging, generate questions and predictions, and encourage thinking aloud (Allington, 2001).

With this in mind, we will discuss six strategies to strengthen reading interest along with comprehension:

Text without pictures

Learning frames

Retelling a story

No right and wrong answers

Questioning the author

Self-checking

Teachers using these dynamic comprehension strategies keep children on task during reading periods and help organize their memory systems to store and retrieve information.

Text Without Pictures

By providing decodable text without pictures, discussed earlier in this chapter with cautions, teachers activate children's previous experience and knowledge. Children read the pictureless text and then talk about what they see in their minds. Teachers prompt thinking by asking questions such as, "How old was Raul in this story?" "Can you describe him?" or "Tell how Raul's face looked when he found out the bully was waiting for him after school?" Using informational text, for example *Look Inside Your Brain* by Heather Alexander (1991), a series of teacher questions could be, "What does your brain have to do when you button your shirt?" "What are you doing right now that your brain controls without you having to think about it?" and "Name some things that you have learned by practicing or repeating." By using this query technique, students are not influenced by interpretive illustrations that may interrupt or alter their comprehension. Questioning this way is elaborative practice that locks conceptual thinking strategies into long-term memory for automatic response. The illustrator's pictures can be shown at the conclusion of the interaction and may stimulate even further discussion about what the artist was thinking.

Learning Frames

Ed Ellis (2001) of the University of Alabama developed another sensible and powerful approach to developing skills of understanding and idea expansion, called *learning frames*. Learning frames help organize big ideas, major concepts, and important implications. A basic frame is a series of boxes organized on a student's work paper. A key topic is identified and inserted at the top of the worksheet. Initially, the teacher directs students' thinking as two or three main ideas, each with several details, are identified and recorded. The entire process culminates with a summary statement. The resulting frame looks like a chart and often fits on a single page.

This strategy directs students to think deeply about the topic rather than to simply identify facts. The frame technique is accompanied by robust instruction, as the teacher introduces the process for developing the frame and completes one for the students to use as a model. With each succeeding exposure to learning frames, the teacher supplies less of the information, and the children fill in more, until students can use the frame independently. Children can use learning frames to organize a report, summarize a story or expository text, or take class notes in the upper elementary grades.

This learning frame comprehension strategy can be used as early as first grade. Learning frames appeal to a child's developing brain by structuring thinking, supporting connections between new ideas and previous knowledge, and developing new patterns for complex thoughts.

A companion strategy is to teach vocabulary and word concepts through semantic mapping. A map of sorts results as children brainstorm ideas and the teacher records their responses on a blackboard or overhead transparency. While the students respond, the teacher also adds words that are targeted to learn. When the brainstorming session is finished, the teacher and the class develop a map to show relationships between the words. Semantic mapping looks like a mind map with categories and is most effective when accompanied by discussion (Stahl, 1999). Framing thoughts and different semantic mapping structures can be used in tandem with the next teaching technique, story retelling.

Story Retelling

A comprehension skill builder, retelling a story, requires imagining, then thinking aloud. Children, either as readers or listeners, must pay attention to a story in order to integrate meaning and reconstruct parts of the story when it is finished. Teachers using retelling as an instructional strategy must pay as much attention to what they do to set up the story and to follow the story as they do for the actual reading. When teachers choose a chapter book, such as *Charlotte's Web* (White, 1952), they make the read-aloud activity meaningful when they prime students' attention with questions, identify new words, or pose ideas to think about during the reading. After children hear the chapter, they engage in discussion or another activity to demonstrate their understanding of what they heard. The focused time before and after the story demands more teacher preparation but ensures that the experience is an efficient use of instructional time.

Children's ability to talk about complex ideas, define new vocabulary, comprehend oral and written text, and understand story structure improves when children know that they will be responsible for participating in follow-up activities. Children may be asked to talk about the story or text, act out specific parts, draw what they picture in their minds, or write about the text's content.

As children engage in these activities, they recount the reading activity in their own words. Rather than recalling what they heard, they capitalize on their own conceptual ideas. This type of work demands not only memory but also a deep understanding of the written

> Rather than recalling what they heard, they capitalize on their own conceptual ideas.

piece to synthesize and manipulate information. It blends comprehension from a reading experience and conceptual information from life experiences through oral language.

Questions With No Right or Wrong Answers

Moving beyond concrete, expected student responses, this more intense questioning strategy is structured by teachers to accept answers that are not predetermined. When there are no wrong responses, the only corrections a teacher may request are to incomplete answers. For this type of cognitive thinking, teachers help children use what are generally called higher-order thinking skills. In terms of building a reading brain, we know that this

> When there are no wrong responses, the only corrections a teacher may request are to incomplete answers.

type of cognitive processing occurs in many different brain structures and is highly dependent on memory strategies and the ability to organize information into categories.

The more vocabulary words a reader has and the larger the chunks of information stored in long-term memory, the greater the potential for concept development. The better the organization of storage systems, the more intense and complete a student's response can be. Children involved in strategic thinking during reading may be asked to follow directions, such as "Write a new ending," or "Think about a time that you were afraid, and tell how you worked to find a solution," or "The text introduced you to an animal called a mule. What do you know about mules?"

Question the Author

Another comprehension strategy teachers can use requires children to challenge what they read and question what the author has written. Children may not recognize that writers are sometimes imperfect in their understanding of a topic. Helping children to see authors as fallible or capable of making errors is a strategy used by Beck and her colleagues (Beck & McKeown, 1998). They call their instructional strategy "Questioning the Author." The technique was field-tested with 14 classrooms over a six-year period.

Teachers led discussions with students that were prompted by questions, such as "What is the author trying to say in the second paragraph?" or "How could you word that sentence so that it makes more sense to you?" Children learned to focus more intensely on the deeper meaning of the text (p. 48). These instructional strategies force students to surpass traditional thinking that simply looks at the literal language of text. Through an active search for meaning, children validate their own experience and knowledge and learn to become thoughtful readers who question rather than passively accept information from textbooks and other expository text.

Student Self-Checking Process

Students can be taught to use a list of questions for self-monitoring during independent reading. As early as second grade, children can learn to respond on their own to questions that the teacher posts on a chart or a bulletin board. Self-questioning begins with "understanding what I read" and continues to higher-level strategies as the year progresses. This strategy includes the following areas and inquiries:

1. Understanding what I read
   - What and who is the story about?
   - What do I need to know more about?
   - What do I need to do with the story's information?

2. Predicting, verifying, and deciding
   - What will happen?
   - How accurate was my prediction?
   - What information supports or changes my prediction?

3. Visualizing, verifying, and deciding
   - Did I form a good picture?
   - How accurate was my picture?
   - What information supports or changes my understanding?

4. Summarizing
   - What has happened so far?
   - Am I missing any important information?

5. What to do if I don't understand
   - Stop reading and reread.
   - Look back for details.
   - Continue to read.
   - Decide why I am confused.
   - Check to see if the reading is too difficult—do I understand almost all of the words on each page? (Allington, 2001)

Questioning with this level of progressive intensity prompts students to self-check their progress during reading and to maintain attention to their reading task.

Students Achieve at Different Levels of Comprehension

Reading comprehension depends on word recognition. Furthermore, vocabulary strongly depends on early oral language experiences. There is significant evidence that children who have decoding problems devote an inordinate amount of time and cognitive energy to the sounds of words, so they are not able to concentrate on meaning (Goldsworthy, 1996; Hirsch, 2003; Lindamood, Bell, & Lindamood, 1997).

Although some comprehension deficits spring from weak instruction, other problems result from a lack of prior knowledge. In a classroom of 20 or 30 children, there may be several who lack background knowledge about almost any new topic. Teachers use a variety of techniques to pretest children's knowledge of a new topic. As we discussed earlier, if the background experience is not there, teachers must provide the experience and prompt the development of neural connections that will allow the new information to be integrated into the child's memory systems.

As children broaden their vocabulary, develop new skills, and grasp important concepts, they progress toward increased comprehension. Children who are able to comprehend text are more likely to be accomplished at a companion skill, fluency.

REFLECTIVE QUESTIONS

1. It is suggested in this chapter that teachers occasionally withhold illustrations for some of the stories they read to students. Why would this strategy strengthen the brain's ability for comprehension?

2. Chunking information helps children to put more information into each available memory slot. How is chunking related to the development of reading comprehension?

3. Many adults prefer that children read hard, academically based books for their leisure reading. What are your thoughts on this preference?

4. If you are reading this book as part of a study group, assign some members to study and reflect upon Table 8.1, the sensory input and memory-related output aspects of learning.

5. What strategies for teaching vocabulary do you find to be most useful with your students? In what ways are these strategies brain compatible?

9

Putting Reading Skills to the Task

Expectations for Third Grade and Beyond

S uccessful readers at third grade and beyond are able to rapidly scan lines of print and see every word but stop for few. These students seem to have an effortless ability to read. We know that they are spontaneously recognizing familiar words and quickly, almost unconsciously, identifying unfamiliar ones by applying their understanding of the orthographic nature of the English language. Students with reading proficiency additionally subvocalize appropriate verbal inflections to enhance the meaning of the sentences. Certainly, each teacher who contributed to the mastery of skills for this level of reader must be delighted.

A student who reads with fluency, accuracy, and prosody is able to concentrate on the meaning of the section read. Brain circuits for word decoding in working memory systems are not being stressed, as word recall is handled almost automatically. The frontal lobes are free to concentrate on what the selection is about, not how it is constructed with individual words and their sounds. Generally, reading experts agree that three principles have importance for successful reading comprehension: reading fluency, vocabulary, and domain knowledge. The latter two were addressed in earlier chapters. In this chapter, we focus on the speed at which the child's brain processes words during reading.

Processing speed is currently receiving its due share of interest. The skill, which is acknowledged by more and more researchers, is rapid automatized naming (RAN). It is defined as the ability to look at objects, such as pictures, colors, single digit numbers, letters, or sight vocabulary, to name the object, to disengage from the object, and to move to the next object to begin the sequence again. Identifying RAN with that complex sequence helps us to know what the brain is doing during rapid naming. Just as this series of neuron networks become active to name an object, this same set needs to quiet down or stop the connections for the child to stimulate a new set of neurons for the next object to be identified and then verbalized. Looking at the process of naming through the activities of the brain helps us to understand that there are different rates of processing—different rates of stimulating neuron connections and then quieting them. What's more amazing is that we have no conscious control over how fast or slow this process is. Some children are fast processors naturally or have learned to process quickly with practice. Other children just do not think with speed. Educators can provide activities that prompt the brain to make connections more rapidly, but realize that for most children who process slowly, changing their thinking speed happens with a lot of practice.

Third grade is the year for all the areas of reading competence to come together—cognition, decoding, comprehending, and fluency. Ideally, children master decoding during the first two years of formal education, then move on to develop networks of information and vocabulary for comprehension so that by third grade, children's fluency, the focus of this chapter, has improved. However, we cannot wait until third grade to address the rate and accuracy of reading, because fluency is so critical to the reading demands of upper elementary grades and beyond.

> We cannot wait until third grade to address the rate and accuracy of reading, because fluency is so critical to the reading demands of upper elementary grades and beyond.

After third grade, instruction no longer focuses on learning to read. Rather, it shifts to using reading as a tool for learning, expanding children's knowledge bases, and making information connections for high-level thinking, reasoning, and analysis. This is not to say that word analysis instruction does not occur in the upper elementary or middle school years. However, the emphasis on reading instruction changes. More time is spent on what is read, and less time is devoted to how to read.

READING AND LANGUAGE ARTS GUIDELINES FOR THIRD GRADE

One of the expectations of our educational system is that every child will leave third grade with an enthusiasm to read and with the ability to read fluently, effortlessly, and independently. Oregon has been recognized as a leader in establishing reading standards. Reading aloud with unpracticed grade-level text at a target rate of 110 to 120 correct words per minute is a specific standard for Oregon's students in third grade. Another goal is for children to read text fluently across all subject areas (Oregon State Department of Education, 2008). While this chapter targets the development of fluency and reading processing speed, content and proficiency standards for third-grade students cover the entire range of language arts skill development. They include the following:

Decoding and word recognition

Listening to and reading informational and narrative text

Systematic vocabulary development

Reading to understand and perform a task

Examining content and structure of informational text

Developing skills in writing conventions (communication, grammar, spelling, and punctuation)

Writing narrative and research reports, and listening with accompanying speaking skills

To address reading fluency, Oregon's third grade standards prominently and specifically require that a child be able to read fluently with expression and without stopping to figure out what words they are reading.

FACTORS AFFECTING READING FLUENCY

When students can read aloud with speed, accuracy, and proper expression, they can concentrate on the meaning of the text and are more likely to understand and remember what they read (Wolf, 2003). Children who are not fluent readers, on the other hand, must devote considerable energy to the mechanics of reading, which decreases their focus on the meaning of a text. Attaining fluency depends on many factors, including automaticity in decoding, orthographic knowledge, and the degree to which the brain has become wired to process print information.

> Attaining fluency depends on many factors, including automaticity in decoding, orthographic knowledge, and the degree to which the brain has become wired to process print information.

What Is Fluency?

Fluency, which literally means *flowing*, has several components. In the context of reading, fluency means the ability to read fast (Hirsch, 2003) or to read a passage where the words are spoken without hesitation, with comprehension, with accuracy, with prosody, and with a lack of effort (Kame'enui & Simmons, 2001). A truly fluent reader is able to adjust the rate of reading to match the vocabulary load, the linguistic complexity of the passage, or the information that needs to be obtained from the text (Rasinski, 2000). In terms of what is happening in the reading brain, reading fluency is a product of

In the context of reading, fluency means the ability to read fast (Hirsch, 2003) or to read a passage where the words are spoken without hesitation, with comprehension, with accuracy, with prosody, and with a lack of effort (Kame'enui & Simmons, 2001).

accuracy and automaticity that accesses perceptual, phonological, orthographical, and morphological processing at the letter and word level (Wolf, 2003). Researchers agree that reading fluency is a skill that children must attain to become independent readers and that fully developed reading fluency produces smooth, relatively effortless oral reading that is accurate and has an appropriate rate, correct stress, intonation, rhythm, and word emphasis—all this and the ability to comprehend text as well.

Orthographic Knowledge

Let us begin with an understanding of orthography. Students' brains, when structured to organize words in orthographic categories, are able to establish visual patterns within written language. They recognize graphemes that represent the sounds of language and are adept at automatically processing words for their structure and for their meaning. This knowledge base is most effectively developed from two techniques that have been supported by research: analytical and anchored. Juel and Deffes (2004), university researchers, found students are least likely to remember words that they identify through contextual clues. Teachers are likely to say, "Look at the rest of the sentence to see if you can identify the word that is puzzling you." This approach may satisfy the current problem, but next time the student sees the word he or she is every bit as likely to be stumped by it. According to these researchers, teachers help students to be

As students become familiar with the orthography of language, not only are they able to recognize words that appear with high frequency, but they can also quickly process less familiar words as well.

more effective readers when they ask the child to *analyze* the word, how it looks, what other words look similar, and how the letters are grouped or ordered. By engaging the child to critically look at the word itself, it is more likely that the next time the word appears the child may be able to identify it. *Anchoring* the word with interest and feeling is equally successful. In this instance, the teacher asks the child how the word makes him or her feel, or if it is it like other words the child already knows, thus involving emotional memory as well as linking it for its orthography. As students become familiar with the orthography of language, not only are they able to recognize words that appear with high frequency, but they can also quickly process less familiar words as well.

The more times a child sees and recognizes words or word combinations, the more likely those words will be instantly identified, allowing reading to become automatic and fluid. However, children do not achieve automaticity with reading solely from constant word exposure. In fact, we prefer that most words not be learned by sight or memorization, as this method for word recall creates a false sense of reading ability. For children to process print with fluency, they begin their journey to become fluent readers by developing an under-

> In fact, we prefer that most words not be learned by sight or memorization, as this method for word recall creates a false sense of reading ability.

standing of the orthographic system that governs words. Fortunately, the orthographic rules for English are reliable and can be taught.

Phonological processing, teaching predictable patterns in their written format, is at the very foundation of reading fluency. Beyond simple phonemes and graphemes, the positions of different graphemes and sylla-bles, particularly at the beginning and at the end of words, are taught through phonics instruction. As children address more complex words, they learn to focus on syllables and come to understand how stress on one syllable rather than another affects word meaning (Abbott, 2001). All the instruction for phoneme awareness, phonics, spelling, and writing in the previous years comes together as children address text with multisyllable words and long sentences. Proficient readers look at each phoneme and syllable that makes up each word, but pause for few, as they automatically recognize words for their orthographic properties and continue effort-lessly reading with speed.

THE BRAIN'S RATE OF PROCESSING

Researchers and reading experts generally agree that three principles have important implications for children's reading comprehension—reading fluency, vocabulary, and domain knowledge. Vocabulary and domain knowledge were discussed extensively in Chapter 8. Here, we focus on their influence on the speed at which the brain processes words when children read.

Three Reasons the Brain Can Process With Automaticity

Children move from being fluent decoders to strategic readers and finally to being expert readers, according to MaryAnne Wolf (2007) in her book, *Proust and the Squid: The Story and Science of the Reading Brain.* From this researcher and author's experience, there are three "brain" reasons readers can read with fluency and comprehension. Following the adage, "Cells that fire together wire together," we learn neurons form cell assem-blies or networks for the shapes, forms, order, and meanings of words. As the word is learned with familiarity, there are concurrent networks linked together and ready to activate as one is able to give recognition and mean-ing as an instant response. Another reason readers experience automaticity is a quite current topic for brain research. Wolf, as well as Simon Liversedge (2007), from the University of Southampton, describes the process the eyes follow during fluent reading. We assume it is a smooth, fluid movement across the page, but research tells a different story. It appears the eyes make small jerky movements to focus on a single word or to go back and reread passages that were elusive during the first glance. An automatic decision to refocus or dart back is executed unconsciously by the frontal lobes using the executive function and the attention systems. Realize these movements vary from 50 to 200 milliseconds, which helps us to understand it is more like a briefly extended blink of the eye and barely discernable (Wolf, 2007). Furthermore, technology applied to the reading process revealed the reader's eyes are not always focused on the same letter or word. They may be two letters apart, but the brain is able to fuse the images to experience a single, clear visual representation (British Association for Advancement for Science, 2007).

While the first two brain reasons for reading fluency result from clusters of quickly responding neuron circuits and rapid, darting eye movements, the third quality identifies a "word form" area in the occipital-temporal areas. Neurons in this specialized area appear to learn orthographic patterns of the writing system for immediate recognition. Wolf identifies Stanislas Dehaene and Bruce McCandliss as researchers who describe changes of the visual cortex in expert readers. Initially, the area is designed for recognizing objects, such as a bus, snowplow, squirrel or star in the sky, but the area is reconfigured to also recognize letters, singularly and together. In this instance, the brain is changed by reading to quickly respond to letters as well as concrete objects. Much as the oral language pathway is co-opted to become the reading decoding pathway, the visual association area is redesigned to accept representational forms, letters, and to place them on the fast tract for identification as words and thoughts.

> While the first two brain reasons for reading fluency result from clusters of quickly responding neuron circuits and rapid, darting eye movements, the third quality identifies a "word form" area in the occipital-temporal areas.

Some Children Are Fast Processors; Some Are Not

Decoding ability is an indicator for success in reading. Whether it is called phonological processing, decoding, or word analysis, the basic skill is being able to put sounds (phonemes) to letters (graphemes) and to apply phonetic rules to recognize words fluently, automatically, accurately, and with meaning. Theoretically, children who understand the rules for decoding and can produce the sounds of phonemes in words with automaticity will be good readers. However, researchers have identified another skill that, when accessed efficiently, works in tandem with phonological processes.

This skill, rapid automatized naming (RAN), is the ability to look at symbols, such as colored squares or simple objects, and rapidly identify them. Reading experts believe that RAN is a very good indicator for reading success. In fact, researchers have recently found that speed of naming, rather than accuracy of naming, differentiated between people who were good readers and those who were labeled as dyslexic (Wolf, Bowers, & Biddle, 2000). Researchers emphasize that when a child lacks skills for automatic naming, comprehension, and speed of word calling, reading suffers.

> This skill, rapid automatized naming (RAN), is the ability to look at symbols, such as colored squares or simple objects, and rapidly identify them.

Recent research has tested and validated the hypothesis that the rate of processing and automaticity of responses are the overarching skill development area and that phonological processing is actually a component of the rate of processing. For example, when children respond to a simple perception task, such as pointing to the color red, there is no significant difference in rate of response between children who are impaired readers and children who are normal readers. However, when children are asked to identify a picture of a common object, recognize the object, determine the name of the object, say the name, and move as quickly as possible to the next object, differences in timing between the two groups—good readers and poor readers—becomes significant (Wolf et al., 2000). These tasks are usually performed with a series of symbols, numbers, colors, letters, objects, or sight words that can be easily identified by the child.

Many neurological activities are occurring rapidly and in tandem during this naming exercise. What we see the child do gives little indication of the intense activity that is happening in the child's brain. There are many points at which this brain activity can stall. Studies are conclusive. Researchers examined naming efficiency with simple objects. The complex process can be impeded at any stage—locating similar objects in memory, identifying the specific object, articulating the name of the object, disengaging from the object, and,

> What we see the child do gives little indication of the intense activity that is happening in the child's brain.

finally, moving attention to the next object to be named (Wolf et al., 2000). Wolf's work gives added value to the working definition of reading fluency. Fluency is not the time it takes to read the words; rather, it is the time it takes for comprehension and making sense of the reading passage.

Assessing Reading Fluency and Automatic Naming

Reading fluency is usually assessed by measuring the speed at which text is read, followed by evaluating the quality of responses to comprehension questions. Teachers using informal reading inventories (IRIs), a graded series of passages with increasing difficulty, can identify children who process slowly when they read. More specific diagnostic information for fluency can help determine when a reading intervention is warranted. There are many tests for decoding and comprehension, and assessment of fluency now gets the attention that it deserves as a continual part of reading development.

One diagnostic tool for reading fluency is the Gray Oral Reading Test (third edition). It has 13 progressively difficult passages, each with five comprehension questions. While this timed assessment is appropriate for third graders, reading sections are leveled too high for children in the lower grades (Torgesen, 1998). Another assessment is the nationally normed Test of Word Reading Efficiency (TOWRE). One section evaluates the number of real printed words that can be accurately identified within 45 seconds. A second section measures the number of pronounceable printed nonwords a student can decode in 45 seconds (Torgesen, 1998). The Woodcock Reading Mastery Test–Revised also contains a section to assess fluency.

An early indicator of reading speed can be predicted by a less formal assessment for rapid naming of objects. The objects include colors, symbols, letters, numbers, or pictures. One simple test involves naming five different objects that are randomly assigned on a page of 50 objects. There are 10 rows of objects with 5 objects in each row. The child is directed to say an object and then to move as quickly as possible to identify the next object and so on. The amount of time, in seconds, it takes to name all 50 objects is recorded (Denckla & Rudel, 1976).

Because of the importance attached to early identification, RAN is suggested as a part of kindergarten screening. Although teacher observation generally provides identification of children who exhibit slow processes for naming and ultimately for slow reading fluency, school psychologists most likely are able to provide an assessment for rapid naming with norms for expected naming speed. Naming assessment is useful for identification of children who, at the onset of reading instruction, show early signs of slow processing.

> Naming assessment is useful for identification of children who, at the onset of reading instruction, show early signs of slow processing.

DEVELOPING READING FLUENCY

> It is interesting that students who are not fluent readers actually benefit from additional oral reading practice, although frequently the quantity of reading they do is less due to the difficulty of their reading material.

It takes only one painful experience with a slow and halting reader in a reading group to understand that this reader is not likely to make the same reading progress as peers who are reading effortlessly. Teachers, in an attempt to be more attuned to the needs of these struggling readers, request that they read aloud, interrupt when a word is miscalled, and tend to give word-by-word feedback. It is interesting that students who are not fluent readers actually benefit from additional oral reading practice (Allington, 2001), although frequently the quantity of reading they do is less due to the difficulty of their reading material. Beyond orthographic instruction, discussed earlier, a key to nurturing fluent reading is to provide appropriate text and to structure successful activities where reading is fun and enjoyable (Rasinski, 2000).

All students, particularly slow, laborious readers, benefit from the three approaches that are discussed in this chapter—repetitive practice for object naming; guided, repeated, modeled oral reading; and independent silent reading at an appropriate reading level. Regardless of the strategies that teachers use, reading fluency can be strengthened through deliberate, planned reading activities.

Repetitive Practice for Object Naming

When children are fluent, accurate readers, they can devote their attention and energy to understanding what they read. RAN using sequentially more difficult letter configurations (e.g., letters, diagraphs, root words, or multisyllabic words) is a precursor to reading with fluency. What are the implications of rapid naming for reading skill development and as a remediation technique? Practicing naming familiar objects and progressing to letter forms, clusters, and words are suggested for practice.

Fluency practice can be turned into a game. Children keep a record of how long it takes to name all the objects on a chart and then attempt to improve their own times. When one set of objects, for example, colors, is mastered within a target time, the child moves on to another set, such as a chart of numbers. Each succeeding set should be mastered with quicker response times than the previous one, and succeeding charts can provide more difficult naming sets. During this process, the brain is primed to develop facilitated neural networks for rapid identification, naming, disengagement, and movement to the next object.

Interestingly, even though flash cards for word recognition have been dubbed by some as "drill and kill," flash cards are useful for practice for reading single words. When words practiced with flash cards are later found in text, children are more able to read with increased fluency (Levy, Abello, & Lysynchuk, 1997). Likewise, pictorial flash cards of objects show promise as one type of remediation practice for children with slow response rates for naming. In this case, children use flash cards with objects, pictures, or words that they already know. Students can work with partners to quiz each other, since demands to turn over the flash cards could interfere with the target process of rapid naming. The desired outcome is certainty, accuracy, and most important, speed. Recording time and engaging children to beat their own best time provides motivation for this type of flash card activity.

Here, also, is a place where the computer is suited to provide repetitive practice. Portions of programs, such as Fast ForWord or Earobics Literacy Launch, are designed specifically to present images for identification at varying speeds. Children learn to respond quickly and to prime their minds to make connections rapidly. Once the concept of naming speed is understood as a developmental skill used by readers to attain fluency, teachers can identify other classroom activities that provide this type of practice through repetition.

Read, Reread, and Read Again

Processing speed for reading is undeniably more complex than it is for object identification. Reading puts demands on the brain structures for memory and complex recall, because reading requires both decoding skills and access to a knowledge base for comprehension. Strategies to strengthen the connections the brain needs to access for increased reading fluency call for guided, repeated, and modeled oral reading. A recent study conducted by O'Connor, White, and Swanson (2007), from the University of California, Riverside, drew on a premise from previous studies, which were based upon isolated word practice. These studies indicated that rote practice for unknown words yielded less than favorable results for increasing reading comprehension.

> Strategies to strengthen the connections the brain needs to access for increased reading fluency call for guided, repeated, and modeled oral reading.

These researchers proceeded to test the effects of long-term practice (15 minute sessions of repeated or continuous oral reading three times a week for 14 weeks) as children in the second and fourth grades read to an adult observer. Study conclusions suggest that poor readers are unlikely to make gains commensurate to gains made by average readers without extensive oral reading practice. Upper-grade teachers are less likely to have students read orally, yet research outcomes indicate this practice will provide successful gains for poor readers in the areas of reading fluency, word identification, and reading comprehension (O'Connor et al., 2007).

Another practice activity to increase reading fluency uses a rereading strategy with one-minute intervals. This system uses a passage that children are able to read at or above a success rate of 95 percent. The entire process uses only five minutes each day and begins anew at the start of each week. The technique can be used either with an entire class or with any group of students who are at a similar independent reading level. Following is the design for this strategy.

On the first day, the teacher reads the selected passage for one minute, while students follow with their own copy of the selection. Next, students read silently for one minute, followed by students in pairs each taking a turn to read for one minute. The listening partner provides corrections, as needed. Students record the last line and the last word that they read each day. This process is repeated every day for a week with the same passage. As children progress in their ability to read with fluency, the teacher monitors passages for progressive complexity. Vocabulary from the current lesson may be interjected into the target passage. Passage selection can include poetry, narrative, or instructional text. The process becomes more challenging as the teacher requires passages be read with accuracy, prosody, and attention to the meaning of the words.

Strategies for reading and rereading can be integrated into classroom schedules as focused activities or to fill noninstructional time. Creating pairs of readers using community volunteers, cross-age tutors, peer partners, or parents (through take-home passages) provides a variety of opportunities to practice reading aloud.

In addition to the strategies described previously, the following partner read-aloud techniques are also helpful:

Set a goal, such as 85 words per minute. Students practice on their own without an audience. When they are ready to perform, they read the passage aloud to as many listeners as they can find. When the reading speed target has been reached three consecutive times, they are "signed off" for this passage.

Pair a student who is a fluent reader with a less fluent reader. Partners read a selected passage several times together until the student who is less fluent feels comfortable reading on his own. Students keep a record of accuracy and time until a target is reached, then a new passage is selected. A variation of this strategy is to pair children from different grade levels, say a second grader and a third-grade student, both who have fluency problems. In this instance, the students work together on second-grade-level passages.

Have a child read a passage into a tape recorder. The child may make the recording several times before selecting one sample to use for repeated practice. The child and teacher then set goals, such as reading with improved accuracy, decreasing time for reading, or reading with expression and prosody. The child reads along with the tape until the goals appear to have been met. At that time, another recording is made and the pre- and post-tapes are compared against the predetermined goals.

Using an echo reading approach, Partner A reads a sentence. Partner B then reads the same words. This first-and-follow routine continues through the selection until each partner can reread the passage individually at an increased rate. This technique is also used when the teacher reads, and the group follows with choral reading of the same passage. A variation of this technique is to use unfamiliar but easy-to-sing songs. The teacher sings or says a significant portion of the lines, so the children need to read the words from the song sheet to echo the response.

> Once attuned to the importance of providing reading practice through individual, pairs, and whole-class activities, teachers can include practice for fluency on a regular basis.

Teachers can easily integrate strategies to build fluency practice into classroom schedules. Once attuned to the importance of providing reading practice through individual, pairs, and whole-class activities, teachers can include practice for fluency on a regular basis.

Independent Reading

The last instructional technique simply, but effectively, helps children increase their reading rate through practice with silent reading at an appropriate reading level. Remember the second-grade classroom that was described in an earlier chapter. One striking feature of the class is the number of books that are available for children to read. Every classroom must be a reader's haven.

School is the best place for children to get books to read, as books can be leveled so that the difficulty of the text matches a student's ability. Evidence is conclusive that children who read more do better in school. Based on current research and what we intuitively know as educators, providing opportunities to engage all students in reading in a positive environment is both fun and productive.

Books, Books, and More Books

Literature-based and expository text instruction makes a perfect contribution to reading development to increase practice and, ultimately, fluency. When schools include activities such as storytelling, reading aloud, poetry parties, book fairs, meeting the author events, puppet shows, writing stories, acting out stories, and other wonderfully engaging book-related activities, children learn that reading is fun.

Children can be exposed to lots of books that capture their attention in whimsical and playful ways. In the early grades, stories such as Scheer and Beck's *Rain Makes Apple Sauce* invite children to play with mouth-wallowing phrases about monkeys that mumble with a jumble of jelly-beans. Young children gain reading confidence with stories that have repetitive phrases, such as the everyone-is-sleeping sequence from Wood's *The Napping House*.

> Children can be exposed to lots of books that capture their attention in whimsical and playful ways.

Children find prose and poems to be appealing through authors such as Shel Silverstein. His style, which combines pictures that are a bit quirky with the unique phrases of his poetry, charm childhood audiences. Likewise, poetry with a magic twist captures the young reader's attention, for example, Dean Koontz's "The Paper

Doorway." Koontz tells how it feels to be engaged and trapped within a book. Books similar to Dr. Seuss's *Cat in the Hat*, known for their appeal to early readers, are now available for primary readers as narrative-informational stories. Bonnie Worth's *Oh Say Can You Seed? All About Flowering Plants*, from the Cat in the Hat's Learning Library, is one such book. It contains the ever-present magic rhymes and has serious scientific information to teach, too.

We cannot resist mentioning Joanna Cole's *The Magic School Bus Explores the Senses*. This series features Ms. Frizzle, a zany, absent-minded teacher. In this story, Ms. Frizzle moves through town, while her class tries to catch up with her in the magic school bus. During the chase, the bus and the children shrink, move inside the heads of different people and animals, and learn about the senses and the brain. J. K. Rowling's Harry Potter series is yet another example of how books can capture young readers' interest. With stories like these that are laden with whimsical words, serious information, and sometimes engrossing pictures, even children who have difficulty with reading can be enticed to pick up a book for independent, pleasure reading.

Sustained Silent Reading

Sustained silent reading (SSR) was developed to provide daily time for children to be immersed in reading. SSR can be very, very good with appropriate implementation. It can be a horrid experience if it is a "drop everything and read" strategy followed by an immediate return to the previous task. This latter less productive interpretation of SSR frequently requires students to be engaged with any available reading material and to sit quietly and read for an extended period. Teacher direction and follow-up are nonexistent. When SSR is used without an instructional intent and without any rules for implementation, it runs the risk of becoming a waste of important instructional time.

> It can be a horrid experience if it is a "drop everything and read" strategy followed by an immediate return to the previous task.

What practices make this reading strategy successful? Author and teacher Janice Pilgreen (2000) studied SSR with high school–aged students who were English language learners (ELs). While our target population is much younger students, Pilgreen made recommendations that speak to all grade levels:

Children need access to huge numbers of books.

Teachers are excellent models to show children how much they love to read.

A home reading program extends the time available for independent reading.

Children are not held accountable for what they read (such as having to write a book report), but time is set aside to share reading experiences and recommend books.

An SSR time may be adopted by individual teachers or adopted as a schoolwide program. In effective programs, students make selections from books that have been previously coded for their individual reading level. Children, however, are given freedom to read books that are more difficult when they have interest and desire to learn more about a specific topic.

Variations to SSR could include "reading friends" who select a book together, read alone or together, and then have a conversation about their common reading experience (Hopkins, 2002). Teachers can also use sustained silent writing (SSW) by following individual reading with journal writing. SSR is a widely used strategy, intended to engage students in reading, to give them practice with materials that are self-selected yet at an appropriate reading level, and to help them get the practice they need to become fluent, confident readers.

Programs for Slow Readers

All children do not learn to read at the expected rate. First, let us define a range of expectance by grade level for how many words are read with a one-minute timing. The first set of numbers, from Shaywitz (2003), gives expected rates specifically for the *spring* of the identified grade, while the second *general* range was established by Harris and Sipay (1990) from several standardized measures (see Table 9.1).

A number of factors may influence reading rates. Although the rate of oral or silent reading may be quite similar during the early grades, for third graders the gap between reading aloud and reading silently may be significant (Allington, 2001). In third grade, some children with slow reading rates

Table 9.1   One-Minute Timing: Word Expectations per Grade Level

	Shaywitz (spring)	*Harris and Sipay (general)*
Grade	*Expected Words Read per Minute*	
First	40–60	60–90
Second	80–100	85–120
Third	100–120	115–140

may need instruction in the basics for phonological and orthographic processing. They may not have mastered the skills to identify, manipulate, produce, and recall speech sounds. Other children may have difficulties with reading rates due to a lack of word recognition, vocabulary, comprehension, or processing speed deficits. Unsuccessful readers at any grade level, as identified in Chapter 7, need assessment to determine a remediation plan that addresses their specific deficits. Although programs for fluency intervention or remediation are not as readily available as those that are designed for children with decoding or comprehension problems, an increasing number of commercial programs address reading fluency. One of these is the Read Naturally program developed by reading teacher Candyce Ihnot (see Instructional Resources). "Read, reread, and read again" shows up again as a strategy in this program, which is designed to intervene when children are identified as at-risk students. Read Naturally includes teacher modeling, repeated reading, and progress monitoring. Teachers who implement the program use Oral Reading Fluency Norms to measure the progress made by their students.

Great Leaps (see Instructional Resources) is another program available at all grade levels beginning with K–2. It has remediation for phonics and sight phrases but also includes a section on reading fluency. The intended outcomes for the fluency section are to increase speed for reading, improve motivation, and develop proper intonation during reading. Stories used with Great Leaps were written and designed by Kenneth Campbell, a teacher of students with learning disabilities. Stories include point of view, humor, rhyme, and rhythm as motivation for this reading intervention.

J & J readers (see Instructional Resources) also provide reading practice with decodable text that resembles chapter books but are engaging and appropriate for any age student. These readers are a part of a total reading intervention program called Language! (second edition), but they can be purchased separately. Comprehension, language expansion, and higher-level thinking activities are emphasized with a multiethnic cast of characters. While the J & J readers are not part of a reading-specific program, use of these decodable books or other leveled readers can be built into an instructional plan for increasing reading fluency.

Finally, we mention Fluent Reader, which is part of the Accelerated Reader series (see Instructional Resources). Fluent Reader programs, beginning with grade one, determine students' fluency levels through a computer program. Students practice reading with a variety of reading text that can be delivered to the student with three varying speeds.

FINAL COMMENTS

Students who read slowly and lag behind their peers for reading fluency, students who receive special education services, or those who are in English language programs must be considered and planned for in the

> Although children who are struggling readers may receive supplemental help or may receive the services of an intervention program provided on a pullout basis, they still need the benefit of a complete reading program—not a skill development program only—with their normally progressing peers.

school's reading program. Although children who are struggling readers may receive supplemental help or may receive the services of an intervention program provided on a pullout basis, they still need the benefit of a complete reading program—not a skill development program only—with their normally progressing peers. Students fourth grade and above who are reading two or more grade levels below their expected rates can be gathered for instruction from a replacement, stand-alone reading program. These programs are specially designed to accelerate learning and rapidly remediate struggling reader's deficits so that they can be returned to their age-appropriate class.

All primary-age children benefit when they are a part of the rich and varied classroom conversations that happen naturally between their peers and teachers during reading and language arts instruction. Teachers are the critical force to structure school environments where children construct their reading brain and their attitude about themselves as readers. Talented teachers orchestrate a delicate balance between instruction and student engagement with learning through conversation, practice activities, reading narrative and informational texts, leisure selections read aloud and silently, and through writing experiences that are shared with the class. In a school environment where teachers base their instructional decisions on how children learn to read, children are able to become fluent efficient readers. Reading competencies attained from kindergarten through third grade are critical for all aspects of education in all of the school years that follow.

REFLECTIVE QUESTIONS

1. How do you define reading fluency? From your experience, what skills need to be developed before a child can read fluently?

2. Fluent, accurate reading depends on a child's understanding of orthography, the visual patterns of written language that feature graphemes, phonology, and semantics. Describe some ways a reading program can build teaching orthography into lessons for students in the third grade.

3. Prepare a list of strategies to share with parents that would help children to increase their reading fluency. What could you tell parents to help them understand what needs to happen in the brain for a child to become a fluent reader?

4. If you are reading this book as a part of a study group, have each member explain something known about the reading brain that helps us to understand how children are able to read with automaticity, accuracy, and fluency.

5. Select one of the research studies from this chapter. Describe how the study outcome influences the teaching of reading in a primary classroom.

10

Conclusion

Anyone who has ever been involved in a construction project knows that it's rarely a simple process. The plans need to accurately convey your vision of the final project, the materials must be available, the builder must be skilled, and the cost must be within your means. If there are no unexpected factors—and there always seem to be—the final product will meet the needs for which it was designed, and you will feel the effort and time were well spent.

Building the reading brain is also a construction process, and as in building an edifice, many steps are involved and many factors need to be controlled for the final product—the child's brain—to become one that reads accurately, with fluency and understanding, and also with enjoyment. This final chapter summarizes what has been learned from educational research, the practice of teachers, and more specifically, research from cognitive science and the neurosciences about how to direct a child to best build the reading brain.

Some of what is known comes from scientific brain research about neural structures and their functions, while other knowledge deals more with information gleaned from reading research and practice. Of particular interest is the neurobiological basis for reading that comes from researchers, such as Peter E. Turkeltaub and his colleagues (Turkeltaub, Weisberg, Flowers, Basu, & Eden, 2004), who report from Georgetown University. Their scientific perspective welcomes the protracted time it takes a child to build the reading brain as an opportunity for examining the mechanisms of neural plasticity. One study of 41 healthy readers from the ages of 6 to 22 allowed them to follow and report on the neurological progression for the reading construction process. However, even though other findings may come from research or experience outside the field of neuroscience, the information about the brain and how it learns is helping us to understand why certain instructional processes and strategies are more effective than others.

A CHILD'S BRAIN AND
READING: A DOZEN KEY LEARNINGS

1. The brain is not innately wired for reading; there are no naturally designated neural mechanisms for reading. The brain must co-opt structures designed for other purposes.

   Children are born with a brain that has a built-in pathway for oral language. If they are exposed to a language, barring any neurological disability or disorder, they will learn to speak that language with little difficulty. The same is *not* true of reading. In a sense, reading is an unnatural act for the brain. There is no built-in pathway for reading. While raising children in print-rich environments is important—especially in the early years—most children do not learn to read through exposure; they must be taught.

2. Neuroplasticity is a characteristic of the brain that allows it to be shaped by experience.

   How can a brain not wired for reading eventually accomplish this extremely difficult task? The answer lies in a unique characteristic of the brain called *neuroplasticity*. The reason we can learn habits and skills that are not innate is that the brain is "plastic" throughout life. This means that it can adapt to new circumstances and requirements, literally changing the function of certain cells. This ability to adapt to its environment, to sculpt itself depending on the demands of the environment, is one of the most amazing characteristics of the brain.

3. Many factors have been shown to be strong predictors of eventual reading success.

   Because language is a precursor to reading, the size of children's vocabulary, their expressive language, recognition of the letters of the alphabet, the ability to name the letters rapidly, and their knowledge of the purposes of books are all key predictors of later reading success. Reading aloud to children with interactive dialogue is one means to help children develop these skills before they are able to read well on their own. Writing, reading's reciprocal action, supports the development of skills that will be important in learning to read. Listening to and repeating songs, jingles, or rhymes are additional ways to develop children's emerging literacy.

4. Priming skills for reading, which include paying attention, being able to focus and concentrate, putting order and organization to thinking, and holding information in working memory become critical attributes that need to be in place in the early school years.

Teachers find that when they identify children who struggle with these attributes, they can make relatively simple instructional adjustments to encourage and essentially force children to become better at listening and holding information in their conscious memory. Instructional adjustments for priming skills also affect students' motivation to learn and ultimately how well they store and retain information critical to successful reading.

5. Essential to learning to read is the understanding that the sounds (phonemes) of spoken language can be represented by print and that phonemes can be arranged to make many different words.

   We call this concept *phonemic awareness,* and children can pick up this understanding on their own through a language-oriented preschool environment, or it can be taught explicitly. It appears to be essential to decoding print, to learning to read. In addition to phonemic awareness, children must be able to recognize and produce rhymes, break words into syllables, distinguish parts of syllables (onsets and rimes), and determine root words, prefixes, and suffixes of words. *Phonological awareness* is the umbrella term given to this broader array of skills, which usually includes phonemic awareness.

6. Some strategies commonly used to teach children to decode have proved to be less effective than others. Information on how the brain learns best can assist teachers in selecting the most brain-compatible strategies.

   The content that children practice needs to make as much sense as possible since the brain seeks patterns to make sense of the task with which it is engaged. Many commonly used word walls, letter-to-sound approaches, and orthographic rules seemingly have no patterns or logical sequence. They are confusing to the young child's brain. Word walls need to be sound-to-letter(s) based. Orthographic rules with examples, discussion, and jingles or songs with meaningful practice are more likely to be stored in and retrieved from long-term memory.

7. Early assessment in kindergarten has proved to be effective to determine which children are ready to read and which ones will require early intervention.

   The conventional wisdom has been that some children are ready to read in kindergarten while others won't be ready until later, indicating that we should wait until they are ready. We now understand that many factors determine whether or not children appear to be ready to read.

Children who have limited exposure to print, who have not been read to, learned nursery rhymes, or been exposed to a language rich environment may enter school without the emergent literacy skills necessary to learn to read. Neurological factors may also play a role. Early assessment to identify these environmental and biological factors is essential to select an appropriate reading intervention program from the many that are available.

8. Difficulty in learning to read (e.g., dyslexia) can be the result of several factors.

Some reading problems are the result of a neurological decoding "glitch" in the reading pathway of the brain. This problem either can be a genetically programmed error—generally an underactivation in the angular gyrus and Wernicke's area—or may be more environmentally influenced, such as by a lack of early stimulation or intermittent schooling. Other problems seem to stem from physiological, socioeconomic, ethnic, and/or second-language factors. Regardless of the source of the reading problem, nearly all deficits can be overcome with a reading program that is matched with the child's assessed reading deficit and based upon direct, explicit instruction.

9. Recognizing whole words (and eventually some phrases) automatically is essential for fluent reading and comprehension.

As children become more proficient in decoding print, they begin to see common groups of letters as words. How does this happen? When a certain configuration of letters is processed numerous times, the brain begins to store this configuration as a single bit of information, a word. This chunking process is how the brain overcomes its limited processing space, identified as working memory. Without this ability, there would be insufficient "space" in conscious memory for comprehension of what is being read.

10. Because we read for a purpose, comprehension can be considered an end product of reading.

As important as it is to develop the ability to decode print, it is not of much use if we do not comprehend what we read. In order to comprehend what is being read, children's brains must be able to decode automatically and unconsciously so that the conscious processing functions of the brain are totally available for connecting the words being read to previously acquired information. As the brain instantaneously accesses associations in memory, the reader is able to understand the content of the print. However, this does not mean that we should wait until all decoding is automatic before addressing comprehension.

11. The size of children's vocabulary and their comprehension of what they read are highly dependent on their school and personal experiences.

   Recall that the brain sculpts itself based on the input it receives from the environment. Children who are actively engaged with learning by practicing, rehearsing, talking, experiencing, responding, creating, or making products are more likely to remember words and develop expansive vocabularies. Additionally, they are able to attach new learning to neural networks that were previously established. Teachers help children to organize their thinking by giving them activities that require the children to organize, sort, compare, list, find differences or similarities, mind map, or develop schemas. Through these activities, children's minds form a way to store information important enough to remember.

12. Attaining fluency and comprehension in reading by the end of the third grade is the ultimate goal of reading instruction.

   When children can read with speed and accuracy, they are able to concentrate on the meaning of the text. However, if they must devote considerable energy to the mechanics of reading, their focus on the meaning is diminished. The ability to read fluently is dependent, therefore, on how automatic decoding is (using the decoding reading pathway), how familiar children are with the orthography of language (accessing the visual association areas of the brain), and how quickly neural activity happens among the structures of the brain that have been developed and reinforced for reading.

Finally, we repeat from the introduction to this book: Reading well is more than a legislated priority; it's an ethical and professional imperative. It is our hope that this book will provide an understanding of how neuroscience gives a broader understanding of the complex reading process. Furthermore, outcomes from studies that include neural imaging of both learning and reading tasks are supportive of and match with results-based research from education's behavioral science. May this book be a guide to both parents and teachers as we strive to give our children the reading legacy they deserve.

Glossary

Academic language The ability to use general or content-specific words or terms for acquiring understanding, knowledge, or skills and to be able to interact with others using the terms to impart information to others.

Alliteration Reoccurring sounds, often consonants or cluster at the start of a string of words.

Alphabetic principle The basic understanding that segments of speech are represented by letters.

Angular gyrus A brain structure located at the junction of the occipital, parietal, and temporal lobes. It is here that the letters of written words are translated into the sounds of spoken language.

Arcuate fasiculus A band of neural fibers connecting Wernicke's area with Broca's area.

Attention A cognitive act of focus on a particular object, event, or happening while ignoring other environmental or personal stimuli.

Auditory memory The ability to listen to sounds or words, hold them in working memory, and complete a task, such as repeating a string of words or putting the sounds together to make a word.

Automaticity The ability to perform a skill or habit automatically or unconsciously.

Broca's area The central region for the production of speech and processing of syntax. It is generally located in the left hemisphere.

Cerebellum Often called the "small brain," this structure is located at the base of the cerebral cortex and is a super support system for automatic movement, balance, and many learned actions, such as writing, reading, and walking, for example, that happen without conscious direction from the frontal lobes or motor cortex.

Cerebral cortex The deeply folded outer layer of the cerebral hemispheres that is responsible for perception, awareness of emotion, planning, and conscious thought. Also called the neocortex.

Comprehension The process of attaching meaning to written or spoken language by accessing previously stored experience or knowledge.

Computed tomography (CT) A type of x-ray that provides computer-aided images of various planes of the head or other parts of the body.

Concentration An extended period of attention in which the brain focuses on information and enters into a state to develop understanding or remembering.

Concepts of print The understanding of written language, including reading from left to right, from the top to bottom of the page, that spaces separate words, and that writing conveys a message.

Corpus callosum A large bundle of myelinated fibers (axons) that connects the left and right hemispheres of the brain.

Cueing systems Processes that indicate what a word or group of words is and includes use of semantics, syntax, and graphemes.

Declarative memory Explicit memory to allow storage of information in an organized manner so it can be subsequently recalled by speaking or writing.

Decoding The ability to recognize a sound-symbol relationship when translating a written word to speech or to decipher a new word by sounding it out.

Decontextualized text A developmental skill, which develops during the preschool years, allowing a child to talk about what is being thought, including events and objects that are not visibly present.

Dialogic reading A nontraditional adult/child reading activity where the adult asks questions, prompts the child for additional information, and describes pictures.

Dyslexia A cognitive deficit relating to phonological processing, particularly the ability to decode and recognize words.

Emergent literacy Skills that begin to develop during early infancy through meaningful activities with adults and include oral language, print knowledge, and phonological processing.

Encoding Writing and spelling words using sounds to attach to letter patterns.

Episodic memory Long-term memory of a happening or occurrence that is accompanied by strongly felt emotions.

Explicit instruction Programs that provide precise, systematic directions for teaching.

Expository text Written selections that include essays, paragraphs, textbook chapters, professional articles, and newspaper editorials that are used for reading instruction.

Frontal lobes The largest of four major divisions of each hemisphere of the cerebral cortex located in the front part of the brain and responsible for higher-level cognition. These structures are directly involved with every other functional unit in the brain for response and recognition activities.

Functional magnetic resonance imaging (fMRI) A technique for imaging brain structure and activity by measuring oxygen use of the cells.

Glial cells Provide a vast system of support for the neurons in the brain. One particular type, oligodendrocytes, wrap themselves around an individual neuron's axon to restrict sodium from slowing down messages between neurons.

Grapheme Printed representations, letters, that represent a phoneme.

Heschl's area A small left temporal region where sounds are rapidly processed as speech or language, rather than other sounds.

Hippocampus A pair of structures located under the surface of the temporal lobes that hold information temporarily until it is dropped or moved to long-term memory for storage and recall.

Individualized instruction Instruction responsive to the unique needs of each child in a classroom regardless of the lesson setting (whole class, small group, or one-to-one).

Inhibitory neurons Brain cells designed to siphon, detain, and drop unnecessary sensory stimuli from memory as if it had not been received.

Letter-sound relationship The relationship between the grapheme and its corresponding phoneme.

Lexile Two measures that forecast the level of comprehension that a reader can accomplish and the level of comprehension that a reading measure contains.

Long-term memory A term given to unconscious storage of information for long periods of time, which can be recalled through a memory flash or conscious effort.

Memory How and where the human brain stores information to be recalled at will or automatically. Declarative memory is consciously sought and produced, while nondeclarative memory is located by rote response or by engaging in a procedural action. The very essence of teaching is to encourage the learner to hold information or actions for practice and rehearsal in working memory so the brain can develop neural pathways to the declarative or nondeclarative system for recall.

Metalinguistic skills Development of an ability to view language as worthy of focus and attention.

Mirror neurons A specific type of neuron, discovered unexpectedly within the last decade, which is amply present in the language system as well as other parts of the human brain. These nerve cells allow a person to activate brain areas while watching another person, as if the observer is actually performing the act.

Morpheme The smallest unit of language that has meaning.

Morphology The study of the language of words and how they are ordered to have meaning.

Motor cortex The lateral part of the frontal lobes that extends from ear to ear across the roof of the brain. It governs coordination of movement and some cognitive processes. The motor cortex may also be referred to as the *motor strip*.

Myelination A maturation process in structures and areas of the human brain where one type of glial cell wraps itself around axons and results in speedy transmission of neuron connections.

Narrative text A written selection that tells a story and includes children's picture books, fairy tales, fables, myths, tall tales, short stories, and novels.

Neuron A nerve cell in the brain containing a cell body, which metabolizes and synthesizes proteins, numerous dendrites, which receive chemical messages, and one axon, which transports impulses to excite other nerve cells with proteins.

Neuroplasticity The term given to the characteristic of the brain that allows it to reorganize itself by forming new neural connections and to adjust their activity in response to new situations or changes in the environment.

Nondeclarative memory Memory consisting of habits and skills that have been practiced to the point that they can be performed automatically without conscious thought (procedural) or with a prompt (priming).

Occipital lobe One of the four major divisions of the cortex located in the back of the brain and responsible for the processing of visual stimuli.

Oddity tasks Activities for building phonemic awareness that require a child to "find the one that is different" from a series of sounds or words. Generally the list contains three examples, one of which does not belong.

One-to-one instruction Instruction delivered to one student at a time, not necessarily based on individualized learning needs.

Onsets The initial consonants or blends in the syllable; not every word has an onset.

Organization This term used in relationship to brain development refers to the way the brain is connected among neural networks and brain structures for long-term memory recall.

Orthography Written language's visual patterns that account for features of graphemes, phonology, and semantics.

Parietal lobes One of the four major divisions of the cortex, located in the upper back part of the brain between the occipital lobes and the frontal cortex. They are responsible for sensory integration and give humans their sense of opportunities and dangers.

Phoneme The smallest sound of speech that corresponds to a particular letter of an alphabetic writing system.

Phonemic awareness Conscious understanding that words are made of individual sounds (phonemes) from speech and that these sounds are representative of the alphabet. Phonemic awareness activities include rhyming, alliteration, oddity tasks, phoneme segmentation, phoneme blending, phoneme manipulation, and syllable splitting.

Phonetics The study of articulation of speech sounds.

Phonics A system used in alphabetic writing that is representative of speech sounds, which can be referred to as instruction for sound-symbol reading or a phonics approach to reading.

Phonological awareness Awareness at all levels of the speech/sound system, including stress patterns, onset-rime units, syllables, and phonemes. It includes both phonemic awareness and a systematic approach to phonics instruction systems.

Phonological processing An inclusive term representing the process used to identify, manipulate, produce, and remember speech sounds, which includes word pronunciation, use of memory for naming word, syllable, and rhyme, and phoneme segmentation blending and manipulation.

Phonological sensitivity Breaking the code for how written language represents oral language; an indication of the understanding that words are made up of smaller sounds, such as phonemes and syllables.

Phonology The study of rules that govern how speech is identified for individual sounds and bringing the understanding to a conscious level.

Positron emission tomography (PET) A technique for imaging physiological activity in the brain using radioactive dyes injected into the bloodstream.

Pragmatics A rule system for communication that tells speakers how to choose words.

Print conventions The organizational scheme for writing, which goes from left to right, top of the page to the bottom, and has different forms for different writing genres.

Print form During the development of understanding writing a child identifies units, letters, and words as having names and being organized in specific ways.

Print function An awareness that printed materials provide meaning

Print interest This developmental stage is attained when a child realizes print is stimulating and worthy of attention.

Print knowledge Understanding that words are represented by print, that letters of the alphabet are represented in different ways (e.g., upper- and lowercase letters), and that letters can represent multiple sounds or that the same sound can be represented by different letters.

Print part-to-whole relationships A final stage to understand print function, as the child realizes letters can be combined to make words and words are grouped together to create larger meaningful units.

Procedural nondeclarative memory This term defines a long-term memory system that allows one to perform a task with automaticity and without involving language systems.

Processing speed The rate at which a task, such as reading, occurs through accessing brain structures that are developed for this function.

Prosody The stress and intonation patterns, rhythm, and emphasis given to words during oral reading.

Rhyme The correspondence of ending sounds or lines.

Rime A vowel and the following consonants that make a syllable—letter combinations previously referred to as phonograms or word families.

Semantic memory Words, phrases, sentences, or other forms of text recalled and articulated through speech or writing, which are reflective of the individual's background information and experience.

Semantics The meaning of words, phrases, sentences, and text as reflective of the individual's background information and experience.

Sensory memory A term given to the initial processing of stimuli coming into the brain from internal or external sources.

Somatosensory cortex An area of the brain located behind the motor cortex that receives information through the five senses.

Source memory Episodic memory that retrieves what happened, where an incident happened, and when it happened following a highly emotional experience. Details, although vivid in the mind, may lack accuracy.

Synapse The physical space or void that allows an electrochemical connection between neurons.

Syntax A rule system that functions unconsciously to order words in phrases and ultimately in sentences that correspond to accepted rules for grammar.

Systematic phonics instruction A plan for teaching that is carefully designed around a set of sound-letter relationships following a logical order for introduction.

Temporal lobe One of the four major divisions of the cerebral cortex, located on the sides of each hemisphere. It is responsible for auditory processing and some aspects of memory.

Thalamus A relay station in the central, inner area of the brain for incoming signals from all the senses, except the sense of smell, and an output mechanism for sensory stimuli as it is sent to areas of the cerebral cortex for interpretation.

Visual memory The ability to receive images through the vision center of the brain and hold the images in working memory to complete a task, such as identifying a word from its letters or identifying a series of symbols.

Wernicke's area The language center responsible for comprehension of speech. It is typically located in the left hemisphere.

Word recognition Identifying groups of letters or meaningful units, morphemes, such as prefixes, suffixes, and inflectional endings to determine an unknown word.

Working memory A term given to the conscious processing of information.

Instructional Resources

Accelerated Reader, Fluent Reader Software, Renaissance Learning. www.renlearn.com. (800) 338-4204.

Alphabetic Phonics, Educational Publishing Service. www.epsbooks.com. (800) 225-5750.

Destination Reading, Houghton Mifflin Harcourt. hmlt.hmco.com/DR.php.

Earobics Literacy Launch, www.earobics.com. (888) 242-6747.

Fast ForWord, Scientific Learning. www.ScientificLearning.com. (888) 358-0212.

Fluency Formula and Interactive Phonics Readers, Scholastic. http://teacher.scholastic.com/ips. (877) 511-0005.

Great Leaps, Diarmuid, Inc. www.greatleaps.com. (877) 475-3277.

Interactive Phonics Readers, Scholastic. http://teacher.scholastic.com/ps. (800) 724-6527.

J & J Readers, Sopris West. www.sopriswest.com. (800) 547-6747.

Language Tune-Up, Orton-Gillingham. www.jwor.com. (888) 431-6310.

Leapfrog Literacy Center, Leapfrog Enterprises, Inc. www.leapfrogschoolhouse.com. (800) 883-7430.

Lindamood Phonemic Sequencing, LiPS, Lindamood-Bell. www.lindamoodbell.com. (805) 541-3836.

Phonemic Awareness in Young Children: A Classroom Curriculum, Marilyn Jager Adams, Barbara R. Foorman, Ingvar Lundberg, & Terri Beeler (Baltimore: Brookes Publishing, 1998). http://www.pbrookes.com. (800) 638-3775.

Read Naturally. www.readnaturally.com. (800) 788-4085.

Read Write & Type, Educational Software Cooperative Net Ring, Talking Fingers, Inc. www.readwritetype.com. (800) 674-9126.

Road to the Code: A Phonological Awareness Program for Young Children, Benita A. Blachman, Eileen Wynne Ball, Rochella Black, & Darlene M. Tangel (Baltimore: Brookes Publishing). www.pbrookes.com. (800) 638-3775.

Seeing Stars, Lindamood-Bell. www.lindamoodbell.com. (805) 541-3836.

Test of Word Reading Efficiency (TOWRE), Joseph Torgesen, Richard Wagner, & Carol Rashotte. Ags.pearsonassessments.com/group.asp?GroupInfo10=99676. (800) 627-7271.

U.S. Department of Education free publications for parents to promote early reading preparation, National Institute for Literacy at EdPubs. edpubs.ed.gov. (877) 433-7827.

Visualizing and Verbalizing for Language Comprehension and Thinking, Nanci Bell (San Luis Obispo, CA: Gander Publishing, 1991). www.lindamoodbell.com. (805) 541-3836.

Waterford Early Reading Program, Pearson Digital Learning. www.pearsonschool.com. (800) 627-7271.

Woodcock Reading Mastery Test—Revised, American Guidance Services. ags.pearsonassessments.com/assessments/bibliography/wrmt.asp. (800) 627-7271.

Words Their Way: Word Study for Phonics, Vocabulary, and Spelling, Donald R. Bear, Marcia Invernizzi, Shane Templeton, & Francine Johnston (Columbus, OH: Merrill/Prentice-Hall, 1998). www.pearsonschool.com. (800) 321-3106.

CLASSROOM LIBRARY (LIMITED TO BOOKS REFERENCED IN TEXT)

Charlotte's Web, E. B. White (author) & Garth Williams (illustrator) (New York: HarperCollins, 1952).

Harry Potter and the Chamber of Secrets, J. K. Rowling (author) & Mary GrandPré (illustrator) (New York: A. A. Levine, 1999).

Harry Potter and the Deathly Hallows, J. K. Rowling (author) & Mary GrandPré (illustrator) (New York: A. A. Levine, 2007).

Harry Potter and the Goblet of Fire, J. K. Rowling (author) & Mary GrandPré (illustrator) (New York: A. A. Levine, 2000).

Harry Potter and the Half-Blood Prince, J. K. Rowling (author) & Mary GrandPré (illustrator) (New York: A. A. Levine, 2005).

Harry Potter and the Order of the Phoenix, J. K. Rowling (author) & Mary GrandPré (illustrator) (New York: A. A. Levine, 2003).

Harry Potter and the Prisoner of Azkaban, J. K. Rowling (author) & Mary GrandPré (illustrator) (New York: A. A. Levine, 1999).

Harry Potter and the Sorcerer's Stone, J. K. Rowling (author) & Mary GrandPré (illustrator) (New York: A. A. Levine, 1998).

Look Inside Your Brain, Heather Alexander (author) & Nicoletta Costa (illustrator) (New York: Grosset & Dunlap, 1998).

The Magic School Bus Explores the Senses, Joanna Cole & Bruce Degen (New York: Scholastic, 1999).

Moses Supposes His Toeses Are Roses, N. Patz (San Diego: Harcourt Brace Jovanovich, 1983).

The Napping House, Audrey Wood (author) & Don Wood (illustrator) (San Diego: Harcourt Brace, 1984).

Oh Say Can You Seed: All About Flowering Plants, Bonnie Worth (author), Alice Jonaitis (editor), & Aristides Ruiz (illustrator) (Cat in the Hat's Learning Library, 2001).

The Paper Doorway, Funny Verse and Nothing Worse, Dean Koontz (author) & Phil Parks (illustrator) (New York: Harper/Collins, 2001).

Rain Makes Applesauce, Julian Scheer (author) & Marvin Bileck (illustrator) (New York: Holiday House, 1985).

There's a Wocket in My Pocket, T. S. Geisel (Dr. Seuss) (New York: Random House, 1974).

FAMILY SUPPORT

Between the Lions: Get Wild About Reading, PBS Preschool Education Program: Ready to Learn. Contact for Los Angeles: pbskids.org/lions (323) 953-5202.

Linda Clinard, *Family Time, Reading Fun* (2nd ed.) (Dubuque, IA: Kendall/Hunt, 2002).

Siegfried Engelmann, Phyllis Haddox, & Elaine Bruner, *Teach Your Child to Read in 100 Easy Lessons* (New York: Simon & Schuster, 1986).

WEB RESOURCES FOR BUILDING A READING BRAIN

http://aft.org. The American Federation of Teachers sponsors this site. It includes the latest news, publications, a press center, a parent page, among others. Noteworthy is the availability of articles on research-based reading programs and instructional practices. Issues of *American Educator* are available on a quarterly basis.

http://www.adihome.org. This site gives information about the Association for Direct Instruction. Of particular interest is the availability of articles from the *Journal of Direct Instruction*.

http://www.allkindsofminds.org. All Kinds of Minds is an organization with a mission to help students who struggle to be successful in school. The foundation, launched in 1995, has a school-attuned program, regional training for teachers, and an active Web site and monthly newsletter. Articles and related information lead to cognitive information for clinicians, educators, and families.

http://www.coreknowledge.org. An organization dedicated to identifying core knowledge as a specific, shared content across the grades. Grade-level guides provide content that is solid, sequenced, specific, and shared. Parent information is provided in resources, such as "What Your Kindergartner Needs to Know."

http://www.crayola.com. This company offers activities for parents, educators, and "Crayola kids." A free registration is required. A guide is produced each year for teachers with lessons that encourage visual literacy, reading, writing, storytelling, and "thinking outside the box."

http://www.mcrel.org. A site dedicated to making a difference in the quality of education through applied research. A large number of resources are available that include products, services, and educator resources for content area teaching. Of particular interest is a lesson-plan library that includes the arts, behavioral/social sciences, civics, economics, health/PE, and seven others.

http://www.pattan.k12.pa.us/teachlead/EffectiveInstruction.aspx. Effective instruction is presented in a primer-type format. This Web site comes from the research and work of Edward Kame'enui, Martin Kozloff, and Doug Carnine. It has technical guidelines that range from cognitive strategies for student learning to explicit help for how to teach. A toolkit is available for in-depth information about any facet of instruction. The site contains a plethora of information for teachers at any stage of their career.

http://www.readingrockets.org. This Web site, provided by WETA, a public television station in Washington, DC, gives research-based information about the process of reading. There is a wealth of practical activities for classrooms and for parents to use that encourage children to do more reading, such as "Moving Into Reading: Preschool Through Grade Two."

http://www.rethinkingschools.org. Sponsored by the National Council of Teachers of English, this Web site provides different views of the teaching of reading, teaching children with diverse needs, and the efficacy of teachers.

http://www.uoregon.edu/~bgrossen. A Web site through the University of Oregon, from the Center for Applied Research in Education (C.A.R.E.). This is a nonprofit organization formed by Bonnie Grossen to support schools that serve students who are at risk of failure. The C.A.R.E. team includes teachers and principals who have achieved excellent results with students who are traditionally low-achievers. This site gives up-to-date information that includes a direct instruction model for middle school students as they seek to reach academic expectations and standards.

References and Further Reading

Aaron, P. G. (1995). Differential diagnosis of reading disabilities. *School Psychology Review, 24*(3), 345–360.

Abbott, M. (2001). Effects of traditional versus extended word-study spelling instruction on students' orthographic knowledge. *Reading Online, 5*(3).

Ackerman, S. J. (2003). News from the frontier, an unfelt filter. *Brain Work, The Neuroscience Newsletter, 13*(3), 7–8.

Acredelo, L., & Goodwyn, S. (2000). *Baby signs.* Chicago: Contemporary Books.

Adams, M. J. (1990). *Beginning to read: Thinking and learning about print.* Cambridge: MIT Press.

Adams, M. J., Foorman, B. R., Lundberg, I., & Beeler, T. (1998a). The elusive phoneme. *American Educator, 22*(1–2), 18–29.

Adams, M. J., Foorman, B. R., Lundberg, I., & Beeler, T. (1998b). *Phonemic awareness in young children: A classroom curriculum.* Baltimore: Brookes.

Alaska State Board of Education. (1999). *Reading performance standards.* Retrieved August 04, 2008, from www.eed.state.ak.us/standards

Alexander, A., Anderson, H., Heilman, P. C., Voeller, K. S., & Torgesen, J. K. (1991). Phonological awareness training and remediation of analytic decoding deficits in a group of severe dyslexics. *Annals of Dyslexia, 41*, 193–206.

Alexander, H. (1991). *Look Inside Your Brain.* New York: Grosset & Dunlap.

Allington, R. L. (2001). *What really matters for struggling readers: Designing research-based programs.* New York: Longman.

Allington, R. L. (2002). You can't learn from books you can't read. *Educational Leadership, 60*(3), 16–19.

Ambruster, B., Lehy, F., & Osborn, J. (2006). *A child becomes a reader: proven ideas from research for parents.* Portsmouth, NH: National Institute for Literacy.

American Academy of Pediatrics. (2007). *A systematic review for the effects of television viewing by infants and preschoolers.* Retrieved August 04, 2008, from http://pediatrics.aappublications.org/cgi/content/abstract/118/5/2025

Anbar, A. (1986). Reading acquisition of preschool children without systematic instruction. *Early Childhood Research Quarterly, 1*, 69–83.

Antunez, B. (2002). Implementing reading first with English language learners. *Directions in Language and Education, 15.* Retrieved August 11, 2008, from http://www.ncela.gwu.edu/ncbepubs/directions/15.pdf

Archer, A. (2000). *Expository writing.* Presentation for Sonoma County Office of Education.

Baddeley, A. D. (1986). *Working memory.* Oxford, UK: Oxford University Press.

Bailey, A. L. (Ed). (2007). *The language demands of school: Putting academic English to the test.* New Haven, CT: Yale University Press.

Baker, L., Serpell, R., & Sonnenschein, S. (1995). Opportunities for literacy learning in the homes of urban preschoolers. In L. M. Morrow (Ed.), *Family literacy: Connections in schools and communities* (pp. 236–252). Newark, DE: International Reading Association.

Barton, M. L., Heidema, C., & Jordan, D. (2002). Teaching reading in mathematics and science. *Educational Leadership, 60*(3), 24–27.

Bear, M. F., Conners, B. W., & Paradiso, M. A. (1996). *Neuroscience: Exploring the brain.* New York: Lippincott/Williams & Wilkins.

Beck, I. L., & McKeown, M. G. (1998). Comprehension: The sine qua non of reading. In S. Patton & M. Holmes (Eds.), *The keys to literacy* (pp. 40–52). Washington, DC: Council for Basic Education.

Beck, I. L., & McKeown, M. G. (2001). Text talk: Capturing the benefits of read-aloud experiences for young children. *Reading Teacher, 55*(1), 10–21.

Beck, I. L., McKeown, M. G., & Kucan, L. (2003). Taking delight in words: Using oral language to build young children's vocabularies. *American Educator, 27*(1), 36–41, 45–48.

Bee, H. L., & Mitchell, S. K. (1980). *The developing person: A life-span approach.* New York: Harper & Row.

Bell, N. (1991). *Visualizing and verbalizing for language comprehension and thinking.* San Luis Obispo, CA: Gander.

Berninger, V. W. (2002). *Revealing the secrets of the brain: Neuropsychologist Virginia Berninger studies brain images before and after instruction for clues to the mystery of learning disabilities.* Retrieved August 04, 2008, from http://www.nwrel.org/nwedu/08–03/brain-t.asp

Berninger, V. W., & Richards, L. R. (2002). *Brain literacy for educators and psychologists.* San Diego: Academic Press.

Berninger, V. W., & Whitaker, D. (1993). Theory-based branching diagnosis of writing disabilities. *School Psychology Review, 22*(4), 623–642.

Betts, E. A. (1946). *Foundations of reading instruction.* New York: American Book.

Biemiller, A. (2003a). Oral comprehension sets the ceiling on reading comprehension. *American Educator, 27*(1), 23.

Biemiller, A. (2003b). Teaching vocabulary in the primary grades: Vocabulary instruction needed. In J. Baumann & E. Kame'enui (Eds.). *Reading vocabulary: Research to practice,* pp. 28–40. New York: Guilford Press.

Billman, L. W. (2002). Aren't these books for little kids? *Educational Leadership, 60*(3), 48–49.

Blankenburg, F., Taskin, B., Ruben, J., Moosmann, M., Ritter, P., Curio, G., et al. (2003, March 21). Imperceptible stimuli and sensory processing impediment. *Science, 299*(5614), 1864.

Bloom, F. E., Beal, M. F., & Kupfer, D. J. (2003). *The Dana guide to brain health.* New York: Free Press.

Bloom, P. (2000). *How children learn the meaning of words.* Cambridge: MIT Press. Abstract. Retrieved August 04, 2008, from www.spencer.org/publications/abstracts/abstract.children.learn.htm

Bock, R. (2002). *Why children succeed or fail at reading.* Retrieved August 04, 2008, from www.completelearningcenter.com/whychildren.shtml

Bond, G. L., & Dykstra, R. (1967). The cooperative research program in first-grade reading instruction. *Reading Research Quarterly, 2,* 5–142.

Bookheimer, S. Y., Zeffiro, T. A., Blaxton, T., Gaillard, W. D., & Theodore, W. H. (1995). Regional cerebral blood flow during object naming and word reading. *Human Brain Mapping, 3*(2), 93–106.

Brabham, E. G., & Villaume, S. K. (2001). Questions and answers: Building walls of words. *The Reading Teacher, 54*(7), 700–702.

Bredekamp, S. (1987). *Developmentally appropriate practice in early childhood programs serving children from birth through age 8.* Washington, DC: National Association for the Education of Young Children.

Bredekamp, S., & Rosegrant, T. (1992). *Reaching potentials: Appropriate curriculum and assessment for young children* (Vol. 1). Washington, DC: National Association for the Education of Young Children.

British Association for the Advancement of Science. (2007). Reading process is surprisingly different than previously thought, technology shows. *Science Daily.* Retrieved December 1, 2007, from http://www.sciencedaily.com/releases/2007/09/070910092543.htm

Bucuvalas, A., & Juel, C. (2002). The limitations of over-emphasizing phonics: The research of Professor Connie Juel. *HGSE News.* Retrieved August 04, 2008, from http://www.gse.harvard.edu/news/features/juel12012002.html

Bus, A., Van Ijzendoorn, M., & Pellegrini, A. (1995). Joint book reading makes for success in learning to read: A meta-analysis on intergenerational transmission of literacy. *Review of Educational Research, 65,* 1–21.

California Department of Education. (1999). *Reading/language arts framework for California public schools, kindergarten through grade twelve.* Sacramento: Author.

California Department of Education. (2000a). *California 2002 K–8 reading/language arts/English language development adoption criteria.* Sacramento: Author.

California Department of Education. (2000b). *Prekindergarten learning development guidelines.* Sacramento: Author.

Caplan, D. (1995). Language and the Brain. *The Harvard Mahoney Neuroscience Institute Letter, 4*(4).

Carey, B. (2007). Bad behavior does not doom pupils, studies say [Electronic version]. *New York Times.* Retrieved May 01, 2008, from http://www.nytimes.com/2007/11/13/health/13kids.html?

Carter, R. (1998). *Mapping the mind.* Los Angeles: University of California Press.

Center for the Improvement of Early Reading Achievement (CIERA). (2001). *Put reading first: The research building blocks for teaching children to read.* A joint publication with the National Institute for Literacy, the National Institute of Child Health and Human Development, and the U.S. Department of Education. Jessup, MD: National Institute for Literacy.

Chall, J. S. (1983). *Learning to read: The great debate.* New York: McGraw-Hill.

Chow, P., & Chou, C. (2000). Evaluating sustained silent reading in reading classes. *The Internet TESL Journal* [On-line], *6*(11). Available: http://iteslj.org.

Chugani, H. (1998). A critical period of brain development: Studies of cerebral glucose utilization with PET. *Preventive Medicine, 27,* 184–188.

Clachman, B. Z. (1991). Phonological awareness: Implications for prereading and in literacy instruction. In S. A. Brady & D. P. Shankweiler (Eds.), *Phonological processes in literacy* (pp. 29–36). Hillsdale, NJ: Erlbaum.

Clarke, L. K. (1988). Invented versus traditional spelling in first graders' writings: Effects on learning to spell and read. *Research in the Teaching of English, 22*(3), 281–309.

Collins, M. F. (2005). IRA Outstanding Dissertation Award for 2005: ESL preschoolers' English vocabulary acquisition from storybook reading, *Reading Research Quarterly, 40*(4), 406–408.

Cummins, J. (2000). *Bilingual children's mother tongue: Why is it important for education?* Retrieved August 07, 2008, from www.iteachilearn.com/cummins/mother.htm

Cunningham, A. E., & Stanovich, K. E. (1998). What reading does for the mind. *American Educator, 22*(1–2), 8–15.

Cunningham, P., Hall, D. P., & Heggie, T. (1994). *Making words: Multilevel, hands on developmentally appropriate spelling and phonics.* Torrance, CA: Good Apple.

Curriculum & Instruction Steering Committee, California County Superintendents Educational Services Association. (2007). *Creating a systemwide literacy plan for student success.* Sacramento: California State Department of Education.

Dahlberg, C. P. (2007). In study, bilingual brains stay sharp longer. *The Dana Foundation's Brain in the News, 14*(2), 1–2.

Dana Alliance for Brain Initiatives. (2007). *The 2007 progress report on brain research.* New York: Dana Press.

Deacon, T. W. (1997). *The symbolic species: The co-evolution of language and the brain.* New York: W. W. Norton.

Denckla, M. B., & Rudel, R. G. (1976). Rapid automatized naming (RAN): Dyslexia differentiated from other learning disabilities. *Neuropsychologia, 14,* 471–479.

DeTemple, J., & Snow, C. (2003). Learning words from books. In A. V. Kleeck, S. A. Stahl, & E. B. Bauer (Eds.), *On reading storybooks to children: Parents and teachers* (pp. 16–36). Mahwah, NJ: Lawrence Erlbaum.

Diamond, M., & Hopson, J. (1998). *Magic trees of the mind: How to nurture your child's intelligence, creativity, and healthy emotions from birth through adolescence.* New York: Penguin Books.

Dickinson, D. K., Cote, L., & Smith, M. W. (1993). Learning vocabulary in preschool: Social and discourse contexts affecting vocabulary growth. In C. Daiute (Ed.), *The development of literacy through social interaction: No. 61. New directions for child development: The Jossey-Bass Education Series* (pp. 67–78). San Francisco: Jossey-Bass.

Dickinson, D. K., & Smith, M. W. (1994). Long-term effects of preschool teachers' book readings on low-income children's vocabulary and story comprehension. *Reading Research Quarterly, 29*(2), 104–122.

Dobbs, D. (2006). A revealing reflection. *Scientific American Mind, 17*(2), 22–27.

Duke, N. K. (2000). 3.6 minutes per day: The scarcity of informational texts in first grade. *Reading Research Quarterly, 25*(2), 202–223.

Duke, N. K., Bennett-Armistead, V. S., & Roberts, E. M. (2003). Filling the great void: Why we should bring nonfiction into the early-grade classroom. *American Educator, 27*(1), 30–35.

Durkin, D. (1996). *Children who read early.* New York: Teachers College Press.

Dykstra, R. (1967). *Continuation of the coordinating center for first-grade reading instruction programs* (Report of Project 6–1651). Minneapolis: University of Minnesota.

Eden, G., Phil, D., et al. (2007). Atypical brain activity detected in people with dyslexia. *Science Daily.* Retrieved August 07, 2008, from http://www.childdevelopmentinfo.com/research/dyslexia-research.htm

Eden, G., Turkeltaub, J. Weisberg, D., Flowers, L., & Basu, D. (2004). *The neurobiological basis of reading: A special case of skill acquisition.* Paper from Georgetown University Medical Center. Retrieved August 07, 2008, from http://www.nature.com/nature/journal/v382/n6586/abs/382066a0.html

Eden, G., Van Meter, J., Rumsey, J., Maisog, J., Woods, R., & Zeffiro, T. (1996). Abnormal processing of visual motion in dyslexia revealed by functional brain imaging. *Nature, 382,* 66–69.

Eimas, P. D., Siqueland, E. R., Jusczyk, P., & Vigorito, J. (1971). Speech perception in infants. *Science, 171,* 303–306.

Eliot, L. (1999). *What's going on in there?* New York: Bantam Books.

Ellis, E. (2001). *The makes sense strategies model.* Retrieved August 07, 2008, from http://www.graphicorganizers.com/Sara//ArticlesAbout/MSS%20overview.pdf

Faber Taylor, A., & Kuo, F. E. (2006). Is contact with nature important for healthy child development? State of the evidence. In C. Spencer & M. Blades (Eds.), *Children and their environments* (pp. 124–140). Cambridge, UK: Cambridge University Press.

Farstrup, A. (2000, May 21). Reading is more than phonics. *Tallahassee Democrat.*

Farstrup, A. (2006). IRA comments on new report. *Webpage of the New Conversation on the Skills of the American Workforce.* Retrieved August 07, 2008, from http//blog.reading.org/archives/week_2006_12_10.html

Fletcher, J. M., & Lyon, G. R. (1998). Reading: A research-based approach. In W. Evers (Ed.), *What's gone wrong in America's classrooms.* Stanford, CA: Hoover Institution Press. Retrieved August 07, 2008, from www.Idinstitute.org/approachesreading.shtml

Florida Department of Education. (2001). *Just read, Florida!* Retrieved August 07, 2008, from www.justreadflorida.com

Foorman, B. R., & Connor, C. (in press). Primary reading. In M. Kamil, P. D. Pearson, & E. Moje (Eds.), *Handbook of reading research, Vol. 4.* New York: Longman.

Foreman, J. (2002). The evidence speaks well of bilingualism's effect on kids. *The Brain in the News, 9*(19), 3.

Frackowiak, R. S. J., Friston, K. J., Frith, C. D., Dolan, R. J., Price, C. J., Zeki, S., et al. (2004). *Human brain function* (2nd ed.). San Diego, CA: Academic Press.

Francis, D. J., Shaywitz, S. E., Stuebing, K. K., Shaywitz, B. A., & Fletcher, J. M. (1996). Developmental lag versus deficit models of reading disability: A longitudinal growth curves analysis. *Journal of Educational Psychology, 88,* 3–17.

Francis, D. J., Shaywitz, S. E., Stuebing, K. K., Shaywitz, B. A., & Fletcher, J. M. (1997). Early intervention for children with reading disabilities: Study designs and preliminary findings. *Learning Disabilities: A Multi-Disciplinary Journal, 8,* 63–71.

Fuchs, L. S., Fuchs, D., Hosp, M. K., & Jenkins, J. R. (2001). Oral reading fluency as an indicator of reading competence: A theoretical, empirical, and historical analysis. *Scientific Studies of Reading, 5*(3), 239–256.

Gazzaniga, M. (1998). *The mind's past.* Berkeley: University of California Press.

Gogner, D., Raphael, L., & Pressley, M. L. (2002). How Grade 1 teachers motivate literate activity by their students. *Scientific Studies of Reading, 6*(2), 135–155.

Goldman, S. R., Hogaboam, T. W., Bell, L. C., & Perfetti, C. A. (1980). Short-term retention of discourse during reading. *Journal of Educational Psychology, 68,* 680–688.

Goldsworthy, C. (1996). *Developmental reading disabilities: A language based treatment approach.* San Diego: Singular.

Goldsworthy, C. (1998). *Sourcebook of phonological awareness activities: Children's classic literature.* San Diego: Singular.

Gopnik, A., Meltzoff, A., & Kuhl, P. (2000). *The scientist in the crib.* New York: William Morrow.

Greenfield, S. (2000). *Brain story: Unlocking our inner world of emotions, memories, ideas, and desires.* New York: Dorling Kindersley.

Greenspan, S., & Lewis, N. B. (1999). *Building healthy minds: The six experiences that create intelligence and emotional growth in babies and young children.* Cambridge, MA: Perseus Books.

Haan Foundation. (2007). *LD facts and statistics.* Retrieved August 14, 2008, from http://www.haan4kids.org/ld/stats.html

Hall, S. L., & Moats, L. C. (1999). *Straight talk about reading: How parents can make a difference during the early years.* Lincolnwood, IL: NTC/Contemporary.

Hamaguchi, P. M. (2000). *Practical therapeutic strategies for central auditory processing disorders.* Presentation to Region 10 Coordinating Council, Language and Speech Committee, Apple Valley, CA.

Harris, A. J., & Sipay, E. R. (1990). *How to increase reading ability* (8th ed.). New York: Longman.

Hart, B., & Risley, T. R. (2003, Spring). The early catastrophe. *The American Educator,* 4–9.

Healy, J. (1985). *Endangered minds: Why our children don't think.* New York: Simon & Schuster.

Healy, J. (1987). *Your child's growing mind: A guide to learning and brain development from birth to adolescence.* New York: Doubleday.

Heilman, K., Voeller, K., & Alexander, A. (1996). Developmental dyslexia: A motor–articulatory feedback hypothesis. *Annals of Neurology, 39,* 407–412.

Herron, J. (2007). *Backwards and boring: Phonics instruction has got to change!* Retrieved August 13, 2008, from http://sbsl.org/docs/BackwardsBoring.pdf

Herschkowitz, N., & Herschkowitz, E. C. (2002). *A good start in life: Understanding your child's brain and behavior.* Washington, DC: Dana Press.

Hettleman, K. R. (2003). *The invisible dyslexics: How public school systems in Baltimore and elsewhere discriminate against poor children in the diagnosis and treatment of early reading difficulties.* Baltimore: Abell Foundation.

Hirsch, E. D., Jr. (2003). Reading comprehension requires knowledge and words and the world. *American Educator, 27*(1), 10–22, 28–29, 48.

Honig, B. (2001). *Teaching our children to read.* Thousand Oaks, CA: Corwin Press.

Hopkins, G. (2002). Sustained silent reading helps develop independent readers (and writers). *Education World* [On-line]. Available: www.education-world.com/a_curr/curr038.shtml

Hotz, R. L. (2002a, July 29). In dyslexia study, a child's reading is written on brain. *Los Angeles Times*, p. A10.

Hotz, R. L. (2002b, November 8). Neuroscientists mine the depths of emotions. *Los Angeles Times*.

Hudson, R. F., High, L., & Al Otaiba, S. (2007). Dyslexia and the brain: What does current research tell us? *Reading Teacher, 6*, 506–515.

Huttenlocher, J., Haight, W., Bryk, A., Seltzer, M., & Lyons, T. (1991). Early vocabulary growth: Relation to language input and gender. *Developmental Psychology, 27*, 236–248.

Illinois State Board of Education. (2002). *Illinois reads.* Retrieved August 07, 2008, from http://www.isbe.state.il.us/ils/ela/standards.htm

Irvin, J. L. (2001). Assisting struggling readers in building vocabulary and background knowledge. *Voices From the Middle, 8*(4), 37–43.

Juel, C., & Deffes, R. (2004). Making words stick: What research says about reading. *Educational Leadership, 61*, 30–34.

Juel, C., & Minden-Crupp, C. (2000). Learning to read words: Linguistic units and instructional strategies. *Reading Research Quarterly, 35*(4), 458–493.

Jusczyk, P. W. (1999). How infants begin to extract words from speech. *Trends in Cognitive Science, 3*, 323–328.

Justice, L. M., & Ezell, H. K. (2004). Print referencing: An emergent literacy enhancement technique and its clinical applications. *Language, Speech, and Hearing Services in Schools, 35*, 185–193.

Kail, R. V. (1984). *The development of memory in children.* New York: W. H. Freeman.

Kame'enui, E. J. (2002). *Analysis of reading assessment instruments for K–3* [On-line]. Available: http://idea.uoregon.edu/assessment

Kame'enui, E. J. (2007). A new paradigm, responsiveness to intervention. *Council for Exceptional Children, 39*(4), 6–7.

Kame'enui, E. J., & Simmons, D. C. (2000). *Planning and evaluation tool for effective schoolwide reading program.* Eugene: University of Oregon, College of Education, Institute for the Development of Educational Achievement.

Kame'enui, E. J., & Simmons, D. C. (2001). Introduction to this special issue: The DNA of reading fluency. *Scientific Studies of Reading, 5*(3), 2003–2010.

Koralek, D., & Collins, R. (1997). *On the road to reading: A guide for community partners.* A joint project of the Corporation for National Service, the U.S. Department of Education, and the U.S. Department of Health and Human Services. Retrieved August 07, 2008, from www.ed.gov/pubs/RoadtoRead/part2.html

Kotulak, R. (1997). *Inside the brain: Revolutionary discoveries of how the mind works.* Kansas City, MO: Andrews McMeel.

Kuhl, P., Williams, K., Lacerda, F., Stevens, K., & Lindblom, B. (1992). Linguistic experience alters phonetic perception in infants by 6 months of age. *Science, 255*, 606–608.

Leach, P. (1997). *Your baby and child: From birth to age five* (Rev. ed.). New York: Knopf.

Levine, M. (2003). Getting at getting it: The quest for comprehension. *All kinds of minds.* Retrieved August 07, 2008, from http://www.allkindsofminds.org

Levy, B. A., Abello, B., & Lysynchuk, L. (1997). Transfer from word training to reading in context: Gains in reading fluency and comprehension. *Learning Disability Quarterly, 20*, 173–188.

Liberman, I., Shankweiler, D., & Liberman, A. M. (1999). The alphabetic principle and learning to read. *Read all about it!* (pp. 117–130). Sacramento: California State Board of Education.

Lindamood, P., Bell, N., & Lindamood, P. (1997). Sensory-cognitive factors in the controversy over reading instruction. *Journal of Developmental and Learning Disorders, 1*(1), 143–182.

Linquanti, R. (1999). Fostering academic success for English language learners. What do we know? *WestEd.* Retrieved August 07, 2008, from http://www.wested.org/cs/we/view/rs/514

Liversedge, S. P., & Blythe, H. I. (2007). Lexical and sublexical influences on eye movements during reading. *Language and Linguistics Compass, 1,* (1/2), 17–31.

Locke, J. (1994). Phases in a child's development of language. *American Scientist, 82,* 436–445.

Luce, P. (2002). Untitled presentation at the AASA annual meeting in Boston. Reported in *Brainwork, 12,* 2.

Lundberg, I., Olofsson, A., & Wall, S. (1980). Reading and spelling skills in the first school years predicted from phonemic awareness skills in kindergarten. *Scandinavian Journal of Psychology, 27,* 159–173.

Lyon, G. R. (2001, March 8). *Measuring success: Using assessments and accountability to raise student achievement.* Statement for the Subcommittee on Education Reform, Committee on Education and the Workforce, U.S. House of Representatives, Washington, DC. Retrieved February 20, 2003, from www.plato.com/pdf/teleconference_session3_lyon1.pdf

Lyon, G. R. (2002). Why can't I read? *Northwest Education Magazine, 8*(3). Retrieved August 07, 2008, from http://www.nwrel.org/nwedu/08–03/read.asp

Lyon, R., & Fletcher, J. M. (2001). Early warning systems. *Education Matters, 1*(2). Retrieved August 07, 2008, from http://www.hoover.org/publications/ednext/3389276.html

MacDonal, S. (1997). *The portfolio and its use: A road map for assessment.* Little Rock, AR: Southern Early Childhood Association.

Maclean, M., Bryant, P., & Bradley, L. (1978). Rhymes, nursery rhymes, and reading in early childhood. *Merrill-Palmer Quarterly, 33,* 255–281.

Marzano, R. J. (2006). *Building background knowledge for academic achievement.* Alexandria, VA: Association for Supervision and Curriculum Development.

Mathes, P. (2003, May). *The Tallahassee and Houston first grade intervention studies.* Presentation at the International Reading Association, Orlando, FL.

McCandliss, B. D., Cohen, L., & Dehaene, S. (2003). The visual word form area: Expertise for reading in the fusiform gyrus. *Trends in Cognitive Sciences, 7*(7), 293–299.

McCardle, P., & Chhabra, V. (2004). *The accumulation of evidence, A continuing process.* In P. McCardle & V. Chhabra (Eds.), *The voice of evidence in reading research* (pp. 463–478). Baltimore: Paul H. Brookes.

McCracken, R. A. (1971). Initiating sustained silent reading. *Journal of Reading, 14*(8), 521–524, 582–583.

McEwan, E. K. (2002). *Teach them all to read: Catching the kids who fall through the cracks.* Thousand Oaks, CA: Corwin Press.

McGee, M. G., & Wilson, D. W. (1984). *Psychology: Science and application.* St. Paul, MN: West.

McPike, E. (1998). The unique power of reading and how to unleash it. *American Educator, 22*(1–2), 4–5.

Mehler, J., & Christophe, A. (1994). Language in the infant's mind. *Philosophical Transactions of the Royal Society (Biological Sciences), 346,* 13–20.

Meltzoff, A. N., & Moore, M. K. (1977). Imitation of facial and manual gestures by human neonates. *Science, 198,* 75–78.

Merzenich, M. M., Jenkins, W. M., Johnston, P., Schreiner, C., Miller, S. L., & Tallal, P. (1996). Temporal processing deficits of language-learning impaired children ameliorated by training. *Science, 271,* 77–81.

Meyer, R. J. (2003). Captives of the script: Killing us softly with phonics, a critical analysis demonstrates that scripted phonics programs hold students and teachers as curriculum hostages. *Rethinking Schools Online, 17*(4). Retrieved August 11, 2008, from http://www.rethinkingschools.org/archive/17_04/17_04.shtml

Moats, L. C. (1998). Teaching decoding. *American Educator, 22*(1–2), 42–49, 95, 96.

Moats, L. C. (2000). *Speech to print: Language essentials for teachers.* Baltimore: Brookes.

Moats, L. C., Furry, A. R., & Brownell, N. (1998). *Learning to read: Components of beginning reading instruction, K–8.* Sacramento, CA: Sacramento County Office of Education.

Morais, J., Bertelson, P., Cary, L., & Alegria, J. (1986). Literacy training and speech segmentation. *Cognition, 24,* 45–64.

National Assessment of Educational Progress. (2007). *Trends in fourth-grade NAEP reading achievement level performance.* Retrieved August 11, 2008, from http://nationsreportcard.gov/reading_2007/r0011.asp

National Association for the Education of Young Children. (1998). Learning to read and write: Developmentally appropriate practices for young children. A joint position statement of the International Reading Association and the National Association for the Education of Young Children. *Young Children, 53*(4), 30–46.

National Center for Education Statistics. (2007). *Digest of education statistics.* Washington, DC: U.S. Department of Education, Office of Educational Research and Improvement. Retrieved August 11, 2008, from http://nces.ed.gov/fastfacts/display.asp?id=64

National Center on Addiction and Substance Abuse at Columbia University. (2006). *CASA releases white paper on substance abuse and learning disabilities.* Retrieved August 11, 2008, from http://www.casacolumbis.org/absolutenm/templates/print-article.aspx?articleid=119&zone1d=56

National Institute of Child Health and Human Development. (2000). *Report of the National Reading Panel. Teaching children to read: An evidence-based assessment of the scientific research literature on reading and its implications for reading instruction* (NIH Publication No. 00-4769). Washington, DC: Government Printing Office.

National Research Council, Institute of Medicine. (2002). *From neurons to neighborhoods, the science of early childhood development.* Washington DC: National Academy Press.

Nemours Foundation. (2007). *Healthy habits for TV, video games, and the Internet.* Retrieved June 23, 2008, from http://www.kidshealth.org/parent/positive/family/tv_habits.html

Neuman, S. B. (2001). *Access to print: Problem, consequences and instructional solutions.* Address to the White House Summit on Early Childhood Cognitive Development. Washington, DC: U.S. Department of Education.

Neville, H. J. (1995). Developmental specificity in neurocognitive development in humans. In M. Gazzaniga (Ed.), *The cognitive neurosciences* (pp. 219–231). Cambridge: MIT Press.

Nevins, J. (Ed.). (2007). Thinking and remembering. *The 2007 Progress Report on Brain Research* (pp. 82–88). New York: Dana Press.

New York State Department, Office of Bilingual Education. (2000). *The teaching of language arts to limited English proficient/English language learners: A resource guide for all teachers.* Albany: Author.

Nolte, J. (2002). *The human brain: An introduction to its functional anatomy* (5th ed.). St. Louis, MO: Mosby.

O'Connor, R. E., White, A., & Swanson, H. L. (2007). Repeated reading versus continuous reading: Influences on reading fluency and comprehension. *Exceptional Children, 74*(1), 31–46.

Ogle, D. M. (1986). K-W-L: A teaching model that develops active reading of expository text. *The Reading Teacher, 40,* 564–570.

Oregon State Department of Education. (2008). *English/language arts grade level standards.* Portland, OR: Author.

Ortiz, A. (2001, December). English language learners with special needs: Effective instructional strategies. *ERIC Digest.* Retrieved August 13, 2008, from http://www.eric.ed.gov/ERICDocs/data/ericdocs2sql/content_storage_01/0000019b/80/1a/71/21.pdf

Paglin, C. (2002). *Double dose* [On-line]. Available: http://www.nwrel.org/nwedu/08–03/dose-t.asp

Pascual-Leone, J. (1970). A maturational model for the transition rule in Piaget's developmental stages. *Acta Psychologica, 32,* 301–345.

Patoine, B. (2008). Research consortium finds new evidence linking arts and learning. *BrainWork, the Neuroscience Newsletter, 18*(2), 1–2.

Pence, K. L., & Justice, L. M. (2008). *Language development from theory to practice.* Columbus, OH: Pearson, Merrill Prentice Hall.

Pennington, B. F. (1989). Using genetics to understand dyslexia. *Annals of Dyslexia, 39,* 81–93.

Perfetti, C. (1995). Cognitive research can inform reading education. *Journal of Research in Reading, 18,* 106–115.

Pianta, R. C. (1990). Widening the debate on educational reform: Prevention as a viable alternative. *Exceptional Children, 56*(4), 306–313.

Pilgreen, J. L., (2000). *The sustained silent reading handbook.* Portsmouth, NH: Heinemann.

Pinker, S. (1997). *How the mind works.* New York: W. W. Norton.

Posner, M. I., & McCandliss, B. D. (1999). Brain circuitry during reading. In R. Klein & P. McMullen (Eds.), *Converging methods for understanding reading and dyslexia* (pp. 305–338). Cambridge: MIT Press.

Pressley, M. (1998). *Reading instruction that works: The case for balanced teaching.* New York: Guilford Press.

Pressley, M. (2001). Comprehension instruction: What makes sense now, what might make sense soon. *Reading Online, 5*(2). Retrieved August 11, 2008, from http://www.readingonline.org/articles/art_index.asp?HREF=/articles/handbook/pressley/Index.html

Purcell-Gates, V., & Dahl, K. (1991). Low-SES children's success and failure at early literacy learning in skills-based classrooms. *JRB: A Journal of Literacy, 23,* 1–34.

Rasinski, T. (2000). Speed does matter in reading. *The Reading Teacher, 54*(2), 146–151.

Rayner, K., Foorman, B. R., Perfetti, C. A., Pesetsky, D., & Seidenberg, M. S. (2002). How should reading be taught? *Scientific American, 286*(3), 70–77.

Reeves, D. (2008). You know what to do, teachers. Now do it (Speech at the Achievement Gap Summit, Sacramento, CA). *The Special Edge, 21*(2), 3–4.

Restak, R. (2001). *The secret life of the brain.* Washington, DC: Joseph Henry Press.

Ritter, M. (2007, March 19). New research is mind-wandering. *North County Times,* p. H8.

Rizzolatti, G., Fogassi, L., & V. Gallese. (2006). Mirrors in the mind. *Scientific American, 295*(5), 54–61.

Road to Reading. (1997). *Emerging literacy.* Retrieved August 13, 2008, from http://www.ed.gov/pubs/RoadtoRead/part2.html

Rossetti, L. M. (1996). *Communication intervention birth to three.* San Diego, CA: Singular.

Scarborough, H. S. (1989). Prediction of reading disability from familial and individual differences. *Journal of Educational Psychology, 81*(1), 101–108.

Schwartz, J. M., & Begley, S. (2003). *The mind & the brain, neuroplasticity and the power of mental force.* New York: HarperCollins.

Shaywitz, B. A., Shaywitz, S. E., Pugh, K. R., Mencl, W. E., Fulbright, R. K., Skudlarski, P., et al. (2002). Functional disruption in the organization of the brain for reading in dyslexia. *Biological Psychiatry, 52,* 101–110.

Shaywitz, S. E. (2003). *Overcoming dyslexia: A new and complete science-based program for reading problems at any level.* New York: Alfred A. Knopf.

Shaywitz, S. E., Fletcher, J. M., & Shaywitz, B. A. (1994). Issues in the definition and classification of attention deficit disorder. *Topics in Language Disorders, 14*(4), 1–25.

Shaywitz, S. E., & Shaywitz, B. A. (2001). The neurobiology of reading and dyslexia. *Focus on Basics, 5*(A).

Sherman, L. (2002). Why can't I read? Current research offers new hope to disabled learn-ers. *Northwest Education Magazine*. Retrieved August 11, 2008, from www.nwrel.org/nwedu/08–03/read.asp

Sherman, P. (2007). Organization uses innovative methods to reach at-risk students. *North County Times*. Retrieved June 13, 2008, from http://singonsandiego.com/news/northcounty/20071109–9999-lz1mc9artes.html

Slavin, R. E. (1994). *Preventing early school failure: Research, policy, and practice*. Needham Heights, MA: Allyn & Bacon.

Slavin, R. E., & Madden, N. (1994, April). *Effects of success for all on the achievement of English language learners*. Paper presented at the annual meeting of the American Educational Research Association, San Francisco.

Smith, F. (1998). *The book of learning and forgetting*. New York: Teachers College Press.

Snow, C. E., Burns, M. S., & Griffin, P. (1998). *Preventing reading difficulties in young children*. Washington, DC: National Academy Press.

Snow, C. E., & Tabors, P. O. (1993). Language skills that relate to literacy development. In B. Spodek & O. N. Saracho (Eds.), *Language and literacy in early childhood education* (pp. 1–20). New York: Teachers College Press.

Southern California Comprehensive Assistance Center. (2002). *Taking a reading: A teacher's guide to reading assessment*. Downey, CA: Los Angeles County Office of Education.

Stahl, S. A. (1999). *Vocabulary development, from reading research to practice: A series for teachers*. Newton Upper Falls, MA: Brookline Books.

Stahl, S. A. (2003, Spring). How words are learned incrementally over multiple exposures. *American Educator*, 18–19.

Stanovich, K. E. (1986). Matthew effects in reading: Some consequences of individual differences in the acquisition of literacy. *Reading Research Quarterly, 21*, 360–407.

Stanovich, K. E. (1988). Explaining the differences between the dyslexic and the garden-variety poor reader: The phonological-core variable-difference model. *Journal of Learning Disabilities, 21*, 590–612.

Stanovich, K. E., Cunningham, A. E., & Cramer, B. B. (1984). Assessing phonological aware-ness in kindergarten children: Issues of task comparability. *Journal of Experimental Child Psychology, 38*, 175–190.

Sylwester, R. (1995). *A celebration of neurons: An educator's guide to the human brain*. Alexandria, VA: Association for Supervision and Curriculum Development.

Sylwester, R. (1998). Art for the brain's sake. *Educational Leadership, 5*(3), 31–35.

Sylwester, R. (2005). *How to explain a brain, an educator's handbook of brain terms and cognitive processes*. Thousand Oaks, CA: Corwin Press.

Tallal, P. (2000). Experimental studies of language learning impairments: From research to remediation. In D. V. M. Bishop & L. B. Leonard (Eds.), *Speech and language impairments in children: Causes, characteristics, intervention, and outcome* (pp. 131–155). Hove, UK: Psychology Press.

Temple, E., Deutsch, G. K., Poldrac, R. A., Salidis, J., Miller, S. L., Tallal, et al. (2003). Neural deficits in children with dyslexia ameliorated by behavioral remediation: Evidence from functional MRI. *Proceedings of the National Academy of Science, 100*(5), 2860–2865.

Templeton, S., & Morris, D. (1999). Questions teachers ask about spelling. *Reading Research Quarterly, 34*(1), 102–112.

Texas Assessment of Academic Skills. (1997). *Texas essential knowledge and skills for English language arts and reading*. Retrieved August 11, 2008, from www.tea.state.tx.us/assessment.html

Torgesen, J. K. (1993). Variations on theory in learning disability. In G. R. Lyon, D. B. Gray, J. E. Kavanagh, & N. A. Krasnegor (Eds.), *Better understanding of learning disabilities: New views from research and their implications for education and public policies* (pp. 153–170). Baltimore: Brookes.

Torgesen, J. K. (1998). Catch them before they fall: Identification and assessment to prevent reading failure in young children. *American Educator, 22*(1–2), 32–39.

Torgesen, J. K., & Burgess, S. R. (1998). Consistency of reading-related phonological processes throughout early childhood: Evidence from longitudinal-correlational and instructional studies. In J. Tetsala & L. Ehri (Eds.), *Word recognition in beginning reading* (pp. 161–188). Hillsdale, NJ: Lawrence Erlbaum.

Torgesen, J. K., Wagner, R. K., & Rashotte, C. A. (1994). Longitudinal studies of phonological processing and reading. *Journal of Learning Disabilities, 27,* 276–286.

Tuma, R. S. (2002). How do we remember? Let us count the ways. *Brain Work, The Neuroscience Newsletter, 12*(6), 1–2.

Tunmer, W. E., Herriman, M. L., & Nesdale, A. R. (1988). Metalinguistic abilities and beginning reading. *Reading Research Quarterly, 23,* 134–158.

Turkeltaub, P. E, Weisberg, J., Flowers, D. L, Basu, D., & Eden G. F. (2004). *The neurobiological basis for reading: A special case of skill acquisition.* Georgetown University. Retrieved August 11, 2008, from http.//csl.georgetown.edu/publications/Turkeltab_et_al

Vaughn, S., Hughes, M. T., Moody, S. W., & Elbaum, B. (2001). Instructional grouping for reading for students with LD: Implications for practice. *Intervention in School and Clinic, 36*(3), 131–137.

Vukelich, C., Christie, J., & Enz, B. (2002). *Helping young children learn language and literacy.* Boston: Allyn & Bacon.

Walsh, D. J., Price, G. G., & Gillingham, M. G. (1988). The critical but transitory importance of letter naming. *Reading Research Quarterly, 23,* 108–122.

Walsh, K. (2003). Basal readers: The lost opportunity to build the knowledge that propels comprehension. *American Educator, 27*(1), 24–27.

What Works Clearinghouse. (2007, March 19). *Intervention report, beginning reading.* Institute of Educational Sciences. Retrieved August 14, 2008, from http://www.readingrecovery.ac.nz/research/download/WWC_Reading_Recovery_031907.pdf

Whitehurst, G. J., Falco, F., Lonigan, C. J., Fischal, J. E., DeBaryshe, B. D., Valdez-Manchaca, M. C., et al. (1988). Accelerating language development through picturebook reading. *Developmental Psychology, 24,* 552–559.

Whitlock, J. R., Heyman, A. J., Shuler, M. G., & Bear, M. F. (2006). Learning induces long-term potentiation in the hippocampus. *Science, 313*(5790), 1093–1097.

Wolf, M. (2003). Teaching fluency with Maryanne Wolf, new research on an old problem: A brief history of fluency. *Scholastic.* Retrieved August 11, 2008, from www.teacher.scholastic.com/browse/article.jsp?id=4468

Wolf, M. (2007). *Proust and the squid: The story and science of the reading brain.* New York: HarperCollins.

Wolf, M., Bowers, P., & Biddle, K. (2000). RAVE-O: A comprehensive fluency-based reading intervention program. *Journal of Learning Disabilities, 33*(4).

Wolfe, P. (2001). *Brain matters: Translating research into classroom practice.* Alexandria, VA: Association for Supervision and Curriculum Development.

Woolfolk, A. (2008). *Educational psychology, active learning edition.* Boston: Pearson Education.

Yopp, H. K. (1985). Read-aloud books for developing phonemic awareness: An annotated bibliography. *Reading Teacher, 48,* 538–542.

Index

CORWIN PRESS

The Corwin Press logo—a raven striding across an open book—represents the union of courage and learning. Corwin Press is committed to improving education for all learners by publishing books and other professional development resources for those serving the field of PreK–12 education. By providing practical, hands-on materials, Corwin Press continues to carry out the promise of its motto: **"Helping Educators Do Their Work Better."**